PUBLIC
EDUCATION
IN NEW MEXICO

For Mayor Chavez, a great Professional + Leader — Best Wishes

PUBLIC EDUCATION
IN NEW MEXICO

Best Wishes. John Mondragón

JOHN B. MONDRAGÓN
ERNEST S. STAPLETON

Sincerely, Ernest S. Stapleton

University of New Mexico Press ⮐ Albuquerque

10 09 08 07 06 05   1 2 3 4 5 6 7

Library of Congress Cataloging-in-Publication Data

Mondragón, John B., 1930–
Public education in New Mexico /
John B. Mondragón, Ernest S. Stapleton.
p. cm.
Includes bibliographical references and index.
ISBN 0-8263-3655-8 (pbk. : alk. paper)
1. Education—New Mexico—History.
2. Education and state—New Mexico—History.
I. Stapleton, Ernest S., 1927– II. Title.
LA334.M56 2005
370'.9789—dc22

2004026285

Cover illustration: "Hora del Cuento~Story Time," an original
painting by Edward Gonzales © 2001. All rights reserved.

Design and composition: Maya Allen-Gallegos
Typeset in Sabon 11/13
Display type set in Americana BT

Contents

Acknowledgments / VIII

Introduction / XI

CHAPTER 1
The Roots of Public Education in New Mexico / 1

CHAPTER 2
Governance of Public Education in New Mexico / 28

CHAPTER 3
Indian Education in New Mexico / 59

CHAPTER 4
Education as a Profession / 83

CHAPTER 5
Curriculum / 109

CHAPTER 6
Financing Schools in New Mexico / 132

CHAPTER 7
School Improvements and Educational Reform / 156

CHAPTER 8
Public Education and Higher Education Connection / 187

CHAPTER 9
Future Trends / 208

Epilogue / 218

Appendices / 221

References and Related Sources / 233

Index / 244

About the Authors / 255

Acknowledgments

This book has been made possible by the assistance, guidance, and inspiration of many colleagues, past and present, as well as friends and members of our families. They have been, in fact, a kind of exalted jury for us.

We acknowledge the dean of the College of Education at the University of New Mexico, Dr. Viola Florez, and other colleagues in the Educational Leadership Program for their support and encouragement. It is incumbent upon us to also thank former and present colleagues in the Department of Educational Administration who encouraged us to undertake this writing challenge. In a very special way, we acknowledge the pioneer scholarship of Dr. Tom Wiley, and other scholars at the University of New Mexico who have contributed to the educational literature of New Mexico.

We want to acknowledge the staff of the New Mexico Research and Study Council, Kris McGill, Gaia Rose McNeil, Sonia de Souza, and Josh Torres, for their technical support and for their infinite patience. Special thanks to Jo Nelle Miranda, our gifted and diligent editor, who shepherded this book from its early stages to its present form, and to her husband, Gil Miranda, for his support.

Our families have been there for us from the initial stages; we thank them for their encouragement, support, and timely critiques. The Mondragóns: my daughter and her husband, Christine and Timothy Johnston, my grandchildren, Elizabeth and Brian Johnston, and my son, Thomas Mondragón. The Stapletons: my wife, RoseMary, my daughter and her husband, Dawnelle and Travis Askew, my granddaughter, Alexandria Askew, my granddaughter and her husband, Maya and Dan Gallegos, and my daughter and her husband, Leslie and John Gonzales, and their children, Patrick and Caitlan.

The editor-in-chief of the University of New Mexico Press, Dr. David Holtby, and his staff provided expert professional support. We very much appreciated the talented and able critiques offered by our professional reviewers.

Passion for education was instilled by our ancestors and by the peoples of New Mexico. We owe them our gratitude for instilling in us this passion.

We believe the oral history and tales told by our elders illustrate and give life to the facts of history. Therefore, this time with you will be punctuated with tales, most fact, some fiction, to bring life to the characters and events surrounding the history of public education in the state of New Mexico. We encourage you to share your "stories" to bring your unique view of education as you now see it and as you have experienced it.

Introduction

Public Education in New Mexico is about the history, operations, and issues of the public schools in New Mexico. In it we explore information, significant data, ideas, events, historical antecedents, critical policies and practices, governance and legislation, and management and operation of schools. Knowledge gained from experience in the field of education in New Mexico is shared; folklore and folktales enlighten situations; and our personal reflections, opinions, and challenges are presented to encourage the reader to develop interest and ask more questions.

Public Education in New Mexico is primarily designed as a resource for university students preparing for careers in education and educational leadership in the state. Content is expanded by the use of related readings. Another important purpose is to provide educational leaders, educational administrators, legislators, school board members, and the interested public an abbreviated resource about the history and status of education in the state.

University faculty involved in the preparation of teachers, principals, superintendents, and other educational leaders may benefit from the information generated here. The information may provide insight for administrators unfamiliar with New Mexico who need information about their new location and may be beneficial for recently appointed practicing administrators. The general public may benefit, as this publication will provide brief, but crucial, information about our New Mexico public school system and will encourage more in-depth exploration and study.

Understanding the general history of New Mexico and of education in New Mexico, we must acknowledge the uniqueness and importance of this history to our communities and to the development of our youth. With informed knowledge and understanding, there is hope for greater support for education and increased recognition of the social and economic impact of education in New Mexico.

The information presented in this book may provide increased understanding of the system of education found in New Mexico and specifically, of the policies that helped shape educational standards, the equitable finance system, and the research and understanding of the diverse, multicultural population in rural and urban areas—research that can reveal concepts that may benefit others.

For those citizens of New Mexico who are interested in the history of education in the state, this book will review that history from the early Native American to the Spanish colonial, Mexican, and U.S. territorial periods to the present statehood era. It will also briefly consider such issues as governance, the curriculum, education as a profession, public school finance, state versus local autonomy, religious education and its impact on the public schools, and Native American education. Ongoing evolutionary changes such as charter schools, high stakes testing, accountability, and other educational reforms will be addressed. The characteristics of the state, the multicultural makeup of the population, the unique social development of the peoples, and the role of governments will be woven into the text.

Certain themes or patterns repeat throughout the 400 years of documented educational history in New Mexico. The Spanish, Mexican, and American periods and the imposing presence of "federalism" are all lasting imprints in New Mexico. The endemic multicultural diversity provides a unique foundation for government and schools and has been impacted by the powerful interplay of religious forces (Catholic, Protestant, Jewish, Native American, and others). The economic interests created by new peoples in a new world rich with ancestral history, land, mountains, rivers, forests, and minerals helped to shape the destiny of education in New Mexico.

Curriculum has evolved from the early basic educational needs of young men and women at the family and tribal level, through the industrial period, to the high-technology era. Education of Native American children has evolved from the efforts of the early friars to combine religion and learning with the wisdom of the elders, to government boarding schools, to contract schools, to enrollment in public schools, to Pueblo and tribal students enrolling in prestigious private schools.

Financing of the public schools in New Mexico has grown from each community planting a cornfield to a highly sophisticated system that uses an equitable formula to disperse state dollars to each school district. The growth in teacher and administrator preparation over the years and the process of financing schools, which include the issues of salaries, growth plans, and recognition of the value of wise and experienced educators, are constant variables.

Diverse leadership styles have impacted education as conquerors, local and national leaders, citizens, governors, superintendents, legislators, elected and appointed officials, boards of education, and parents have ultimately developed a system of checks and balances for the governance of education.

The system is responsive to state and federal educational involvements, while maintaining autonomy at the local level. New Mexico schools are both beneficiaries and advocates of federal knowledge and largesse and of state involvement in enhancing education. Political acuity and skills, political opportunism, and rivalries (yes, even shenanigans and corruption) have impacted the fortunes of education in this state. Leadership has come from pioneers and from a variety of parents, citizens, educators, government officials, and students. Only a few are identified here, some by name as leaders or heroes, some as figures in situational scenarios. It is left to the readers to list their heroes, both public and private, who have impacted the educational system in New Mexico. Certainly support staff must be celebrated and acknowledged, for they too make education happen for students in New Mexico.

Educational reform in New Mexico appears to be a cyclic phenomenon, starting with the inception of the first public schools; however, never before in the history of education in New Mexico has there been such emphasis on immediate and imperative reform. Reform movements have been a mixture of political, professional, and public drama at the local, state, and national levels. The complexity of such movements makes this book "a work in progress."

We, the authors of this book, are two native New Mexican educators whose cultural and experiential backgrounds reflect education of and in the entire state. We are products of the New Mexico education system. Our professional careers each span over five decades in education at both the public school and university level. We have held teaching as well as administrative positions, including those of assistant principal, counselor, principal, assistant superintendent, deputy superintendent, and district superintendent. We have taught graduate students in the Educational Leadership Program at the University of New Mexico, preparing future school administrators, and we also have held administrative positions at the university level.

We believe in a concept of "wisdom of practice" which stems both from our intellectual practice and from the circumstances we experienced in active involvement in the educational arena. We believe that the lessons learned from a wide range of educational experiences provide credibility for us as we share ideas, opinions, history, and tales. That credibility, we believe, allows us the chance to express opinions and thoughts in an effort to encourage your thoughtful concern for public education in New Mexico.

Above all, and most importantly, we are passionate about education in New Mexico. We believe that a sound education for each student is a key to the economic growth of our state. It is our belief that New Mexico's young people deserve quality education, and we believe that the strong leaders that we help prepare and an educated citizenry will provide this quality education for New Mexico youth. *Public Education in New Mexico* has provided us with another avenue for sharing knowledge and history.

And, oh! The stories we can tell!

The Roots of Public Education in New Mexico

The history of public education in New Mexico took several paths in its journey to the twenty-first century. Historical antecedents of the state's educational system can be traced to the sixteenth century as Native American traditions of teaching and learning and extending knowledge mix with early colonization efforts to reveal an educational mosaic. Roots of the Native American educational system before the sixteenth century still exist today. The history of the development of the educational system in New Mexico is also as varied as the populations it has served. The evolving system has existed and operated under three national flags: Spanish, Mexican, and American. The concept of public education varied dramatically in each of these three periods. From each period came aspects of diversity, equity, equality, excellence, and accountability, impacting the educational system in New Mexico.

Certain historical events and beliefs also color the history of education in New Mexico. Certainly the struggles of the Native American populations impacted that history. Histories of New Mexico show that the area was often discounted and ignored; education and development suffered from institutionalized neglect and indifference from governing authorities, first from Spain, then from Mexico, and later from the United States of America. Religious and philosophical influences of governing authorities, distances, challenging topography, and the ethnic diversity of New Mexico may have influenced this neglect and indifference.

Historians have portrayed New Mexico as having a tumultuous political life and clearly, the political forces in New Mexico have influenced education. The legacy of the Spanish, Mexican, and American governance and political systems persist in the twenty-first century in the customs, laws, political influences, and attitudes toward support for education. The continuing interest and participation of Hispanics in educational matters, the resistance to taxation for public schools, the long struggle for bilingual education, the stamp of Hispanics on legislation, and the more recent influence of Native Americans attest to that legacy.

Additional characterizations of this state known as the "Land of Enchantment" revolve around perceptions of New Mexico as a frontier state whose "wild and woolly" history, especially in the middle and late 1800s, impacted its development. It has been noted that some of the earliest Protestant missionaries may have been on their way to the gold fields of California and were accidentally detoured into New Mexico; the history of the Protestant missions is discussed later. Early railroad enterprises were headed west to connect with Arizona and California, with New Mexico only an afterthought. In recent times, New Mexico has been viewed as merely a conduit for neighboring Texas in the ongoing battle for access to water coming from northern resources. It has also been noted that in the early years of New Mexico's mining industry, some of its mineral wealth was taken without sufficient financial remuneration for the good of the state and its citizens.

Religious and ethnic issues contributed to New Mexico's unique nature and directly affected the development and operation of schools. A significant factor in New Mexico's uniqueness is found in its varied and rich Native American cultures. The education provided by and for the Native American population requires examination and analysis if education in New Mexico is to avoid the errors of the past.

Early Native American Period

Native American practices for teaching and learning and for transmission of the respective cultures were in place before the Spanish arrived. These practices included teaching about their religious, economic, medical, and social life. Formal teaching and informal education were part of that Native American system marked by learning through oral recitation and performance.

Gregory Cajete says that oral histories are a rich part of Native American cultures (Cajete 1994). Family and communal activities also constitute an important part of the culture. The apprenticeship of young people to the trades, and the notion of learning from the elders, both directly and through their roles (medicine men, warriors, clowns, homemakers) are yet another expression of Native American culture and education. These and other basic elements continue to be reflected in the educational system, albeit in different forms in the curriculum.

The Spanish Colonial Period (1540–1821)

The Spanish colonial period in New Mexico began in 1540 and lasted until 1821, a period of over 280 years. Franciscan friars were involved with the Spanish conquistadors in the initial exploration and conquest of New Mexico. History of education in what was then part of New Spain in the Americas indicates that the Franciscan Order was preeminent in providing education and evangelization (the two concepts were inseparable) for the Native American population. In New Mexico, two Franciscan missionaries, Fray Juan de Padilla and Fray Luis de Escalona, were likely the first "teachers" to enter what is now New Mexico; they established the first schools at Quivera and Cicuye.

Undoubtedly there was a clash of cultures and educational methods when the Spanish initiated their efforts. Historians have noted that the Native Americans were originally resistant to Spanish influences, especially to their educational and religious practices. Those first two teachers, Fray Padilla and Fray Escalona, were killed. Fray Padilla served at Quivera and initially experienced a positive welcome and found the inhabitants "well disposed and teachable." Sometime later, he died at the hands of those he was serving. Fray Escalona, who served at Cicuye and who struggled from the outset, made a few converts before he, too, was killed. S. P. Nanninga in his pioneer work *The New Mexico School System*, R. A. Moyers in *A History of Education in New Mexico*, Rufus Palm in *New Mexico Schools from 1581–1846*, and other historians refer to Padilla and Escalona as New Mexico's first teachers, for teaching was their primary mission.

There are reports that a Father Rodriguez attempted to establish a mission school at Bernalillo as early as 1581. Nanninga and Palm indicate that Father Rodriguez was another of the early teachers. By 1598, there were five mission schools established in the area. Basic goals pursued by the mission schools were to Christianize and to educate the native population. It appears that

education of the Spanish military and the civilian population
(non-Native Americans) was, at best, a secondary consideration.
(See Figure 1 for early mission schools.)

Although instruction in the Catholic faith was the primary
objective in mission schools, the Franciscan Fathers, in their
reports, noted the teaching of reading, writing, and singing.
Manual arts such as tailoring, shoemaking, carpentering, black-
smithing, metal working, weaving, and painting were also
taught. Fray Alonso de Benavides, reporting to the King of Spain
in 1626 on the condition of the missions of New Mexico, noted
"The religious, besides instructing their people in our Holy Faith,
have their schools in which reading, writing, music, and several
trades are taught" (Salpointe 1898, 62). Catholic historians
report that the Franciscan Fathers were instructing thousands of
religious converts and that there were industrial schools in the
main Pueblos in each of the eleven districts organized by the
Spanish government in New Spain.

In 1630, Fray Alonso de Benavides, who had been elected *cus-
todio* for New Mexico, wrote an important report which included
information on New Mexico's schools. His report is best known
for the condition of the missions, but school data are included.
He writes of three monasteries and churches that were "costly
and beautiful" and that the Indians were "dexterous in reading
and writing and playing all music instruments and craftsmen in
all the crafts" (Moyers 1941, 57). Benavides wrote extensively
about the missions at Jémez, Taos, and Zuni. Some controversy
has arisen about the Benavides report with scholars like Dr.
France V. Scholes and others claiming that Benavides overstated
the condition of the missions and the schools. Scholes writes that
"formal education (in New Mexico) was practically non-exis-
tent" (Scholes 1935). Moyers offers his own criticism of the
Scholes research by suggesting that the schools and missions may
have been in reasonable order and condition at the time of
Benavides's report, but a few years later may have fallen into "bad
times." It is interesting to note that Benavides wrote a second
report in 1634 and offered additional details about the missions
and the schools. Moyers, in a concluding statement about the
period before 1680, writes "The educational status of the distant
'Kingdom of New Mexico,' while not on a par with that of
Mexico, compared favorably with that of the English, French,
and Dutch colonies on the Atlantic seaboard" (Moyers 1941, 71).

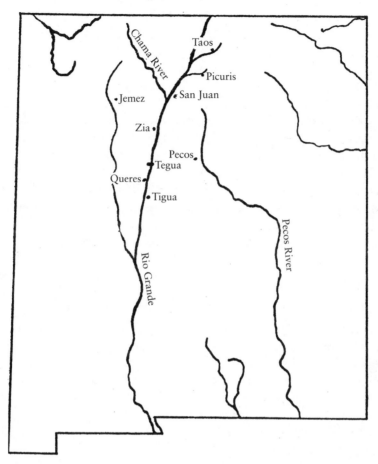

Figure 1. Early mission schools established by Franciscan brothers in New Mexico.

A positive linear view of education in that early period does not emerge from the records, but the Pueblo Revolt led by Popé in 1680 clearly interrupted the work. At that time there were forty-six Pueblos with a mission school or learning center; at the same time, there were also nomadic tribes—Ute, Navajo, and Comanche—and other indigenous groups south toward Mexico. The Spanish were driven out of New Mexico by the Indians, under the leadership of Popé of Taos during the revolt. Churches and their church mission schools were burned or torn down, and government records were destroyed or lost. Spanish colonists were killed, and an effort was made to destroy all material influence of Spanish life.

⟵⟶

Who Survives?

A human interest story emerges from the pages of that
violent history. In the earliest stages of the revolt, many
priests died at various places. However, one priest,
Father José de Espoleto from the mission at Oraibi,
was apparently spared their fate. Missing and unac-
counted for by Spanish and Church authorities during
that time and for many years after the revolt, it appears
that Father Espoleto may have been taken as a slave
among the Picuris. Labeled more hostile than other
tribes by one Catholic historian, the Picuris gave Father
Espoleto refuge, albeit he was hidden among them as
a slave.

⟵⟶

Reconquest by Diego de Vargas began in 1692 and was completed by 1694, although de Vargas had to work rigorously
through both military and political means to fully reestablish
Spanish rule. By 1694, the Spanish had reestablished missions in
at least eighteen Pueblos. Limited or lack of knowledge of the
Native American languages was a handicap in both the governance and education of the people of the Pueblos. Salpointe indicates that some Franciscan Fathers were outstanding in acquiring
language skills, enhancing their ability to teach and work with
the Pueblos (Salpointe 1898, 52).

Clearly mission schools and teachers in Spanish colonial
New Mexico reflected the mission and the doctrine of the
Catholic Church and transmitted a substantial legacy over the
next 150 years.

Cultivate a Cornfield

The concept of free public schools was born on those colonial
frontiers. In 1721, free public schools were established in the
Pueblos and in all the Spanish settlements by decree of the King
of Spain, to be administered by the Franciscans (Hallenbeck
1950). Pueblos or Spanish settlements during this period were
Socorro, Alamillo, Sevilleta, Santa Fe, San Juan, Taos, Santa
Cruz de la Cañada, Zuni, Laguna, and Sandia (Jenkins and
Schroeder 1974, 18).

One provision that stands out among others was that each Pueblo and Spanish colony would cultivate a field of corn to provide remuneration for the teacher. This proviso supports other reports of how teachers of the time were rewarded for their instructional services. Although teachers often were not paid, when they were, it was in the form of *los pesos de tierra* (fruit of the land: livestock, crops, harvests). Perhaps from this time on, the implication for finance, poverty, distance, and philosophy began to be evidenced.

Lack of funds and perhaps lack of will limited the establishment and support of "free public schools" (Simmons 1968, 131). According to historian Nanninga, "Education remained stagnant," and "backward all through the 18th century" (Nanninga 1942, 4). Poverty repeats as a theme for the condition of schools from that early time through the later territorial history of New Mexico. Benjamin Read, in his illustrated history, wrote " . . . nothing in the territory is in a more pitiable condition than the schools" (Read 1912, 535). In 1812, Pedro Bautista Pino observed in his reports of Spanish governance of New Mexico that only children whose parents could contribute to the salary of a teacher were receiving a primary education (Simmons 1968, 18). In his famous report to the crown after the journey of the Spanish Hernando Cortes in 1812, Pino made specific pleas for the establishment of schools (Pino 1995). However, at the beginning of the nineteenth century, there was little evidence of schooling in New Mexico except that which was privately established. A private school in Santa Fe existed for a time in which Spanish grammar, Latin, and philosophy constituted the curriculum. "There were a few private schools established in New Mexico prior to Mexican independence, but just where they are located is not known" (Moyers 1941, 94). With Santa Fe, Santa Cruz de la Cañada, Albuquerque, or Taos as prominent villas, it is likely that the private schools were established there, with Santa Fe the most likely location. The circumstances surrounding the condition of the schools or the absence of educational institutions are illustrative of the severe poverty of the territory and its times. Cornfields and crops were not enough to sustain schools and schoolmasters.

Schoolmaster and Soldier of the Cross

Education under Spanish colonial rule ended on a very sad note, with one major exception. While a few private schools struggled to survive, Father José Antonio Martinez, described by both admirers and detractors as an imposing figure, established a school in Taos. His school and his life merit special attention, for they provide a bright spot in the history of education during those years. Father Martinez and his contemporary, Bishop Jean Baptiste Lamy, are the stuff of legend, and their work, their clashes, and their educational achievements became a part of the history of the Mexican and American territorial periods.

The Mexican Period (1821–1846)

In the early nineteenth century, revolutions swept Central and South America. Mexico gained its independence from Spain in 1821, and New Mexico, for so long a province of the Spanish crown, became a part of the Mexican Northern Province. History records that the independence movement did not bring about major changes because Mexico and its society retained its immutable form: privilege survived. The church retained its *fueros* (special rights or exalted status) and its wealth; the military retained its fueros. The Mexican peasantry felt it was "the same priest on a different mule" (Lynch 1973, 329). In the Northern Province (New Mexico), changes were slow and subtle, but they were real; government and other institutions felt the impact of independence.

An Early Vision of Public Education

The establishment of free public education for the Mexican citizens or Spanish-speaking population of New Mexico under the new government of Mexico throughout the province was created on April 27, 1822, by the new government of Mexico in its first meeting in Santa Fe (Prince 1913, 164–69). A free public education plan was to be carried out by each *municipalidad* (town or village) according to its own means, perhaps establishing the disparities among those who "have and those who have not." Another law passed in 1823 established secondary schools, although only one high school existed in the El Paso (now Texas) area. On May 19, 1826, Father Sebastian Albarez opened the College of Santa Fe; and, in the same year, Father José Antonio Martinez opened his school in Taos.

Nanninga says that at the outset of the Mexican period, schools were in a deplorable state. However, the Mexican government gave more attention to general education than had been the case before independence from Spain. The year 1821 marked the end of the Spanish period in New Mexico and the beginning of a new era in many ways. Independence from Spanish domination opened up trade between Santa Fe and the United States via St. Louis, Missouri. This was the beginning of the flourishing Santa Fe Trail. "Some changes were enormous; others were quite specific and individual" (Gallegos 1992, 20). Eyes that had been directed south to Mexico now began turning to the east; wealthy Spanish families began sending their sons to be educated in Durango, Mexico, St. Louis, and even New York (Prince 1913, 164). Nepomuceno Alarid of Santa Fe was one of the first students to go to school in Missouri (Salaz 1999, 189).

By 1827 there were nineteen schools located in Santa Fe, Vado, Cochiti, San Juan, Zia, Sandia, Alameda, Albuquerque, Tome, Belen, La Cañada, Laguna, Abiqui, San Miguel, Taos, and Santa Fe. (There was more than one school in some villages.) The schools at Taos and Santa Fe received more recognition than the others, and it was reported by historian Benjamin Read (Read 1911, 5) and others that some of the earliest leaders of the time were educated in these schools. Education in New Mexico during the Mexican period was primarily Catholic education; the Franciscan Order offered a presence and dedication to the educational scene so strong and significant that without those clerics, education in the new Northern Province would have been practically nonexistent (Defouri 1930, 80). It is true that the Franciscan order changed roles. According to Moyers and Catholic historians Shea and Salpointe, the secularization of the missions in New Mexico was ordered by the Spanish Cortes in a decree of September 13, 1813 (Shea 1892). When this was carried out, the Franciscan missions of New Mexico became parishes; control was taken from the religious order and placed in the hands of the Bishop, who appointed parish priests to take charge. Secularization, however, took place over a thirty-year period (Bloom and Donnelly 1933; Coan 1925). The Franciscans withdrew from New Mexico in the 1820s, but their control had started to end in 1813, according to Moyers, Scholes, and Bloom.

A strong commitment to free education supported by public funds did not exist during the Spanish or the Mexican colonial periods. Efforts for financing education in each community that did provide schools followed three distinct strategies: tithing, subscription, and appropriations. The entire period was also marked by a lack of commitment to any of these strategies, and the financial resources were seldom available. This shadow of neglect was to continue to plague the New Mexico system of education throughout the American territorial period and into the early stages of statehood. The Catholic Church offered a continuing measure of support for schooling, even though the Church itself was experiencing resource problems. In 1832–33, Bishop Laureano Zubiría of Durango, Mexico, visited the New Mexico Territory and reported that only sixteen priests were available to minister to the churches and the schools.

Lay teachers were few, although, according to historian Jenkins, the first known discipline case involved a lay teacher at a school in Santa Fe. The teacher, Guadalupe Miranda, disciplined the son of a military officer (*caballero*) to such an extent that the teacher was forced to leave Santa Fe and return to the El Paso area (Jenkins 1977, 5–11). Pay, materials, and other kinds of support for education remained meager or nonexistent.

By 1832, when Bishop Zubiría made his journey through New Mexico, there were eight primary schools in the six communities of Albuquerque, Belen, San Miguel, Santa Cruz, Santa Fe, and Taos. Textbooks from Mexico or Spain were difficult to obtain, and the curriculum remained limited to basic reading, writing, and religious instruction. The arts and sciences were generally neglected, although some evidence of music education was reported from early sketches of school life. Father Martinez's school in Taos was one of the few to record significant achievements because the students had the benefit of basic primary textbooks written and printed by the enterprising priest. Figure 2 reflects sites of public schools in 1832.

In 1840, the census counted only eighteen teachers; these teachers and schools were established only in the larger communities. Rural areas appear not to have been served by an educational program; it appears that if the villas were having trouble supporting schools, the rural areas must have had no schools. Population, money, privilege, distance, and availability of teachers and materials were early problems that continue to plague education in New Mexico.

The Mexican Period provided another subtle impact on education in New Mexico. Historians have written that New Mexico's society was gradually being altered from a way of life

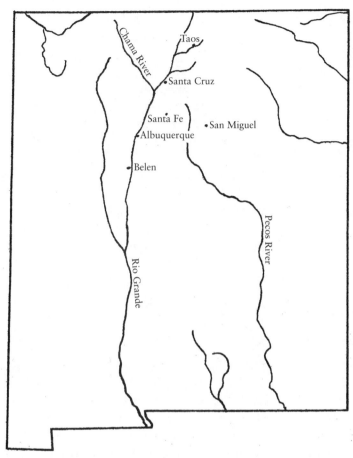

Figure 2. New Mexico public schools in 1832.

dominated by the Spanish to a new and robust Mexican domination. According to Jenkins, the presence of Spanish-born teachers, known as *gachupines*, was resented and barely tolerated in the schools (Jenkins 1977). Those Spanish teachers or priests who did not survive the rigors and pressures in the Northern Province made their way back to El Paso and points south. Other institutions of the territory were impacted by the Mexican Independence movement when Mexican-born government officials replaced those of Spanish descent. The quality of the language and the mastery of Spanish were compromised in the new regime (Gallegos 1992, 43–60).

Informal education no doubt presented significant value for the educational system in New Mexico. The Catholic Church with its ceremonies and feast days, oral histories, plays, puppet shows, a few books owned by families, some children sent to school in St. Louis and other points east—all these and more— offer meager, but significant, evidence that both formal and informal educational activity was ongoing.

Lack of commitment and resources, issues of governance, issues of support from the church and the diocese of Durango, and the psychological and physical distance from seats of power in Mexico diminished the success of the schools. Simmons, in his history of Spanish governance in New Mexico, challenges the notion that New Mexico was isolated from either Spain or Mexico during those periods. He argues that New Mexican authorities closely followed the changes in policy that occurred between 1810 and 1822, after the Treaty of Cordova (Spain ceded territory, including what is now New Mexico, to Mexico) and Mexican Independence. Other historians have written about New Mexico's isolation from the seats of government in Spain, Mexico, and the United States.

Church and Schools

The governments of both the Spanish and Mexican periods functioned as if it were the responsibility of the Catholic Church to advance education in the territory. During the Mexican period, this became, in effect, a philosophy that supported education. The Catholic Church was seen as the instrument for carrying out that mission of education, and this philosophy was to be a legacy for the rest of the nineteenth century. The issue of schooling, Catholic or secular, would continue to be a dominant one in the American territorial period.

The American Occupation (1846–1848)

America's Manifest Destiny cast its giant shadow over the New Mexico Territory in 1846 when an Army of the West was formed under the command of Stephen W. Kearney, who was to capture New Mexico and proceed to California. The Army of the West took possession of New Mexico on August 19, 1846. Brigadier General Kearney issued the Organic Laws and the Constitution for the government of the new American territory in what became known as the "Kearney Code." General Kearney's initial proclamations in the name of the United States of America stressed civil order and obedience. That bloodless conquest of New Mexico and the issuance of laws would bring about tumultuous changes in governance and commerce. New Mexico would undergo subtle, but dramatic, changes. However, what passed for schooling in New Mexico would not change in any significant way for at least another fifty years.

The American Territorial Period (1848–1912)

The military governance of the newly conquered territory did not view schools as a priority. A dynamic New Mexican Hispanic, Donaciano Vigil, Secretary of State in the new administration, gave voice to educational needs. His promotion of education for the general populace was a ray of light in an otherwise barren period of educational development (Stanley 1963). Perhaps it is too much to expect civility in the arts and educational enlightenment at a time when the mere survival of people and institutions was paramount.

THE LAND OF SHALAM

The territory of New Mexico after the American occupation in 1846 attracted not only the mainline Protestant missionary groups, Baptists, Methodists, Presbyterians, Lutherans, and others; seeing utopian possibilities in this western hinterland, a group known as the Shalamites settled in the Mesilla Valley (Las Cruces area). Communal settlers, the Shalamites were a quiet, independent, and self-sufficient community; they remained in existence until the turn of the century. They were also called Faithists and became the subject of ridicule in their waning years because of charges of fraud due to land deals that went "sour" (Priestly 1988).

Executive actions, governance, and legislative initiatives of the 1850s and the 1860s offered some promise for the establishment and financial support of schools, but these efforts fell short of establishing a stable school system. Several of the major themes impacting public education in New Mexico were born in the

fledgling years of the American territorial period, while some
themes transcended the Spanish and Mexican periods of governance and continued into the American territorial period, even
into the twenty-first century. The meager support of schools from
a fiscal point of view is clearly one of those themes. The language
issue, the hovering presence of federalism, the role of Hispanics
in politics, the role of religion, and the influence of religion on
schools are other themes, some of which were carried over from
earlier periods. Poverty, distance, and negligence were evidenced;
the provision for monies for schools was anemic in the 1850s
and the 1860s. That trend continued for the first fifty years under
the American flag. Educational institutions fared no better financially than they had under the Spanish and Mexican banners.

The Saints and the School

New Mexico was genuinely fortunate that the Catholic Church,
from the Spanish period through the Mexican period, had established schools. The concept of schooling as established in the mission schools traveled up the Camino Real from Mexico, conceived
and attempted in early New Mexico by the pioneer priests of the
Franciscan Order of the Catholic Church. Pedro Bautista de
Pino's dream of a school seminary was a seed planted as early as
1810; the Treaty of Cordova and the First Mexican Constitution
helped to reinforce the notion of schooling in the Territory.

DOÑA BLONDIE AND THE DEIST

Territorial New Mexico witnessed an interesting mix of
religious and philosophical developments. Not the typical story was the one about a certain Old Town
Albuquerque-Atrisco family whose matriarch, Doña
Güera (Blondie) and her husband, as rich as rich can be,
befriended a certain Mr. Jesus Martinez. This man
named Jesus, ironically, was a Deist. Deism (believing in
a supreme power or creator, but not a personal God)
had its followers in the territory. These religious or
philosophical stances were as much a part of the New
Mexico Territory as were concerns for survival and
land. These ideas had come up from Mexico and South
America via France, England, and other European
sources. Born of the French Revolution and transmitted

to the Americas that were also in ferment, Deism was but one of many ideas that were adopted by a few New Mexicans.

⟵

The American occupation was accompanied by an unanticipated change in the governance of the Catholic Church in New Mexico. Jurisdictional authority was changed from the Bishopric in Durango, Mexico, to Cincinnati, Ohio, and heralded the arrival of Bishop John Baptiste Lamy, a French Jesuit. The ensuing conflict between Lamy and the leaders of the Franciscan Order, primarily Father José Antonio Martinez of Taos, is epic in its historical significance. Horgan, Mares, and De Aragon, among others, have brilliantly written about Lamy and Martinez (Horgan 1975; Mares 1983; De Aragon 1978). Many consider Bishop Lamy the father of education in New Mexico because he not only espoused schooling, he was also a doer; he founded major Catholic schools, including Loretto Academy for Girls and St. Michael's College.

Lamy's opponent, Father Martinez, was an imposing figure, a teacher and a political and religious leader of great repute and accomplishment. He produced the first textbooks printed in New Mexico, established coeducational schools in Taos, and was an educational force in the territory of New Mexico. The end result of the clash between Martinez and Lamy "was the excommunication of Padre Martinez sometime between 1858 and 1860." The exact date is unknown because, as Father Angélico Chávez (Chávez 1954) has pointed out, Bishop Lamy "left no official record of the excommunication." According to Ray de Aragon, excommunication was "a pseudo affair" (Mares, et al. 1988, 143). Padre Martinez's excommunication from the Catholic Church was landmark religious politics; however, Father Martinez may be viewed as one of the leaders who helped make educational history in New Mexico.

The Men on Horseback

The vanguard of Americans coming to the New Mexico Territory after the initial American occupation included another set of religious pioneers. Protestant missionaries arrived in the territory of New Mexico in 1849. The stereotype of the missionary on horseback riding across the West best describes these pioneering preachers. The roll call suggests both religious zeal and a kind of denominational rivalry that makes for interesting stories. The Baptists were first; the Methodists a close second by a few months; and the Presbyterians were third, followed by the Congregationalists, the Episcopalians, and the Lutherans (Anderson 1907, 481–510). Other Protestant denominations made their presence felt later in the nineteenth century. These pioneer preachers were also teachers and, as they attempted to establish their first parishes or churches in the territory, they also opened schools. The Baptists under Reverends Hiram Read, John Milton Shaw, and Samuel Gorman opened a number of schools (Foote 1990, 23–24). Most of these schools were later closed because of lack of resources and because of opposition by local Catholic authorities. Nonetheless, both Catholic and Protestant efforts helped to establish a New Mexico school system.

⌐

The Dueling Clerics

Competition of a most civil nature occurred during the 1860s between Catholic and Protestant clergy. Harriett Bidwell Shaw, wife of Baptist missionary John Milton Shaw, recorded in her letters that well-known Father Truchard of the Tomé Catholic Church and John Shaw of the Socorro Baptist Mission engaged in a kind of "spiritual duel" where each one countered the other's arguments and positions on religion. Unique to the religious jousting of the two men was the fact that they posted arguments and responses on the church doors of their respective chapels (shades of Martin Luther and the 1500s theses nailed to the door of All Saints Church in Wittenberg).

⌐

Money and the Schools

The question of public versus private education and whether public funds would be used to support church-sponsored schools became an issue that would not be resolved in New Mexico until 1951, when it was resolved by the courts (Wiley 1965, 23–24). The struggle for tax-supported monies for schools would affect both Catholics and non-Catholics in the Territory. The growing strength of the so-called secularists who championed nonsectarian education was to be seen after 1873 (Atkins 1982, 344–51). In

1890, Congress appropriated monies to religious groups to operate schools. Political leaders of both Democratic and Republican persuasions were confronted with this burning issue. More prosaic topics such as the multitude of school districts, the role of educational leaders (county superintendents and others), and the nature of the school program were almost forgotten in the struggle for funding and position.

⟶

A Shotgun Wedding

Tom Wiley notes briefly in his classic study that schools along the railroad lines received some extra assistance from the railroad authorities. The coming of the railroad to New Mexico in the late 1880s was a boon to both schools and churches. In fact, a wag named Somoski refers to it as a shotgun wedding of churches, schools, and the railroad. Where a school was opened, a church followed; where a church was built, a school opened. The railroad lines came to be known as "Bible Tracks" and could just as well have been called "Little Red Schoolhouse Tracks." (Wiley 1965)

⟶

Rural and Urban Realities

Educational historian Tom Wiley wrote knowingly about the conflicts that have risen historically in New Mexico between rural and urban schools and school districts. Referred to in his book as an intramural conflict, the roots of this issue are to be found in the Spanish and Mexican as well as the territorial periods of New Mexico. The Spanish settlements had their version of urban centers in Santa Fe, Albuquerque, perhaps Santa Cruz de la Cañada, and others. Resources and authority for using those resources tended to flow to those centers. This was to remain true throughout the three cultural periods. It was the case even with private schools, which would have been established in the larger towns and villages. Attempting to cover all of the mission areas was one of the goals of the Catholic Church in early New Mexico history.

In more recent times, the rural/urban issue has been quite pronounced because of such issues as equity in funding and availability of resources for schools, for school buildings, and for a host of other needs. Issues of dominance by the larger school districts versus the smaller districts existed in school policymaking at the state level. The problem of urban overload (transportation, special education, crime, and other urban social problems) concerned larger districts; availability of personnel and other needs concerned smaller districts. These issues in education in New Mexico have roots in a multiplicity of historical causes, including that of statehood.

Statehood and Schools

The entire issue of education was caught up in the question of statehood. Among the obstacles to achieving statehood for the territory of New Mexico were objections and perceptions about New Mexico that revolved around ethnicity, religion, slavery, language, and the level of education. The Native American and Spanish-speaking population were suspicious of the American influence.

NM—BACKWARD?

Senator Arthur Beveridge of Indiana influenced a major statehood vote in the U.S. Congress because of a damaging congressional report he made on New Mexico's schools. The report was the result of Senator Beveridge's fact-finding mission to the New Mexico Territory. While visiting Socorro County, he spoke with the county superintendent who (in some format) declared with pride and sincerity that he did not know Christopher Columbus had died. Beveridge, already skeptical about New Mexico's statehood quest, used that incident as an example of New Mexico's "backward condition."

During the territorial period, New Mexico's people and its leaders made several attempts to achieve statehood. There were efforts in 1850, 1867, and during the 1870s; all were in vain. The citizens of New Mexico voted down a constitution that was developed in 1889.

Congressional objections and obstacles at the national level were strong and reflected a prejudice against New Mexico because of its large Native American and Hispanic population, the prominence of the Catholic Church, the different languages, and the slavery issue. The continuing questions of statehood and of funding for education in New Mexico were further complicated by strong ranching and mercantile interests opposed to property taxes for schools (or for any other public purpose). The "land barons" helped establish a pattern of meager or no support for school funding that was to carry over to statehood and into the rest of the twentieth century (Wiley 1965, 34–35). Countless other factors sidetracked statehood, among them the poor showing of educational systems in New Mexico at the time.

THE SANTA FE RING

There were significant opportunities which opened up in New Mexico after the Civil War. One situation involving land speculation resulted in the rise of a group of enterprising businessmen, large ranchers, and attorneys who came to be known as the "Santa Fe Ring." They influenced political parties, federal decisions, and educational matters. Wiley calls them "land barons" (Jenkins and Schroeder 1974, 73). Jane Atkins highlights the nature of this struggle as follows: "Land fraud and political corruption further impeded the achievements of peaceful civilian government and community development, and with them, the Common Schools" (Atkins 1982, 2).

A Few Heroes, Leaders, and Special Citizens

The struggle to establish a school system in New Mexico was not without its heroes. Donaciano Vigil was an early proponent of education in the 1850s and 1860s. Bishop Lamy, Father Martinez, and other Catholic clergy were also major contributors in attempting to provide education for the citizens of New Mexico. The first missionaries of the Protestant denominations should be credited for their work, and leaders like John and James Menaul, Thomas and Emily Harwood, and others who helped establish schools that continue even today deserve special mention. Political figures like Governors Edmund Ross and Bradford Prince, Hiram Hadley, William G. Ritch, and others provided distinctive leadership.

⌐

HUNTER LEWIS AND THE HORNY TOAD LINE

Reverend Hunter Lewis, first a Baptist preacher and
later an Episcopalian clergyman, was among those
very active missionaries who ministered to people
from Taos to Las Cruces. Hunter Lewis has been
described as an independent fellow with a ministry
that was at times eccentric, but always interesting.
Among his hobbies was that of riding the train from
one town to another, all the while knitting baby
clothes, sometimes interrupted by a visit to a local
saloon to preach the gospel. Hunter Lewis, and perhaps other early teachers, preachers, and priests, took
advantage of the coming of the railroad. They rode the
line from Albuquerque to El Paso, a line known for a
time as the "Horny Toad Line." The story goes that
there were so many horny toads on the tracks,
squashed to a point where the tracks were slick and
fast as could be, that the train could make it all the way
south without steam power . . . so said a storyteller
about the horny toad epidemic.

⌐

Amado Chaves, a prominent New Mexican and Catholic,
emerged as a special hero in the effort to build a strong school
system that was both public and secular and that would receive
financial support conducive to success. The modern era of a
strong school system for New Mexico began in 1895.

⌐

THE CROSS AND THE EAGLE

Legislative struggles and defeat of fair and supportive
educational bills were the rule in the 1870s. So active
was the presence of the Roman Catholic Church in
New Mexico and its schools that, in 1878, a celebrated Jesuit priest by the name of Gasparri (called a
Neapolitan adventurer by the attorney general of the
Territory) was able to influence the legislature to pass
an act incorporating the Jesuit Fathers or Society of
Jesus, of New Mexico, conferring upon them general

powers to establish educational institutions throughout the territory, as well as the right to own an
indefinite amount of property, all forever free from
taxation. Governor Sam Axtell vetoed the measure; it
was, in turn, passed over his veto, but subsequently
annulled by the U.S. Congress on February 4, 1879.
Thus the influence of the clergy in New Mexico col-
lided with the secular influence of the American Eagle
and the doctrine of separation of church and state.
This telescoped significant reform in New Mexico
education in 1891 and heralded the critical appointment of Amado Chaves as state superintendent and
the emergence of the public school system.

⤸

   Neglect of Native American children in New Mexico's schools
was not addressed; the needs of those children for education,
which had been first in the hearts and minds of the Franciscan
priests, were being essentially ignored as the nineteenth century
closed. It was left to the federal government to continue a chapter of educational service that many have challenged. This federal
shadow not only touched Native American children, it was a controlling factor in the New Mexico statehood effort. Federal oversight was felt in New Mexico's first constitution as a state in 1912.
   As New Mexico reached the statehood period, a great growth
in public schools began. The school population increased from
53,008 in 1901 to 68,400 in 1904, and to 100,045 in 1911. The
enrollment in public schools in 1901 was 31,500; ten years later,
it had almost doubled to 61,027. The average attendance more
than doubled (from 19,451 to 40,018); the number of teachers
increased from 713 to 1598. Total expenditures for schools
increased from $258,226 to $954,407. The average length of the
school term increased from 87 days to 125 days. The amount
spent for teachers' salaries increased from $174,000 to
$623,000, and the number of public schools increased from 599
to 1007 (Moyers 1941, 324).

Statehood Period(1912–)

The chronology of statehood attempts reveals a tortured journey from 1850 to 1910. Following the failed first effort to call a

constitutional convention in 1850, a second attempt occurred in
1872. The issue was clearly approved by vote of the citizenry;
however, Governor Marsh Giddings permitted the issue to die.
The U.S. Congress displayed very little interest in the New
Mexico statehood quest.

The history of the state constitution began immediately after
New Mexico became a territory of the United States. Statehood
efforts throughout the territorial period took place under military governorships, the first being under Colonel John Monroe.
Two main features of the first document produced by the
Constitutional Convention were declarations against slavery and
a strong statement regarding the value of education. The cen-
trality of education was a hallmark of the statehood fight for the
next sixty years.

The United States Congress was reluctant to admit New
Mexico to statehood because of a whole series of issues, such as
opposition to taxes, religious and racial prejudice against Spanish
and Native American citizens, big business interests, slavery factors, and others. Approval of New Mexico as a U.S. Territory
was one thing; admission to statehood was another. In 1906,
during the administration of President Theodore Roosevelt, an
attempt was made to admit New Mexico and Arizona as one
combined state called Arizona. Although approved by Congress,
signed by the President, and subsequently approved by the
people of New Mexico, the Arizona territory rejected it; and the
effort failed again. Statehood would remain an elusive goal for
the citizens of the territory until 1910.

During the 43rd U.S. Congress in 1910, Senator Stephen B.
Elkins of New Mexico introduced an enabling act, but the
requirement for a two-thirds majority in the vote by the House
of Representatives sounded the death knell for this bill. Governor
Bradford Prince of New Mexico Territory made another attempt,
but this undertaking was rejected.

Statehood and Control

An Enabling Act finally was approved and signed on June 20,
1910. This historic moment in the history of New Mexico was
the culmination of many efforts by a host of leaders beginning
with Donaciano Vigil in the 1850s, continuing with political
leaders and educators like Charles Hodgin, Amado Chaves,

Francisco Baca, and Governor Bradford Prince, and further enhanced by leading citizens like Charles Speiss of Las Vegas, a legislative leader. Their personal stories and sacrifices remain legends in this struggle for statehood.

In September 1910, President William Howard Taft called for an election for a state constitutional convention. The recommendation for statehood was approved; and despite some delays in the U.S. Congress, it was finally signed by the President. On August 21, 1911, New Mexico came into the Union as its 47th state. The constitution was officially adopted on January 21, 1911. New Mexicans celebrated statehood on January 6, 1912.

Battles have been waged over the years for amendments to the New Mexico State Constitution but, for the most part, the constitution has remained historically intact as approved on January 21, 1911. Strong measures of control reflecting the federal presence stand out in Article XII of the constitution, and the history of those controls has been captured most eloquently in the writings of Tom Wiley, pioneer educator. A significant democratic safeguard is the requirement that amendments to the New Mexico Constitution that have been approved by a majority vote of the state legislature must then be approved by the citizens. Given the tremendous efforts expended by the leaders and the people of New Mexico in achieving statehood, this democratic safeguard is understandable and important to the educational history of New Mexico. Figure 3 reflects the current eighty-nine school districts in the state of New Mexico.

Summary and Reflections

Public education in New Mexico since the sixteenth century has been influenced by poverty, isolation, language, religion, politics, leadership, privilege, and philosophy, and governance. The educational history of New Mexico must be read and understood through the prism of historical evolution. John Lewis Gaddis, an American historian, has written: "The past is something we can never have. We can only represent it" (2002). Representing New Mexico's educational history requires sensitivity to its rich and complex multicultural heritage.

Public education in New Mexico had its historical antecedents in the Spanish and Mexican periods, and in the precolonial period when a great Native American culture dominated the

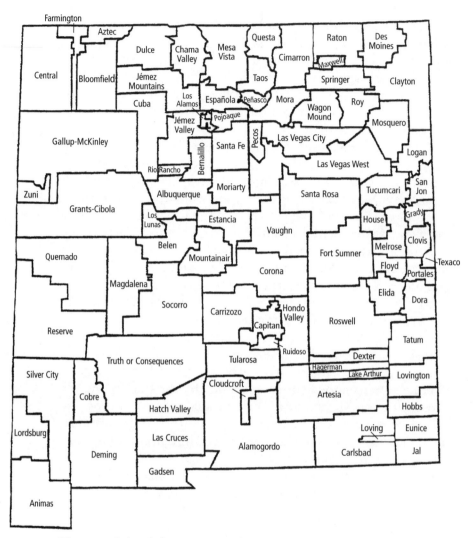

Figure 3. School district map of New Mexico. The New Mexico K-12 public school system is comprised of eighty-nine school districts.

landscape. Credit for the system we have must be shared by all of these cultural entities. The missteps as well as the progressive steps are a part of the history of the system. When compared to Europe's old world history, New Mexico's may pale by comparison. In terms of the New World, however, New Mexico's educational experiences stretch back over 400 years; this is, by far, a uniquely long educational history in the United States.

This educational history has been influenced by the landscape of towering mountains, desert vistas, and verdant valleys; New Mexico's schools, rural, urban, and in between, bear the markings of that landscape. This influence of geography has been reflected in myriad ways; historically, it impacted the earliest Native American and Spanish settlements, where homes, churches, and schools would dot the landscape. The first schools were built where the people found appropriate geographical resources for homes and survival, and demographics in the twenty-first century continue to provide evidence of that geographical influence.

Art and music have been influenced by native populations, both Native American and Hispanic. From an instructional point of view, the focus on fine arts and support for them in New Mexico (art and music at the K–12 and university levels) is a reminder of that influence. The attitude of appreciation for our cultures, our environment, and our history reflects this geographical influence.

Economically, the resources available to the educational sector represent those geographical features that either fuel and sustain or fail to support public education—bond issues, population growth and new schools, or population loss and closing of schools. The consolidation of schools and school districts from over 800 early in the twentieth century to the present eighty-nine is a stark reminder of New Mexican topography and its economic impact. The Native American roots, which were deep long before the arrival of the first Spanish conquistador, have been a treasure not always appreciated and understood, but they must become a more positive part of the educational scene in New Mexico.

Political forces of different persuasions have made their presence felt in promoting support of the public schools. At times, political acrimony has worked against the best interests of our schools; at other times, coalition elements of all political interests have forged important and positive educational legislation.

Historically, New Mexico's educational system has been impacted quite dramatically by religious institutions. Both the Catholic Church and the Protestant churches made their presence felt in the state against the historic backdrop of a Native American religious reality.

From the beginning of the colonial period, commercial interests have woven their threads into the educational and cultural

life of New Mexico. Modern times have only accentuated that
influence with a major scientific and technological presence blos-
soming in New Mexico in the twentieth century.

Albeit more nebulous, New Mexico's school history has been
framed by a kind of western culture, a frontier spirit at work. It
comes to mind as one thinks of the American territorial period
when fledgling schools, churches, and railroad tracks intersected.
The people who created and established those first schools
(Spanish, Mexican, or American) were pioneers.

Quite evident in the history of our schools has been the imposing, sometimes distant, sometimes hovering, presence of a
national "big brother." In the Spanish and Mexican periods, the
American territorial period, through the statehood battles, and
into the twenty-first century, that national presence has impacted
education in many ways. All of these historical forces have
influenced and created the public education system in New
Mexico, a system much in the mainstream of American education, yet original and unique.

As we struggle to record and capture key issues and events in
the history of education in New Mexico, there is something of a
risk of glorifying some aspects and inadvertently failing to honor
other elements. The challenge has been to record events as accu-
rately as possible and to separate (but share) opinion and edito-
rial comments from factual history. We hope that, from a
historical point of view, we offer up history that the learner can
use and that is instructive and, perhaps, even a bit memorable.
Again, John Lewis Gaddis writes: "Learning from the past lib-
erates the learner from . . . earlier constructions of the past"
(2002). The challenge in telling the New Mexico story has been
to make it feasible to appreciate our colorful and distinguished
history and to make it possible for the reader to study and assess
current school issues with a basic knowledge of that history. A
most intriguing challenge is to make that history come alive.

Chapter 1 Questions and Related Materials

Discuss the "concept of public education" in terms of the Spanish, Mexican, and American territorial periods.

For the public schools in New Mexico, what might be considered the most significant development of the American territorial period?

What would you consider to be some of the "unique" characteristics of the New Mexico educational system as that system developed from the early teachings of the elders through the statehood period?

Anderson, George (1907)
Atkins, Jane (1982)
Moyers, R. A. (1941)
Palm, Rufus A. (1930)
Read, Benjamin (1912)
Sanchez, George (1940)

CHAPTER 2

⟿

Governance of Public Education in New Mexico

There have been many changes in the roles of each of the governing elements of public education in New Mexico, but since the system was formalized in 1891, the intent has been, directly or indirectly, designed to provide a system that includes checks and balances and broad involvement and representation from the citizens of the state. The constitution has been amended several times in attempts to facilitate this involvement and to create efficient participation. One of the major premises of the governance system has been the philosophy that local boards of education, administrators, and citizens will have a voice in how individual districts provide educational programs for students.

The Role of Governance

Formal governance of K–12 public education in New Mexico evolved over the years into a pattern fairly typical of that of other states, involving both elected and appointed officials. The New Mexico State Constitution identifies the secretary of public education, appointed by the governor to the cabinet-level position, as the person primarily responsible for the operation of the public schools. Other agents or agencies such as the governor, the legislature, and the ten-member Public Education Commission have roles in the operation of schools. Each of these also has a role in financing and managing public schools.

The New Mexico State Board of Education was originally given the responsibility to oversee the operation of the schools in the state, leaving as much autonomy as possible to the local boards, citizens, administrators, and professional staff. Local boards of education were patterned after the Common School concept, which provided for a free and public education for all students. Power and authority were decentralized, providing opportunity for dialogue between the local communities and the state. Vehicles for this dialogue are facilitated by elected representatives at the local and state level. Community involvement at the local district level is crucial to the equitable implementation of policies developed at the state, federal, and local levels.

The initial formal governance system that was developed and implemented began during the U.S. territorial period using the Common School model. Major entities now involved in the governance of education include the governor's office, the legislature, the judicial system, the secretary of public education, the Public Education Commission, the local boards of education, the district superintendent, the principals of the schools and their instructional staffs, and local councils. There has also been a significant, but sometimes controversial, role of the federal government in the public schools of New Mexico.

Federal Role in Education in New Mexico

The state of New Mexico, like all states, has been the beneficiary of largesse from the executive, legislative, and judicial branches of the federal government. The relationship between the federal government and the state governments has been referred to by some as a love-hate relationship. Since education is not mentioned in the U.S. Constitution and the responsibilities for educating citizens belong to the individual states, the role of the federal government is complex and sometimes controversial.

However, the federal government has impacted the public education system in specific ways, such as compensatory education for disadvantaged students through Title I of the Elementary and Secondary Education Act (No Child Left Behind [NCLB] Act). The General Welfare Clause of the Constitution, when construed broadly, affects educational matters. There are other constitutional clauses affecting education, such as Article 1, Section 10, which prevents the states from enacting laws that impede the obligation of contracts, for example, collective bargaining in the schools. The First Amendment deals with freedom of religion, speech, and assembly. The Fourth Amendment deals with unreasonable searches and seizures and, even more directly, the Due Process and Equal Protection clauses of the Fourteenth Amendment have preoccupied school administrators for many years. Major elements of that federal role are to be found in the funds allocated and the regulatory powers that are applied in following the expenditure of those federal funds.

The President of the United States proposes, vetoes, or approves legislation. The President also appoints a cabinet-level secretary of education who is responsible for overseeing the educational budget and who oversees and regulates the education statutes that apply.

Equally powerful and active is the United States Congress that enacts the laws and appropriates the funds. The role of the federal government in following its financial allocations, its educational priorities, and its legal prerogatives is extensive and heavily researched and reported. (See Figure 4 for a brief look at the role of the federal government in the structural development of education in New Mexico.) Surprisingly, notwithstanding the awesome presence of the federal government in the educational theatre, the share of funding has never been very large. According to one report, the highest point was approximately 10 percent in the 1980s.

New Mexico's education system is, in reality, an intergovernmental system with very distinct powers at the federal, state, and local levels, and those responsibilities and influences are often changing. In addition to the executive and legislative roles, judicial decisions have had a role in shaping the design of governance of our schools.

In brief, Uncle Sam has been a demanding parental figure, absent at times, but a benevolent figure most of the time. It is unlikely that the twenty-first century will bring about a diminished role of the federal presence; instead, with the scientific and technological activities and interests that abound in New Mexico, the federal role will undoubtedly be enhanced.

The Governor and Public Education

The office of the governor has existed since the Spanish colonial period. One hundred thirty-six men have served in this office over the history of the state: sixty-one under Spanish colonial rule (1540–1821), sixteen during the Mexican period (1821–1846), six under American occupation (1846–1848), twenty-four during the U.S. territorial period (1848–1912), and twenty-nine since statehood (Salaz 1999).

Several governors in the territorial and statehood periods have been influential in New Mexico education, but Governor Bradford

I. Federal Land Grant Policies
   a. 1785, Land Ordinance
   b. 1787, Northwest Ordinance
   c. 1848, Oregon Territory becomes a state
   d. 1898, Ferguson Act
   e. 1912, Statehood

II. Impact of World Events
   a. World War I
      1. 1914, Smith-Lever Act
      2. 1917, Smith-Hughes Act
      3. 1917–on, Other Vocational Education Acts
      4. 1968–on, Modernization of Vocational Educational Acts
   b. World War II
      1. 1941, Lanham Act, Aid to Federally Impacted Areas
      2. 1944, Servicemen's Readjustment Act
   c. SPUTNIK
      1. 1958, National Defense Education Act

III. War on Poverty
   a. 1963, Vocational Education
   b. 1965, Elementary and Secondary Education Act (and variations on the themes)
      1. Impact on State Departments of Education
      2. Impact on Parental Involvement
      3. Impact on School Boards, School Administrators, and School Teachers

IV. Other Federal Legislation
   a. 1934, Johnson O'Malley
   b. 1973, Indian Education Act
   c. 1935, School Lunch Program
   d. 1960s and 1970s, Americans with Disabilities Act, PL 94-142
   e. 1970s, Title VII, Bilingual Education

V. Recent Federal Initiatives
   a. The Reagan Revolution
   b. The Bush Proposals, America 2000
   c. The Clinton Initiatives
   d. Re-authorization of ESEA 2002

Figure 4. Role of the Federal Government in the structural development of education in New Mexico. Compiled by Luciano R. Baca, PhD.

Prince is given credit for establishing a workable educational system in 1891. One of Governor Prince's major contributions was the appointment of Amado Chaves as the first territorial state superintendent of schools.

Article V of the New Mexico Constitution established the office of the governor with limited involvement in public education. (See Appendix 1 for an early summary of education-related articles.) The governor's office became significantly more involved in education in 1974 with Governor Bruce King's support for the state equalization guarantee funding formula for public schools. After 1986, control of public school funding came under the governor's office. Governor Jerry Apodaca became known as the "education governor" because of his strong support for education, and in the past twenty-five years, the governor has become a more involved player in the field of education. This changing involvement parallels the increase of state financial support for public education. (In New Mexico, about 97 percent of the K–12 operational budget, which includes federal and capital outlay resources, is derived from state resources; approximately 47 percent of the total New Mexico state budget goes for public school operations.)

The major role of the governor's office includes three areas: (1) proposing legislation, including funding levels, (2) appointing the secretary of public education to a cabinet-level position, and (3) approving or vetoing laws proposed by the legislature including those affecting education and specifically the budget.

Over the years, there were efforts to delegate to the governor the power to appoint the State Board of Education and the state superintendent of public instruction, in effect, giving budget and oversight of education in New Mexico to one individual, the governor. Citizens, through a constitutional amendment, revised this concept of budget control by the governor in 1986 when the budget office for public schools was moved to the State Board of Education and the state superintendent of public instruction, a response that indicated that citizens wanted more control of their educational system and would achieve this through their elected officials, the state board members, the legislature, and their local boards of education. In recent years (1994–2002), the governor has exercised the veto power to control education. In 2003, an amendment to the state constitution, approved by the citizens, changed the structure and role of the State Board of Education to a public education commission, which serves in an advisory role to the secretary of public education, who is appointed by and responsible to the governor.

↼

WHO'S IN CHARGE?

In matters of school governance, there are always tensions that arise between levels of government (local, state, and federal). Directing and controlling the budget-making process in New Mexico's schools has always been an arena for school gladiators. Early on, school auditors and later, school finance chiefs delighted in making their annual tour of all the school districts to review and approve budgets; with those visits inevitably came clashes between school personnel and finance chiefs. Educational historians will record that local school boards were often ignored or as Tom Wiley wrote "treated almost as though they were intruders at budget hearings for their school district." These school board members were representatives elected by the people in their districts.

↼

The New Mexico State Legislature

Article IV of the New Mexico Constitution provided for the establishment of the New Mexico State Legislature. The legislative body is composed of a senate and a house of representatives. There are seventy members of the house of representatives and forty-two members of the senate. Representatives must be at least twenty-one years old; senators must be at least twenty-five years old. All legislators must be citizens of the United States and must live in the districts they are elected to represent.

Before reapportionment in the 1960s, legislators represented counties; now they are elected from defined districts that have approximately equal population. Members of the house of representatives are elected to office for two-year terms, while the members of the senate are elected to four-year terms. Members of the legislature receive no compensation; they are paid per diem for the days the legislature is in session or for the time they attend committee sessions. They also receive the standard mileage rate as they travel to and from the legislative sessions and to the committee meetings established by the legislature.

The legislature convenes in regular sessions on the third Tuesday in January each year. In odd-numbered years, the legislature meets for sixty days; and, in even-numbered years, it meets for thirty days. The governor may call the legislature into special session to handle emergencies or to enable that body to finish work that could not be handled in the regular session. The only matters that may be considered in special session are those contained in the governor's proclamations and financial matters. The legislature may call itself into an extraordinary session if it determines the need great enough; this special session called by legislators must have a three-fifths majority in support in each house.

The speaker of the house of representatives conducts all the sessions of the house and appoints all committees, their chairs, and vice chairs. Other key leadership positions are the majority floor leader, the majority whip, the minority floor leader, and the minority whip. These positions ensure that interests of the respective parties are served. Senate leadership is exercised by committees rather than by a single officer. The lieutenant governor serves as the presiding officer of the senate and can vote only in case of a tie vote of the senate. The legislature is charged with passing all legislation that pertains to education, including the state budget, which includes funding for public education.

The legislature handles all proposed legislation through the committee process. The speaker of the house and the Committee on Committees appoints members to the committees during each session. This process ensures that all proposed legislation gets a fair hearing. There are several standing committees in each house, and there is a standing educational committee in each of the two houses. These standing committees work only during legislative sessions. There are interim committees that work on specific issues and projects between sessions; several permanent interim committees with professional staffs assist the legislature year round by compiling research, drafting bills, preparing fiscal and budget analyses, and doing educational research.

The Legislative Education Study Committee (LESC) is one of the permanent interim committees. This committee is made up of members from both houses. The chair is a member of the majority party and serves on the Senate or House Education

Committee. The LESC has additional legislators who serve in an advisory capacity and meets on a monthly basis between legislative sessions. The LESC is a critical committee for the state educational system. The executive director of this committee has a professional staff that assists the committee year round; that staff is a critical component of the committee's success as they work with budget analysis and research and provide overall direction and expertise. Major responsibilities include

    A. Following up on legislation passed at the regular session,
    B. Conducting research and study on memorials passed by the regular session,
    C. Hearing proposals from the secretary of public education,
    D. Hearing from other state agencies on educational issues,
    E. Drafting an educational budget for the total legislature, and
    F. Drafting education legislation.

The state budget is approved by the legislature and includes appropriations that will support the public school system. The percentage of the state budget that goes for public education varies from 46 percent to as high as 51 percent. (Sharon Ball, in her dissertation proposal *Equity at Risk: An Examination of the New Mexico Public School Funding System, 1974–2003*, presents figures on the percentage of state budget devoted to education; see Table 1.)

The legislature utilizes three types of legislation:

    1. A *bill* is used to propose laws. For a bill to become law, it must pass both houses and must be signed by the governor. A significant bill is the general appropriations bill that originates in the state house of representatives. This is the bill that approximates a budget to operate the state government and includes the budget for public schools.
    2. A *resolution* is a formal declaration of the legislature concerning some subject that it either cannot or does not wish to control by law.
    3. A *memorial* is an expression of legislative desire. It is usually addressed to another governmental body in the form of a petition or declaration of intent. A memorial involving areas of education will usually require research and

Table 1. New Mexico General Fund Appropriation
to Public Education

Fiscal Years 1988–1998

FY 1988	51.5%
FY 1989	50.8%
FY 1990	50.3%
FY 1991	49.0%
FY 1992	49.0%
FY 1993	47.8%
FY 1994	46.7%
FY 1995	46.5%
FY 1996	46.7%
FY 1997	45.6%
FY 1998	45.7%

From Sharon Smith Ball, *Equity at Risk: An Examination of the
New Mexico Public School Funding System, 1974–2003.*

will be addressed by the LESC or the secretary of public
education.

The legislature approves the budget for education, based on
the equalization funding formula. After this budget is incorporated into the state budget, the total budget is submitted to the
governor for approval.

The legislative role in education also includes proposing and
approving other laws that affect education. Laws passed by the
legislature must be approved by the governor. The legislature can
override the governor's veto by a two-thirds majority vote in each
of the two houses. The legislature appears to have been responsive to education over recent years and is sensitive to the educational needs of the local communities, evidenced by the large
proportion of the state budget dedicated to public education.

Legislative action has had tremendous influence on education; different political philosophies, ranging from conservative
to liberal, have impacted legislative action on educational
issues. Coalitions representing different points of view on educational issues have formed at different times. An example of
this is the case in the early 1970s when a group of democratic
legislators known as the "Mama Lucy's" (named after the

owner of the restaurant where the group would informally meet) created a majority to pass several pieces of legislation; among these was the original bill establishing kindergartens in the state of New Mexico.

~

"I'm Glad I Didn't Ask Him for His Credit Card!"

The power of one legislator was demonstrated most dramatically when the La Joya School District, sandwiched between the Belen and the Socorro School Districts, was placed under State Department of Education "receivership," so to speak. The district was "taken over" late Friday by state officials because of reported infractions and was placed under the authority of a neighboring superintendent. State Superintendent Tom Wiley's proxy, the district superintendent, asked for the La Joya keys, school car, and official documents. Over the weekend, the powerful La Joya superintendent, who was also an imposing figure as a state senator, regained leadership and control of the La Joya District. With a few calls to political allies as well as to other school districts, the La Joya superintendent flaunted his power over the state superintendent.

~

The Judicial Branch and Public Education

While the courts are not directly involved in directing or governing education, the judicial branch has affected the educational system through rulings in specific cases. Some of these cases have had great impact on the public school system in New Mexico.

Zeller v. Huff

Zeller v. Huff (1949–50) is the case that determined or had strong influence in removing Catholic nuns from teaching in the public schools. This case, known as the Dixon Case because it involved publicly funded schools in the town of Dixon, was filed and eventually appealed to the State Supreme Court, but it was never heard because the Archbishop removed the nuns from the public schools.

Serna v. Portales Municipal Schools

The Portales case (1965) involved a suit (*Serna v. Portales Municipal Schools*) filed in the city of Portales in which parents indicated that their children were not receiving an appropriate education because they were not being taught in their home language. The court ruled in favor of the parents, giving impetus to legislation soon thereafter that established bilingual education in the state.

Los Alamos v. Wugalter

Los Alamos v. Wugalter (1975) was filed by the Los Alamos school district. The district felt that money received from the federal government because of the presence in the school district of Los Alamos National Laboratory (located in New Mexico by the federal government and whose mission was to do research on nuclear weapons) should not be submitted in the Equalization Funding Formula. The court ruled that the district could keep all the federal money and would not be required to submit those monies to the state as part of the 95 percent local revenue for the Equalization Funding Formula. To this date, that federal money received because of the Los Alamos nuclear research activity is kept by the district above and beyond the amount received from the state under the State Equalization Funding Formula.

Association for Retarded Citizens v. State of New Mexico

In 1980, a coalition of organizations representing students with disabilities filed a suit against the state of New Mexico for discriminating against students with disabilities. The court ruled that the state must provide, under federal law, education in the least restrictive environment for students with disabilities. This ruling forced the state to accept federal money which it had refused in previous years; New Mexico was the last state to accept federal funding for this purpose.

Zuni, Gallup-McKinley, Grants-Cibola County School Districts v. State of New Mexico

The Zuni Case (2000) was filed by the Zuni, Gallup-McKinley, and Grants-Cibola County School Districts. The districts claimed that because a large portion of the property in the district was nontaxable tribal land, they were not able to bond the district and provide capital outlay funding for needed and adequate facilities. Other school districts later joined these three. The districts stipulated that since much of their property was tribal land which cannot be taxed for capital outlay school projects, the districts were not being treated equitably; and therefore the state was not providing an equal education for their students. The court ruled in favor of the school districts and allowed the legislature and the state to devise a plan to address these inequities. A task force was established to work on this issue, and legislation has been enacted to make this funding more equitable.

The State Board of Education

The first State Board of Education was established in 1863 by the territorial legislature. It was a first step towards a statewide system of public education. The same legislation established the office of the state superintendent of public instruction. The state superintendent was to be appointed by the governor; however, the position was under the direction of the State Board of Education. The members of the State Board of Education were the governor, the secretary of state, judges of the New Mexico Supreme Court, and the Catholic Bishop of New Mexico. The composition of the board gave the impression that the judicial and the executive branches of government were the foundation of the educational system; however, the influence of the Catholic Church was most evident. This system appears not to have been placed in operation and, in fact, had very little influence on the education of the youth of the territory.

In 1891, under the leadership of Governor Bradford Prince, the legislature established the State Board of Education again. Under this statute, the state board included the governor, the superintendent of public instruction, and the presidents of the University of New Mexico (UNM), the Agricultural College, and St. Michael's College. The superintendent was appointed by the governor (Wiley 1965, 33), and the board was given wide powers for both organization and control of public schools. This makeup and authority of the board continued until New Mexico became a state.

In 1912, when New Mexico became a state, the State Board of Education was included in Article XII, Section 6a of the constitution, which stated: "The State Board of Education shall control all public schools. It shall consist of the governor, the state superintendent of public instruction, and five other members appointed by the governor with the consent of the senate, including the head of a state institution of higher education, a county superintendent of schools, and another person actually engaged in educational work."

In 1958, a constitutional amendment was passed that required that ten state board members would be elected by judicial districts in the state. The governor and the state superintendent were to serve in an ex officio capacity.

In 1986, through another constitutional amendment, the number of state school board members was increased. There would be ten members elected by the people and five appointed by the governor for staggered four-year terms from five districts substantially equal in population. The five appointees would be qualified citizens of the state of New Mexico; no more than half would be of the same party; and they would be approved by the senate. This amendment transferred the responsibility of school budgeting and finance of schools from the Department of Finance to the office of the state superintendent in the State Board of Education. This was a major step in combining the program of education with the finance of schools as part of the authority and responsibility of the state board. Until this time, the governor's office controlled the budget of the schools and the state board controlled the programs of the schools. Stories abound in educational circles about state and local confrontations over rules and regulations and finances. Over the years, tension and controversy sometimes existed between the State Board of Education and the Department of Finance because of their different roles in the operation of schools.

The Auditor is Coming

In an earlier time, when budget auditors were the state's kingpins in enforcing and approving budgets and more, a classic tale is told about a school district in central New Mexico in which the budget chief was faced with two competing budgets involving school custodians—one from the School District Superintendent and one from the School Board President. The auditor asked for a recess to make a decision. When the meeting reconvened, the auditor announced the decision. He selected the School Board President's budget and list of custodians. His reason? Simple. The School Board President was also the head of the custodial department for the school district. His expertise overrode that of the Superintendent.

⤳

The New Mexico State Board of Education had, until 2003, the governing authority to establish policy and direction for the public schools in the state. The board had the power to publish and enforce policies and regulations under the Public School Code, the collection of state statutes compiled since 1923. This changed in 2003 when, by constitutional amendment, the State Board of Education became the Public Education Commission. The 2004 legislature determined functions and responsibilities of the Public Education Commission. New Mexico School Code 22-2-12 says that money budgeted by a school district shall be spent first to attain and maintain the requirements of a school district as prescribed by law and by standards and regulations established by the secretary of public education.

Duties of the New Mexico State Board of Education
Prior to the constitutional amendment passed in September 2003 establishing a position of the secretary of public education, the duties and authority of the State Board of Education encompassed all aspects of public education. The authority of the state board came from the constitution and legislative statute. Major duties of the state board included (1) law, policy, and regulation; (2) finance; (3) instruction; and (4) strategic planning.

Law, Policy, and Regulation
A. Enforces the School Code.
B. Establishes policy and direction for public schools and vocational education programs.
C. Establishes policy and direction for services for individuals with disabilities served by the Division of Vocational Rehabilitation.
D. Appoints the state superintendent of public instruction.
E. Licenses teachers and other instructional personnel.
F. Suspends and revokes the licenses of school personnel according to law.

G. Reports to the legislature on the consolidation of school districts.
H. Adopts regulations for administering public schools.
I. Requires periodic reports from public schools and attendance reports from private schools.
J. Authorizes and regulates adult education programs in schools.
K. Requires schools under board's jurisdiction that sponsor school programs to have insurance coverage for participating students.
L. Approves all accrediting agencies for public schools.
M. Manages and operates any public school or school district which fails to meet requirements of law or state board standards and regulations.
N. Approves rules regulating public school activities and reviews decisions made by governing boards or officials regulating public school activities.
O. Enforces requirements for home schools.

Finance

A. Controls, manages, and directs funding for public education.
B. Purchases and loans instructional materials for students.
C. Accepts and receives grants from the federal government and disburses the funds.
D. Accepts or rejects charitable gifts or requests.
E. Applies for and disburses special education funds.

Instruction

A. Designates courses of instruction to be taught in public schools.
B. Assesses and evaluates private schools seeking state accreditation.
C. Establishes and maintains regional centers to conduct cooperative educational services.
D. Assesses and evaluates for accreditation at least one-third of all public schools each year.
E. Provides technical assistance to local school boards.

Strategic Planning

The State Board of Education has developed a strategic issues plan for education in New Mexico which is used to implement the educational program for the state. The board uses this plan as they propose legislation, budget, and policy for the schools of the state. These strategic issues are all-encompassing and serve the board effectively. These issues include

A. Academic achievement;
B. Quality teachers, principals, administrators, and educational support personnel;
C. Accountability, choice, and technology;
D. Earning public trust;
E. Safe schools and respectful learning environment; and
F. Constructive engagement with our partners.

The board stated in its strategic plan "There are many excellent teachers, administrators and schools. However, there are inequities in the quality of education delivered to our students. Some students have not been provided with the education they need to meet increased demands of the twenty-first century. It is our goal to seek continuous improvement of our better schools and major improvements among those schools and districts that are not providing quality education that our children need and deserve" (New Mexico State Board of Education 1999).

The State Board of Education has included elected and appointed members over the years that represent the diverse population of the state. This diversity has been represented by different ethnic and gender groups of differing political persuasions from rural and urban sections of the state. These boards have represented varied beliefs about curriculum and program, including science, bilingual education, reading, political science, and extracurricular activities. Balance in belief systems and philosophy has been significant for the benefit of the diverse populations of the schools of the state.

The State Superintendent of Public Instruction

The position of superintendent of public instruction in New Mexico is first mentioned in the proposed Territorial Constitution of 1850. "The supervision of public instruction shall be vested in the state superintendent and such other officers as the legislature

may direct; the powers and duties of these officers shall be prescribed by law. The Secretary of State shall by virtue of his office
be the superintendent, for which he shall receive no extra compensation under any pretense whatever." The next formal mention and actual establishment of the position of state
superintendent of public instruction was in the legislative session
of 1863. The person to fill this position was to be appointed by
the governor to manage the public schools of the state.

Thereafter, there was little activity in the area of public
schools until 1891 when Governor Bradford Prince recommended to the legislature that an office of state superintendent
be created by appointment of the governor. The legislature
approved his recommendation, and Governor Prince appointed
Amado Chaves to be the first territorial superintendent of public
instruction. Another influential state superintendent, Hiram
Hadley, was appointed by Governor Otero in 1905.

The State Constitution adopted in 1912 stated "the board
shall appoint a qualified experienced educational administrator
to be known as the Superintendent of Public Instruction, who
shall, subject to the policies established by the board, direct the
operation of the state department of education" (New Mexico
Constitution 1911, 72). It is significant that even though the state
superintendent was appointed by the governor at first, and later
was elected, the position was to be under the direction of the
State Board of Education. Historically the governor appointed
the individual to the position; later, the individual was elected in
a partisan election. Appointment of the state superintendent by
the State Board of Education came through a 1958 constitutional
amendment. Together with this change in 1958 came the change
in the composition of the board. The board was now to be elected
from the ten judicial districts. In January 1959 the governor
appointed the first interim State Board of Education, which then
appointed the superintendent of public instruction. Dr. Tom
Wiley was the last elected state superintendent and the first superintendent appointed by the state board (Wiley 1965, 117).

The Secretary of Public Education
The constitutional amendment approved in 2003 provided for a
secretary of public education appointed by the governor; this
position will replace the position of superintendent of public
instruction. The secretary will select the staff of the Public

Education Department. The responsibility of the staff includes carrying out and implementing the policies as directed by the secretary of public education. These include regulatory as well as technical assistance to the eighty-nine school districts and the Division of Vocational Rehabilitation. A major responsibility is approving and overseeing the budgets of the eighty-nine school districts in the state. (The 2002 budget for the operation of the school districts was approximately $1.8 billion and represented about 48 percent of the total budget of the state. Figures for the 2003–2004 school year were approximately $1.9 billion.)

The secretary of education and the Public Education Department are charged with carrying out the State Accountability Plan. This includes the rating of schools based on five indicators: (1) student achievement, (2) attendance, (3) dropout rate, (4) school safety, and (5) parent and community involvement. Schools across the state are rated on a system using ratings of (1) exemplary, (2) meets standards, (3) needs improvement, and (4) probationary. (The Public Education Department does not evaluate Bureau of Indian Affairs [BIA] schools, which are federally funded schools.) Implementation of this rating system has caused many communities with schools rated "probationary" or "needs improvement" to seriously explore different ways to assist their schools and their students. The secretary of public education determines corrective actions to be taken by the schools given probationary or low performance ratings. The original accountability law was passed by the legislature in 1989 and was updated and enhanced in 1999. The mandate of the Elementary and Secondary Education Act has been incorporated into this system of accountability.

The secretary of public education will work with the legislature, the governor, and the 89 school districts. The secretary of public education is the school financial officer as well as the instructional leader for the public schools of the state; the position carries both prestige and responsibility. (See Appendix 2 for a list of appointed and elected chief school officials since 1891.)

Local School Boards of Education

Boards of education for each of the eighty-nine public school districts are created by legislative mandate. Local districts normally have five board members, but the local school board may, by resolution, increase the number of members to seven. This resolution must be voted upon and approved in a special election of the district.

The concept of local boards of education emerged when New Mexico was a territory. In 1855–1856, the first attempt at appointing a county board of education was made. This law was repealed the following year. In 1866, the law provided that the county probate judge was to act as county superintendent, and the justice of the peace in each precinct was to appoint the teachers. In 1884, the position of county superintendent was made an elected office, and provisions were made for election of school directors in each school district in the county. The district judge appointed the county board while the county superintendent ran on a partisan ticket in a countywide election. A municipal system evolved later, and the county system was eventually abolished. The present local board of education system evolved over the years from board members being appointed by district judges to a board elected by the citizens of the community.

Politics in the School?

Competing political forces are always present in local school districts. With personal agenda thrown in for good measure, a northern New Mexico school district experienced a clash of wills between the local school superintendent and the principal of a local junior high school. The issue was the reappointment or naming of the school staff and faculty for the coming year. The superintendent had his list; the school principal had his list. The local board of education, in a Solomon-like decision, hired half of the superintendent's nominees and half of the principal's recommendations. Criteria for teaching credentials or placement be damned; this was politics and some kind of local wisdom at work.

The powers and duties of the local school boards are many and varied; the local board is the policy-making body for each school district. The powers and duties of the local boards of education are stated in Section 22-5-4 of the New Mexico School Code 2001. The local boards shall have the following powers and duties:

A. Subject to the regulations of the state board, supervise and control all public schools within the school district and all property belonging to or in the possession of the school district.

B. Employ a superintendent of schools for the school district and fix salary.

C. Delegate administrative and supervisory functions of the school board to the superintendent of schools.

D. Subject to the provisions of the law, approve or disapprove the employment, termination, or discharge of all employees and certified school personnel of the school district upon a recommendation of employment, termination or discharge by the superintendent of schools; provided that any employment relationship shall continue until final decision of the board. Any employment, termination or discharge without prior recommendation of the superintendent is void (Item D was changed by the Educational Reform Act of 2003, HB 212; the superintendent of the school district now has this responsibility).

E. Apply to the state board for a waiver of certain provisions of the public school code in relation to the length of school day, staffing patterns, subject area, and the purchase of instructional materials for the purpose of implementing a collaborative improvement program for an individual school.

F. Fix the salaries of all employees and certified school personnel of the school district.

G. Contract, lease, purchase, and sell for the school district.

H. Acquire and dispose of property.

I. Have the capacity to sue and be sued.

J. Acquire property by eminent domain as pursuant to the procedures provided in the eminent domain code [42A-1-1 to 42A-1-23].

K. Issue general obligation bonds of the school district.

L. Prepare and maintain all property belonging to the school district.

M. For good cause and upon order of the court, subpoena witnesses and documents in connection with a hearing concerning any powers or duties of the local school boards.

N. Except for expenditures for salaries, contract for the

expenditure of money according to the provisions of the procurement code.

O. Adopt regulations pertaining to the administration of all powers or duties of the local school board.

P. Accept or reject any charitable gift, grant, devise or bequest; the particular gift, grant, devise, or bequest accepted shall be considered an asset of the school district or the public school to which it is given.

Q. Offer and, upon compliance with the conditions of such offer, pay rewards for information leading to the arrest and conviction or other appropriate disciplinary disposition by the courts or juvenile authorities of offenders in case of theft, defacement or destruction of school district property; all such rewards shall be paid from school district funds in accordance with regulations that shall be promulgated by the department of education.

The term of office for school board members is four years; the nonpartisan election is held in February. Officers of the board are the president, the vice president, and the secretary. The board usually appoints several committees. The local board of education has broad powers as provided by statutes and by the State Board of Education. Boards of education establish and adopt student codes of conduct; they also develop salary schedules for employees. A major responsibility is the adoption and approval of a budget for the school district. This budget is submitted to the secretary of public education for approval. The district budget must be closely related to the district Educational Plan for Student Success (EPSS) that, in reality, is the strategic plan of the district. A more recent responsibility is that of approving charter schools and overseeing their expenditures.

Local boards of education can be characterized as a diverse group of dedicated individuals. They represent their communities—rural, urban, conservative, or liberal. They are lawyers, farmers and ranchers, business owners, homemakers, educators, and interested citizens. The ethnic makeup of local boards of education is varied and generally representative of their communities; in recent years, the ethnic composition has changed to represent more closely the makeup of the general population of the district.

The District Superintendent of Schools

The local district superintendent of schools position originated as the county superintendent, who was the local probate judge under the supervision of the county boards of education known as the board of supervisors and directors (Atkins 1982, 330). Over time, the position has been known as the elected or appointed county superintendent, municipal superintendent, and district superintendent. The position has always been under the supervision of the local board of education.

Each of the 89 school districts in New Mexico has a school superintendent who is appointed by the respective boards of education. The state license regulation for a superintendent is the same as for all administrators. The licensure includes the following competencies and indicators:

A. *Ethical leadership*—The ethical school leader demonstrates the knowledge and ability to promote the success of the educational community by acting with integrity, fairness, and in an ethical manner.

B. *Visionary leadership*—The visionary leader promotes the success of all students, including students with disabilities and students who are culturally and linguistically diverse, by facilitating the development, articulation, implementation, and stewardship of learning that is shared and supported by the learning community.

C. *Instructional leadership*—The instructional leader promotes the success of all students, including students with disabilities and students who are culturally and linguistically diverse, by maintaining a positive school culture, ensuring a successful instructional program, applying best practices to student learning, and designing comprehensive professional growth plans for staff.

D. *Multicultural leadership*—The multicultural leader promotes the success of all students by addressing the needs of multicultural, multilingual diverse populations.

E. *Disability leadership*—The disability leader promotes the success of all students by addressing the needs of students with disabilities.

F. *Leadership in community relations*—The leader in community relations has the knowledge and ability to promote

the success of all students, including students with disabilities and students who are culturally and linguistically
diverse, by collaborating with families and other community members, responding to diverse community interests
and needs, and mobilizing community resources.

G. *Political leadership*—The political leader has the knowledge and ability to promote the success of all students,
including students with disabilities and students who
are culturally and linguistically diverse, through their
understanding of the political, economic, legal, and
social climate that exists in school settings.

H. *Legal and fiscal leadership*—The legal and fiscal leader
promotes the success of all students, including students
with disabilities and students who are culturally and
linguistically diverse, by managing the organization,
operations, and resources within a legally sound framework to promote a safe, efficient, and effective learning
environment.

I. *Personal and professional leadership*—The personal and
professional leader promotes the success of all students,
including students with disabilities and students who
are culturally and linguistically diverse, by maintaining
a process of continuous personal and professional
development.

Subject to provisions of the law, the district superintendent
employs, terminates, or discharges all employees of the school
district.

These competencies are used by the board of education as the
basis for evaluation of the district superintendent. The superintendent influences the entire community as that person works
with every school in the community. (The American Association
of School Administrators provides a list of major responsibilities
for school administrators, which parallels the responsibilities
designated in New Mexico. The AASA responsibilities identified
for school administrators are listed in Appendix 3.)

The district superintendent is the officer who ensures that an
effective instructional program is provided for the students of
the school district. The division of responsibilities between the
superintendent and the board of education is a delicate and controversial matter at times. Excellent communication between

the superintendent and the board of education is essential for successful operation of the schools in each district. (A profile of the eighty-nine district school superintendents in 2001 is shown in Table 2.)

The School Principal

The principal of each school is the administrator who implements all local school board policies, which are a compilation of state and federal policies, directives of the local board of education, and directives of the district superintendent. The principal in each school is under the supervision of the superintendent and is the administrator who ensures that each student is provided with the most appropriate instructional program. A significant step in assuring a quality instructional program includes hiring an effective teaching and support staff and providing appropriate and sufficient instructional materials to implement an effective instructional program.

Historically, the position of school principal in New Mexico follows the national development of the position, which originated as a teacher who was a master at teaching. Often, the position was a part-time one. As schools became larger and more complex, professional training for leadership in instruction and management was provided at colleges and universities. Many of the first principals in New Mexico were religious personnel rather than trained educational leaders. This changed as colleges of education developed educational administrative preparation programs.

There are approximately 730 principals in New Mexico. The majority of these are full-time positions, but there are some part-time administrators. Some principals fill the position in more than one school. The number of women and minorities selected as school principals has increased over the years, and those numbers continue to grow. Principals must have earned a master's degree in educational administration or other related fields and

Table 2. Profile of New Mexico School District Superintendents
2000–2001

	Anglo			Black			Hispanic			Nat. Am.			Asian			Other			
	F	M	Tot	F	M	Tot	F	M	Tot	F	M	Tot	F	M	Tot	F	M	Tot	Grand
Supers	16	44	60	0	1	1	6	21	27	0	0	0	0	1	1	0	0	0	89

must meet licensure requirements set by the secretary of public education. (A profile of principals in New Mexico in 2001 is shown in Table 3.)

The role of the principal is that of instructional leader and manager of the individual school. The competencies that a principal must exhibit are identical to those stated for a district superintendent. Major administrative competencies and processes for the school principal are often identified as (1) planning, (2) decision-making, (3) organizing, (4) coordinating, (5) communicating, (6) influencing, and (7) evaluating.

Other areas of the principal's responsibility include the school instructional program, pupils, staff, community relations, physical facilities, and overall management and budgeting for the school. New roles for principals have evolved as a result of school reform movements; budgeting expertise, involving teachers and parents in decision making, encouraging professional development, selecting and evaluating personnel, securing additional resources, creating a vision, fostering a culture of success, managing change, and performing as liaison between school community and school district are just some of the responsibilities of the principal.

The principal is the major force in the creation of an effective school, a complex process because the principal cannot do it alone. The principal must be able to involve teaching and support staff, the student body, parents, and the community in developing a vision and mission and in identifying goals for the school. The principal must utilize theoretical bases as well as theories developed from successful practice in leading the staff toward developing a sound instructional program that meets the needs of that particular school and community.

The principal must work with the central office, the board, and the community to find the resources to accomplish goals. The teacher is the one who is the powerful direct influence in the students' learning, but it is the responsibility of the principal to find and cultivate those teachers and provide the resources for

Table 3. Profile of New Mexico School Principals 2000–2001

	Anglo			Black			Hispanic			Nat. Am.			Asian			Other			
	F	M	Tot	F	M	Tot	F	M	Tot	F	M	Tot	F	M	Tot	F	M	Tot	Grand
Elementary	142	93	235	2	1	3	81	62	143	1	1	2	5	2	7	1	1	2	392
High	23	51	74	1	1	2	6	31	37	0	0	0	2	1	3	1	0	1	117
Middle	29	42	71	1	0	1	10	31	41	0	1	1	2	1	3	0	1	1	118

effective and efficient teaching and learning. This includes providing textbooks, supplies, furniture, comfortable classrooms, a safe environment, and professional development opportunities for each teacher and support staff member. The principal is the instructional leader, the manager of the school, and the facilitator of the vision.

An early characterization of the principal was of the imposing figure that came from the coaching ranks; this was especially true at the secondary level. Most new principals now come from the teaching ranks through the assistant principal position, in which they have developed knowledge, skills, style, and political wisdom.

Preparation programs for principals and other administrators are emphasizing and expanding both the managerial and the instructional role. A major component of preparation programs includes greater emphasis on site-based management. New Mexico's five major four-year public universities and two private universities continue to strengthen their administrator preparation programs. The foundation of the university programs is based on the New Mexico competencies for educational administrators. Those competencies are reviewed and revised periodically by university faculty and practitioners through the Professional Standards Commission and the secretary of public education.

There was a time when the principal was not necessarily a strong part of the administrative hierarchy of the school district. With increasing emphasis on accountability, the role of the local school principal as the leader who can rally the faculty and the community to improve the achievement level of students as measured by accountability and other processes has changed.

A major issue that must be addressed is professional development programs for school administrators. The Public Education Department requires a professional development plan from every school district, usually addressing programs for teachers rather than for principals; however, that department requires forty-five contact hours (clock hours) of professional development for administrators, with professional development loosely defined.

Principals have developed their own professional organizations and are affiliated with the New Mexico Coalition of School Administrators. Primary goals for individual organizations are devising professional development opportunities for principals and lobbying legislators and boards of education at the local and state level. Principals have also worked to develop programs for individual school improvement and have encouraged faculty and parent involvement in that process.

Local District Superintendents and School Level Administrators

Superintendents and principals have been increasingly challenged to become strong instructional and change leaders. The issues of curriculum change and reform are complex. Instructional changes may call for significant new approaches for using professional talent, for utilizing and allocating physical facilities, for altering physical spaces, for obtaining financial and other resources, for scheduling instructional time, for providing for evaluative machinery, and for reporting to school board officials, state officials, and communities. All these responsibilities depend upon the initiative displayed by administrators.

School administrators in New Mexico, as in other states, have found it imperative to be knowledgeable about new accountability measures required by the state. They must be knowledgeable about curriculum and instructional materials, even as they work with instructional specialists in the various disciplines; they must know the state-mandated standards; above all, they must know about children and young people and how they learn. In our state with its diverse student population, leaders must find qualified teachers and appropriate materials, as well as specialized resources and strategies to serve a diverse population. A quality school system requires professional in-service education, and administrators in New Mexico must discover and develop the best and most appropriate professional development opportunities.

The diversity administrators seek to address is fraught with promise, but accompanied by controversy. Issues in bilingual education, special education, and physical education and athletics confront all administrators in all school districts. Also requiring attention are curriculum issues in the social sciences; in our state rich with Native American, Hispanic, and other cultures, inclusion of this heritage in curriculum and planning becomes a significant responsibility. In a state with a strong scientific and technological culture, science curriculum issues must be addressed with vision.

School administrators and their work are enhanced by their professional organizations; district, state, and national organizations provide research, in-service education, technical, and other resources. Increasingly, other states and school districts with major concerns for diversity and excellence in education provide sources of direction and assistance. Basic to the success of school administrators is a commitment to involve the community and parents in the affairs of the school district and individual school. Ways must be found to give voice to the needs of children and young people so that administrative decisions are informed by the knowledge of learners—who they are, what their culture and history reveal, and their potential, promise, and possibilities. Administrators must find ways to provide the best possible education for their students and schools.

In providing the best education possible, and preserving and highlighting the natural ingredients of our New Mexico curriculum (historical, social, religious, economic, and geographic), administrators must contend with national and external influences. A home-grown curriculum which reflects our state's bountiful and diverse culture has been compromised by wars of conquest, by the manifest destiny of the American system, by national and international events, by world wars, economic depressions, and scientific discoveries and accomplishments. To some extent, these events have dwarfed local and state developments in education. However, they have also enriched New Mexico school curricula and made it even possible to retain and sustain much of our local cultural wealth. That struggle to balance external and local demands, needs, and desires is a special and challenging responsibility for school administrators at all levels.

Local Councils

Local councils for individual schools are required by New Mexico House Bill (NM HB) 212, passed and signed into law in 2003. This legislation requires that each school have an elected school council composed of parents and teachers. The purpose of the school council will be to assist in the management and operation of the school, its instructional program, and the budget. These groups assist the school in the development and monitoring of the Educational Plan for Student Success, which every school in New Mexico is required to develop. This concept of site-based management has given increased impetus to the charter school movement. Some school administrators and school districts have been utilizing the concept of a local council for many years. One example is in the provision for such a council in the Albuquerque Public Schools contract with teachers.

⟶

THE HOUSE OF MANY FATHERS?

Issues of school governance and school finance are rightfully considered professional technical concerns, notwithstanding the fact that they are concerns which also legitimately must be considered in a public or political context. Thus it has always been a question of determining the source of ideas, plans, and programs which purport to change or impact the governing or financing of education. Dr. George I. Sanchez of UNM, as early as 1932, cautioned that there are "non-professional individuals and organizations to the end that we are now burdened with many illegitimate educational babies fathered by political or economic vested interests." Dr. Sanchez would be astounded to see the welter of interests making their presence felt in New Mexican education today. Educational decision making, whether dealing with governance, finance, curriculum, or what-have-you could be easily described as "the house of many fathers."

⟵

Summary and Reflections

Involvement of so many entities and personalities makes governance of education a complex process; the issue of governance has become contentious at times, and finding balance between state and local control is essential. The state has the legal responsibility for public schools; however, each local district is unique and must have a role in developing policy. A marvelous and wonderful genius of the American system of public schooling has been local control of public schools and utilizing national and state trends, laws, and funding opportunities as required and appropriate. It is essential that local boards elected by the people and the community be given enough autonomy to carry out their responsibilities. Parents must be given a voice through their elected representatives, as well as personally at the local school level. Parents and teachers must work closely for an effective education for students.

Teachers must be given opportunities to develop and implement programs for their students. It is our premise that the educational staff, most directly and formally in contact with students, must be involved in the governance of public schools, particularly in the area of curriculum. The state, responsible for the education of all the students, must be zealous about its role in the governance system. Constant vigilance is needed to ensure that quality education is provided for all students in the state.

Developing a balance of power between state governance and the local school district has been a long-standing objective. Both the state and the local district must keep the education of all students as their primary objective. Goals of equity, equality, excellence, and accountability must be primary.

This goal of balance of power will continue to be the focus as a new form of governance is proposed. The original purpose for creating a separate unit or agency to govern the schools was to enable an elected State Board of Education to be closer to the local communities and separate from the legislature or the office of the governor. This concept has been challenged, and an amendment to the constitution has changed the structure so that the governor appoints a secretary of public education, responsible to the governor, to manage the public school system. The amendment also calls for an elected, ten-member public education commission.

State legislators, other elected officials, educators, and citizens continue to search for the system that will be most beneficial for all students in New Mexico; education is kept in the forefront for community analysis. There is agreement that education is the key to quality of life and economic growth for the citizens of New Mexico. One key to a successful educational system is the qualified and talented classroom teacher, supported with appropriate resources, who will work with parents and students to achieve the highest levels of knowledge and skill. A creative and knowledgeable principal, supported by administrators, parents, community, and sound financial resources, provides direct contact with faculty, support staff, and administration to make schools in New Mexico fulfill the dream of an appropriate public education for every child.

Chapter 2 Questions and Related Materials

Describe the governance structure of the New Mexico educational system. What do you consider to be the most positive
features of the system? What would you consider in need of
improvement or change?

What does it mean when we say that New Mexico citizens
have reflected a passion for keeping governance of the public
schools "close to home"? How does the concept of "local control" of schools in New Mexico compare with the level of
local control in other parts of the country?

Involvement of teachers and administrators on the State Board
of Education, now the Public Education Commission, and in
the state legislature has been a fairly recent phenomenon in
New Mexico. Should this practice continue? Is there a
"conflict of interest"?

Discuss the relationship and import of the educational governance structure and the demand for "accountability" in New
Mexico public education.

Angel, Frank Jr. (1959)
Education Survey Board (1948)
Phillip Gonzales (2000)
Haines, Paul; Garcia, F. Chris; St. Clair, Gilbert (1994)
New Mexico Constitution (1912)

CHAPTER 3

Indian Education in New Mexico

P ublic education for all K–12 students in New Mexico is the responsibility of the state. This responsibility is mandated by the state constitution and by other statutes and includes the education of Native American students. The United States government shares responsibility for the education of these students based upon treaties with tribes entered into between 1778 and 1871. Native American students have the option of attending federally funded BIA schools, New Mexico public schools, or private schools.

During the 2001 school year, 32,011 Native American students were enrolled in twenty-four public school districts in New Mexico, and represented twenty-two independent tribes, four languages, and five dialects. The 32,011 students represented approximately 11 percent of the total state public school enrollment and 70 percent of the total Native American student enrollment. There were 11,278 students enrolled in federally funded BIA schools, and approximately 1,100 students were enrolled in private or mission schools. While many districts had few or no Native American students enrolled in their schools, Zuni Public Schools had the highest enrollment percentage of Native American students with 99.3 percent; Dulce Independent Schools had the second highest enrollment (89 percent); and Central Consolidated Schools (88 percent) had the third highest percentage. Gallup-McKinley County Schools (79.5 percent) had the next highest enrollment percentage of Native American students. (See Tables 4 and 5 for tribes and school districts with enrollment percentages of Native American students over 30 percent, and Figure 5 for Native American languages in New Mexico.)

For the school year 1999–2000, 1,854 Native American students graduated from public high schools compared with 7,554 Hispanic students, 7,910 Anglo students, 416 Black students, 206 Asian students, and 80 Other students. For this same school

Table 4. Pueblos and Reservations in New Mexico

Nineteen Present-day Pueblos:	Four Present-day Reservations:
Acoma	Jicarilla Apache
Cochiti	Mescalero Apache
Isleta	Navajo Nation
Jémez	Ute Mountain Utes
Laguna	
Nambé	
Picurís	
Pojoaque	
Sandia	
San Felipe	
San Ildefonso	
San Juan	
Santa Ana	
Santa Clara	
Santo Domingo	
Taos	
Tesuque	
Zia	
Zuni	

term, the dropout percentage rate was 5.81 percent (Native American), 7.76 percent (Hispanic), and 3.89 percent (Anglo), respectively. Academically, Native American students performed at a lower level than all other ethnic groups on state-mandated testing. (New Mexico Legislature 2001). Testing results are discussed later in this chapter.

History

The early history of Indian education in the state of New Mexico, the methods used by the federal government and the state to fulfill their responsibility to the students, and how students are presently taught in state and government schools includes a series of epic events which reflect conquest, religious education, language issues and instruction, culture clashes, formal and informal culturally irrelevant curriculum, revolt, renewal, neglect, some success, and some failure. The role of the federal government in the education of the Indian student population has been

Table 5. School Districts with 30 to 99 Percent Enrollment of
Native American Students (2001)

Zuni	99.3
Dulce	89.3
Central	88.3
Gallup-McKinley	79.5
Jémez Valley	60.1
Cuba	58.5
Magdalena	45.0
Bernalillo	42.9
Bloomfield	32.2

significant because it accepted responsibility through the different treaties. The diverse native culture of this unique student population is also part of this history.

Early History

The education of Indian students began, centuries ago, with tribal elders and parents teaching the younger members by example or by "storytelling." Young men were included in hunts and were taught how to fish, plant, and develop language skills while in the company of older male members of their community. Young women were taught cooking, planting, weaving, making pottery, and developing language skills in much the same way. The elders and parents also taught younger tribal members (male and female) about their religion and cultural beliefs. Among the Pueblos, the *estufa* (the kiva) was school, clubhouse, and even armory for the male youth. There, around the fireplace in the estufa, during the long evenings of winter the elders taught songs and prayers embodying traditions and myths, first of their clan, then of their tribe (Bandelier 1871, 19).

The Spanish Period

With the arrival of the Spaniards in the 1500s, young tribal members received their formal lessons from the Franciscan friars whose emphasis was on teaching the Catholic doctrine. Jorge Noriega says "The Spanish Jesuits, who had pioneered a system of some 30 mission schools in Paraguay and Uruguay from 1609 onward, termed 'Reductions'—an entirely appropriate description given their intended role in diminishing indigenous cultural

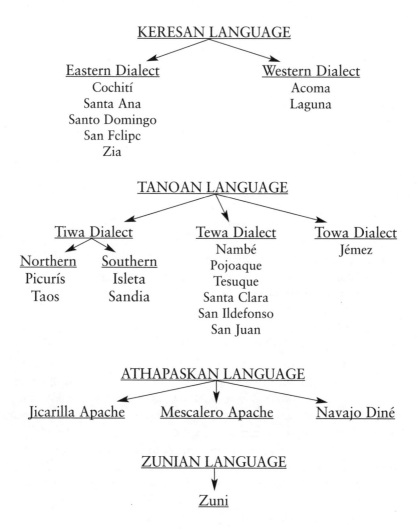

Figure 5. Native American languages in New Mexico.

integrity to the point of nonexistence—passed along the benefits of their experience to the . . . Franciscans who were quick to attempt to duplicate such feats in North America" (Noriega 1992, 371–72). Noriega quotes Evelyn C. Adams, author of *American Indian Education*, as saying "Success came early in New Mexico where tribes were found living in communities. The natives were taught to read, write, sing, and play musical instruments. Crafts and trades were also taught; and in these, many of the Indians were skillful and clever and became tailors, shoemakers, carpenters, and blacksmiths" (Noriega 1992, 372).

The Mexican Period

The education of Native Americans continued pretty much unchanged during the Mexican period, with the Catholic friars expending great effort in Christianizing the students. The friars sometimes served as advocates for the youth against unfavorable treatment by the government. In both the Spanish and Mexican periods, the friars addressed the formal education of the male population; female youth were educated by elders.

The U.S. Territorial Period

Little was accomplished for the education of Native American youth for the first twenty-five years of the territorial period. In the early 1770s, the U.S. government contracted with religious organizations, Catholic and Presbyterian, to provide schools in the tribal communities. These efforts were discontinued when rivalry developed between the Catholic Church and the Protestant groups. The religious denominations had established schools in all areas of the state, including all of the Pueblos and the Apache, Navajo, and Mescalero tribes.

From 1778 through 1871, U.S. government representatives entered into over 370 treaties with the indigenous tribes, nationwide. These treaties were intended to create trust and to establish responsibilities. Under the Northwest Ordinance (1789), property of Native Americans could not be taken away without consent; the U.S. officially pledged itself "to conduct its Indian affairs on the basis of utmost good faith"; this, for the federal government, included health, technical, agricultural, and educational services. When the nation's tribes across the continent entered into treaties with the U.S. government, those treaties included provisions for education of the Native American youth.

⤚

CORNPLANTER (SENECA LEADER) TO
THOMAS JEFFERSON

You, who are wise, must know that different Nations have different Conceptions of things, and you will therefore not take it amiss, if our ideas of this kind of Education [college proposed by the Continental Congress] happens not to be the same as yours. We have had some experience of it; Several of our young men

were formerly brought up at the Colleges of the
Northern Provinces; they were instructed in all your
Sciences; but, when they came back to us, they were bad
Runners, ignorant of every means of living in the
Woods, unable to bear either Cold or Hunger, knew nei-
ther how to build a Cabin, take a Deer, or kill an Enemy,
spoke our Language imperfectly, were neither fit for
Hunters, Warriors, nor Counsellors; they were totally
good for nothing. We are however not the less oblig'd
by your kind Offer, tho' we decline in accepting it; and
to show our grateful Sense of it, if the Gentlemen of
Virginia will send us a Dozen of their Sons, we will take
Care of their Education, instruct them in all we know,
and make Men of them. (Noriega 1992)

Treaties in all states and territories (including New Mexico)
mandated federal government boarding schools operated by the
BIA outside the reservations. One of the most famous of these
boarding schools was the Carlisle Indian School, founded in
1879 in Pennsylvania by Lieutenant Richard Henry Pratt.
Another school was the Haskell Institute in Kansas, which still
remains, but in different format from the original schools. By
1897, more than 14,000 American Indians were in boarding
schools (Bruchac 2003, 152). Pratt's primary goal was complete
assimilation: students wore standard uniforms; boys were
required to wear their hair cut short; students were given new
names; no traditional foods were allowed; and speaking in their
native language, even with each other, was totally forbidden.
"The institution of the school is one that was imposed and controlled by non-Indian society . . . its goal primarily aimed at
removing the child from his aboriginal culture and assimilating
him into the dominant white culture" (Noriega 1992, 371).
    Under the auspices of the Bureau of Indian Affairs, children
were taken from their homes and taught the "white man's" culture and ways. Native American parents did not agree with this
concept of schooling, but they could do very little about it. In
the BIA schools, conversion to Christianity was deemed essential. Football taught the value of winning; national holidays such
as Columbus Day, Thanksgiving, New Year's Day, and Memorial
Day were used to further indoctrinate Indian youth into the white

man's culture. Male students were taught farming and ranching techniques that they would apply to the farming techniques of their tribes. Young women learned about food preparation, weaving, music, childcare, household chores, and language.

⤝

COCHITI PUEBLO, FARMING, AND DAM!

Joe Suina relates a very recent event with the federal government's concept of farming in New Mexico. It was decided that farming could be improved by blading lands on the Cochiti Pueblo used for farming in a style similar to a Kansas flatland farm. Then the government offered seeds and tractors to do the farming. Only a few (two) took advantage of the offer for new-style farming. Other former farmers changed their work patterns. The land no longer allowed the farmers the lifestyle it had provided. (Suina 2003)

⤝

Ultimately, the concept of sending children away from home and family was deemed unsuccessful, in part because of displacement from the family. The ramifications of this practice have had negative effects upon generations of Native Americans. The Bureau of Indian Affairs found that children experienced alienation from family and community and increased stress as they attended boarding schools. This alienation continues in the parents of today's students. The BIA later changed this approach of schooling away from home and built many of its schools in Indian communities.

Recent History

There have been great changes in the education of Native American students since the early colonization period. Goals have gone from merely teaching the Christian doctrine to a Common School concept, and the transition has not always been a pleasant one. The education of Native American students in New Mexico went through a similar process as that suffered by the nation's Native American population: from imposed curriculum, to integration into the state public education system, along with the choice of attending BIA schools. As we look at the history of education in New Mexico, it appears that education of Native

American students has been one-sided, with very little consideration given to Indian culture. Acts of Congress and of the state legislature do not reflect an Indian philosophical orientation. Integration of the "American" way and of the Native American way has been generally nonexistent. It can be said that the educational development of Native American students by both federal government and state public schools was inadequate, inappropriate, and not a priority; it has not been successful for the majority of students.

〜

AN EARLY CASE OF SOCIAL CONSCIENCE

The story of Indian culture and education in New Mexico is enriched by the lives of some early Jewish merchants in the territory of New Mexico. Henry Tobias described one Nathan Bibo, who arrived in New Mexico in 1867, as a man with a social conscience. He cultivated and enjoyed a close relationship with the Indians. Apparently the Indians trusted and admired Bibo, and he served as an advocate for them with the army and with other government agencies. He was very much concerned with the deprivation and neglect he observed. Tobias writes: "For his part, Bibo did his best to teach and advise in any way he could" (Tobias 1990).

〜

Potential increases in enrollment in public schools were created by incentives from the federal government through programs such as the Johnson O'Malley Act, passed in 1934, which allocates limited public funds to schools districts with Native American student enrollment for textbooks, supplies, and other needs. Joe Suina, spokesperson for Native Americans, indicates that little actual increase in enrollment was accomplished with this effort until after World War II because so many Native Americans were involved in the war effort. In 1951, New Mexico began receiving increased federal funding to provide some support for public schools with Native American students enrolled. There is some indication that school authorities may have deliberately avoided receiving funds from legislation such as Johnson O'Malley in public schools. By 1966, 61 percent of the Native American children in New Mexico were attending New Mexico public schools. BIA schools were educating 32 percent, and the other students were in mission schools, schools operated by church-affiliated organizations (Smith 1968, 10). In the same year (1966), 2,300 Native American students between the ages of six and eighteen were not in school anywhere.

In 1975, the New Mexico legislature enacted legislation that created the Indian Education Division in the State Department of Education. There was no additional funding for this legislation because the legislative body felt the Indian Education Division could function within the State Department of Education's existing resources.

In 2002 the great majority of the Native American students in New Mexico (33,000+) attended state public schools. There were also thirty-eight BIA or contract schools (BIA schools operated by the local tribes) in the state, enrolling 10,624 students. The majority of BIA and contract schools are at the elementary level, with a large percentage of the enrollment at the kindergarten level. Examples of schools developed for a new generation of Native American students have been the Institute of American Indian Arts in Santa Fe, which encourages development of artistic talents, and the Southwestern Indian Polytechnic Institute in Albuquerque, which encourages science and technological studies.

Changes, Issues, and Themes

C. David Beers's *Practitioners' Views of Indian Education*, published in 1989 by the State Department of Education and the University of New Mexico, provides some discussion of Native American education and is a compilation of themes that affect the education of Native American students. These issues and themes summarize needs of students and, therefore, what educators need to address.

1. Native American students are culturally different.
2. Most educators do not have sufficient information or understanding about Indian cultures.
3. Teaching methods and daily routines do not match student skills, abilities, and learning patterns.
4. Some Native American students demonstrate low self-esteem within the walls of the classroom and have a high rate of absenteeism.

5. Native American students sometimes experience prejudice, and some educators have low expectations for their performances.
6. Native American teachers do not have enough input into educational matters, and there is not enough research on Native American education.

LANGUAGE AND LOVE

Educators, whenever they find themselves encountering a new and different culture, struggle to unlock the secrets of language and learning of that culture. Joseph Suina, pre-eminent spokesperson for Indian education in New Mexico, recounts a story of being torn between a grandmother's explanation of natural phenomena (thunder and lightning) and a fourth grade teacher who explained the same phenomena as he writes, ". . . simply by science. This conflict tore at me; caught between what was so obviously sensible and what let me touch the Spirits. My mind sided with the teacher; but I could feel my heart tear."

The New Mexico First (an organization of community groups, educators, and legislators addressing an issue) Town Hall on American Indians in New Mexico and their neighbors provided a list of recommendations for Indian education in New Mexico (New Mexico First 1998). Briefly they are

1. Quality education should be consistent regardless of the child's community or location of the school, with particular emphasis on improving American Indian student advisement.
2. Student competencies and understanding of cultural diversity shall be required as part of the State Board of Education Content Standards and local Educational Plans for Student Success.
3. The State Board of Education should be encouraged to adapt and approve curricula prepared by Indian educators that promote Indian history, culture, values, and perspectives as part of the overall educational process.

4. Indians and non-Indians concerned about the quality of education for Indian students must form a statewide coalition to address numerous issues revisited at this Town Hall and develop an implementation plan.
5. Teacher compensation, training, and recruiting should be consistent and improved for all New Mexico schools including a requirement of education for teachers in diversity and American Indian culture and history.
6. Tribal, educational, and all leaders should examine state funding for public schools and the factors taken into consideration to equalize funding for all schools serving American Indian students.
7. Support pending legislation and PL 874 (impact aid) funding that provide for direct support and augmentation of American Indian education.

These recommendations and other research assisted the State Department of Education in developing two bills for the 2002 legislative session.

One bill provided for alternative licensure for teachers of Native American language and culture (New Mexico Senate Bill [NM SB] 126, 2002). The legislature passed the licensure bill, and the governor signed it into law. NM SB 126, on licensure for Native American language and culture, provides for issuing a teaching license on language and culture to persons proficient in a native language and culture of a New Mexico tribe or Pueblo and who meet the established alternative criteria (a bachelor's degree is not required). The major purpose of this act was to provide school districts latitude in hiring Native American adults to teach students in their native language and culture. This bill became effective in 2002 and is considered a major step in improving education of Native American youth.

The other bill, The Indian Education Act, passed in a previous legislature in 2002 but was vetoed by the governor. That bill was later passed and became law in 2003. The Indian Education Act established a position of assistant secretary for Indian education in the Public Education Department and established a formal council composed of representatives of the twenty-two different tribes (nineteen Pueblos and the Apache, Mescalero, and Navajo tribes). It also directed teaching of the language and culture of Native American children. Gregory Cajete advocates developing a contemporary, culturally based, educational process founded upon tribal values, orientation, and principles, while simultaneously using the most appropriate concepts, technologies, and content of modern education (Cajete 1994, 12).

Legislation may be needed to require stronger professional development programs for all personnel working with Native American students. At present, the majority of teachers and administrators working with schools with high enrollments of Native American students are non-Indian educators. A specific educational challenge facing urban schools in particular is the enrollment of large numbers of Native American students and extremely limited numbers of Native American teachers or teachers with special training and skills in working effectively with these students.

Governance of Indian Education

Governance of Indian education is complex because it involves several entities at federal, state, local school district, and tribal levels.

The Federal Government

The federal government is involved with Indian education through the different treaties. In New Mexico, the federal government established the first schools specifically for Indian students through the Department of War and later through the Department of the Interior and the Bureau of Indian Affairs. BIA boarding schools and day schools were built on and off the reservations. The BIA school system continues for Indian students who choose to attend federal government schools. In 2002, almost 11,000 students participated in the thirty-eight BIA and contract schools; these are primarily students enrolled in the primary grades. The Santa Fe Indian School continues to be a boarding school which provides an appropriate education both academically and culturally for students from all over the United States.

The federal government also provides support for Indian students in the state public schools through separate legislation and funding for specific programs. With the federal funding go regulations to assure that the money provided to school districts is used appropriately. Specific federal laws and programs that provide supplemental funding to assist Native American students in the public schools include

1. *Johnson O'Malley Act* This program for services is designed to meet the specific and unique educational needs of eligible Indian students including programs supplemental to the regular public school program and school operations support, where such support is necessary to maintain established state educational standards (Code of Federal Regulations 1934).

2. *Title VII* This program covers services to all Indian students from all tribes enrolled in state public schools. These services can include teaching staff, home school liaisons, and clerks. This program provides for some take-home computers, Indian clubs, newsletters, and a Web site. The primary goal is to improve the academic achievement of Indian students.

3. *Title III* This impact aid program compensates public school districts impacted by enrolled students who reside on the reservations. This funding is in lieu of taxes not paid by the residents of the reservation. In New Mexico, part of this money had traditionally gone into the State Equalization Funding Formula. In 2002, a suit about the legality of diverting this money to the Equalization Funding Formula was filed, and the court ruled against the diversion. The state is in the process of correcting this through legislation.

Over the years, funding for Johnson O'Malley and Title VII programs has been seriously decreased, resulting in less support for Native American students who are enrolled in the public schools.

The federal government attempts to fulfill its commitment to Indian students as specified in treaties entered into with the different tribes. The impact of the latest revision (2002) of the Elementary and Secondary Education Act (No Child Left Behind) which requires disaggregating of district test scores by ethnicity, disability, and socioeconomic level is presently being assessed. Schools with large Native American student enrollments are especially hard hit because of the low achievement levels of those students as measured by norm-referenced tests. Plans are being made to address identified needs such as native language teachers and multicultural education that must be provided by state and local school districts. One proposal is to provide students the opportunity to transfer to higher achieving schools.

The State Government

The state has responsibility for the education of all Native American students enrolled in New Mexico public schools. In 1975, the state legislature enacted NM HB 8, which created the Indian Education Division within the State Department of Education. The purpose of this division is to provide direct assistance to local tribes and school districts so that special needs of Native American children enrolled in New Mexico public schools will be adequately addressed. Prior to 1975, the Indian Education Division was supported solely with federal Johnson O'Malley funds. However, the state legislature provided funds to establish a seven-member advisory council on Indian education under the 2003 Indian Education Act. An appointed representative council with a member from each of the twenty-two indigenous tribes in the state was created. One member is appointed who represents the urban Indian population. One of the main purposes of the advisory council is to promote quality education for Native American students (Status Report on Indian Education, 1998–99, New Mexico State Department of Education).

The legislature also passed NM House Memorial 43 in 1999, which directed the State Department of Education to survey the needs of public school districts with high percentages of Indian student enrollment. The findings included a recommendation that a close relationship between tribes and the Public Education Department be established. The secretary of public education is to provide increased financial support to public schools for the teaching of Indian traditions and culture. Continuing efforts for programs, classes, and conversations must be supported in the areas of cultural sensitivity and cultural and global issues so that teachers, administrators, and citizens learn to respect and appreciate the uniqueness of the Native American culture and its influence on our own society.

The State Board of Education (Prior to 2003)

The State Board of Education adopted a policy statement on Indian education on November 28, 1994, reaffirming its commitment to support quality educational opportunities for Native American students. The purpose of this policy is to emphasize systems reform to be implemented by local school districts. System reforms refer to government-to-government relationships with tribes and the involvement of parents and communities in developing partnerships with school districts. Another of its purposes is to promote a shared responsibility and partnership with tribal entities and Native American parents with a goal of attaining quality education for students (New Mexico State Department of Education 1994).

Local Boards of Education

Local boards of education are responsible for the education of all Native American students enrolled in the public school system. School districts receive regular funding from the State Equalization Funding Formula and also receive federal funding under specific laws. School districts must recognize the uniqueness of Native American students and provide for meeting their cultural needs (language, traditions, and beliefs) within the curriculum, across content areas, in teaching practices, and through the assessment system. Central Consolidated Schools and Bernalillo Public Schools have a limited number of teachers who are using some of the native languages in their teaching. The Indian Education Act passed in 2002 will help some districts provide personnel to teach language and culture through instruction from certified, qualified adults.

The Tribal Government

Tribal governments have had semiformal relationships with the local school boards in district schools attended by Native American students. Tribes unanimously endorsed the Indian Education Act of 2003. One of the provisions of the act would require that each local school district enter into a formal agreement with each tribe enrolling students in public schools. The act also establishes a formal advisory council within the Public Education Department. A more extensive Division of Indian Education staffed with an assistant secretary to work with Indian students and the tribes was established. (See Table 6 for schools and school districts with Native American student enrollments.) Federal and state governments and local boards of education are working together to provide a quality education for Indian students by utilizing these shared governance policies.

As an example of collective efforts, the Native American Student Success Conference, held in November 2002 and sponsored by the New Mexico Research and Study Council, brought

Table 6. New Mexico School Districts with Enrollment
of Native American Students*

District	Tribe	District	Tribe
Albuquerque	Isleta	Jémez Valley	Jémez
	Sandia		Zia
Aztec	Diné	Los Lunas	Isleta
Bernalillo	Sandia	Magdalena	Diné
	Santa Ana	Mesa Vista	San Juan
	San Felipe		
	Santo	Peñasco	Picurís
	Domingo	Pojoaque	Pojoaque
	Cochití		Nambé
Bloomfield	Diné		Tesuque
Central	Diné		San Ildefonso
Cuba	Diné	Rio Rancho	Zia
Dulce	Jicarilla		Santa Ana
	Apache	Ruidoso	Mescalero
Española	Santa Clara		Apache
	San Juan	Santa Fe	Tesuque
Farmington	Diné	Taos	Taos
Gallup-McKinley	Diné	Tularosa	Mescalero
Grants	Acoma		Apache
	Laguna	Zuni	Zuni
	Diné		
Jémez Mountain	Jicarilla		
	Apache		
	Diné		

*These arc New Mexico tribes near the school districts.
   Additionally, there are over 152 tribes throughout the United
   States represented in urban schools.

together educators, legislators, and Native American students and
citizens to discuss the education of Native American youth. During
this conference, a panel of high school students indicated that
encouragement from family, tribal leaders, and school personnel
has the greatest influence on their motivation to stay in school, be
successful, and include a college degree among their goals for the
future. In addition, high academic expectations and positive attitudes toward native cultures and language were listed as indicators
to improve student success and increase student self esteem.

Administrators and teachers were urged to understand the different learning needs of Native American students. Some of the students indicated that it would help them be more successful if administrators and teachers knew about their Native American culture and could treat them as their "own child," if schools employed more Native American administrators and teachers, and if others could recognize that the students want to make a difference.

The goal of achieving quality education also dictates that agencies act in a collective manner when addressing issues and themes that create obstacles to Native American student success.

Present Status of Native American Students

Based upon testing required by the state, the achievement level of Indian children is lower than achievement levels of other ethnic groups in public schools in New Mexico. The state tests students in grades three through nine and administers the New Mexico High School Competency Examination to all graduates. In the High School Competency tests administered in 2001–2002, Indian students lagged behind significantly, with the percentage of students passing in 2001 declining from 71.1 to 48.0 percent. (Some explanation for this extreme decrease may be explained by the change in the testing format.) New Mexico scores on the ACT (college entrance examination) reflected an average of 16.8 for Indian students compared with 20.1 for other students. These results may indicate that the test does not address student language and culture, not necessarily that student achievement is lower.

Results of the Spring 2001 New Mexico Assessment Program (for all New Mexico students and Indian students) California Test of Basic Skills (CTBS) Terra Nova reflected that significant differences existed between New Mexican Native American student percentile scores and all other student scores in grades three through nine in the areas of reading, language arts, and mathematics (see Table 7). In no grade or subject area did Indian students score at or above the 50th percentile (New Mexico State Department of Education 2002).

A review of the research on learning styles of Native American students and teaching styles of the schools may give some indication of the causes of these drastic differences. Tribal leaders, schools districts, and state agencies must work to address the

Table 7. Spring 2001 Achievement Data

	Grade	Reading	Lang. Arts	Mathematics
NM State	3	51.5	51.4	57.7
Indian Students	3	25.9	30.7	36.9
NM State	4	53.1	54.7	59.2
Indian Students	4	31.0	33.8	33.8
NM State	5	51.7	51.1	57.9
Indian Students	5	29.2	33.4	37.7
NM State	6	46.0	51.6	51.4
Indian Students	6	22.9	35.8	35.2
NM State	7	48.0	50.3	51.4
Indian Students	7	26.7	37.0	33.9
NM State	8	54.8	52.0	52.4
Indian Students	8	29.4	36.4	29.2
NM State	9	51.9	49.6	47.4
Indian Students	9	28.7	31.6	25.7

great differences indicated by the test results. The closer relationship required by the 2003 Indian Education Act will encourage and assist appropriate assessment and action.

Dropout data show that Indian students have the second highest dropout rate in New Mexico; Hispanic students have a dropout rate higher than all groups, with more students involved. Major reasons given by the students for dropping out (Kitchens and Velasquez 1998) were teachers' lack of understanding of their culture and lack of student incentives.

It is also interesting to note that of the eighty-three schools assessed by the New Mexico State Department of Education as "In Need of Improvement" in 2001, sixty-five of those schools had a Native American student enrollment of 74 percent of the total enrollment; of the fifteen schools identified as "Performance Warned," eight schools had Native American student enrollment of 53 percent or above (New Mexico State Department of Education 2002, 3).

Darva Chino, former Director of Indian Education, indicates that studies show that Indian students achieve at higher levels in public schools than they do in federal BIA schools, although they achieve at lower levels than other ethnic student groups. (Conversation with Darva Chino, former Director of Indian Education.)

New Mexico schools have become increasingly aware of the problems and issues in the education of Native American students. The Status Reports on Indian Education, published by the State Department of Education in 1999 and in 2001, prompted increased awareness and political willingness to address the academic gaps in the achievement levels of Native American students. A major issue is the lack of Native American teachers and administrators in public schools (see Tables 2 and 3, and Figure 6 for profiles of superintendents, principals, teachers and students). Another issue is that many non-Indian teachers and administrators are not culturally responsive. Another factor includes some of the tribal leaders' feelings about teaching their language in public schools. Some tribal leaders agree that language instruction is desirable; some do not. Recently, some Native American teachers have been attempting to teach students their native language with some success.

PARENTAL INVOLVEMENT/LANGUAGE ISSUE

Some years ago, a high school staff had a grand idea involving working with students from a nearby Pueblo in an advisory period to discuss common issues and to polish their native language. In very polite, but positive, terms, a group of parents representing the Pueblo told the school "You teach the students what they need to know to be successful in this world; we'll teach them our language."

Parental involvement in these areas allows schools to determine positive direction for the public schools. The Navajo Nation now has more trained and educated persons per capita than any reservation in North America (Noriega 1992, 249). Cajete proposes that Indian education be based on Indian philosophies, perspectives, and orientation, and that alternative

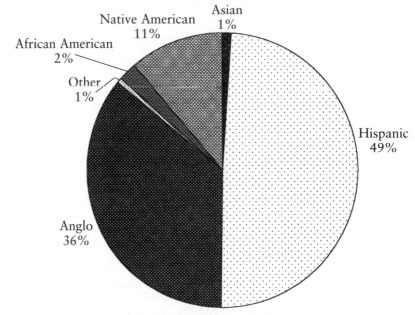

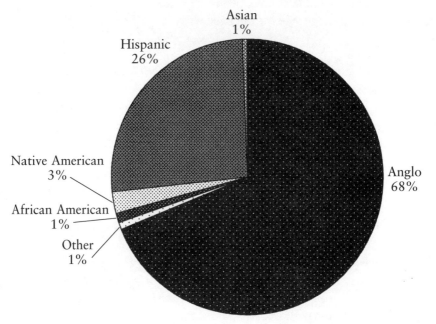

Figure 6. Students and teachers in New Mexico public schools by
ethnicity (from the NM State Department of Education).

education that directly and successfully addresses the requirements of the Indian population be explored. He also indicates that schools can integrate, synthesize, organize, and focus the accumulated materials from a wide range of disciplines about Indian culture and education. Integrating the connections to nature, family, community, and spiritual ecology helps to make learning a creative act. Cultural sensitivity for all educators is a major professional development effort that must be developed, implemented, and continued.

Me? Learn From My Students?

Joe Suina tells of a teacher who wanted to be sure her students understood that the Christmas season was more than glitter and shopping and presents. The class baked a cake, complete with a candle to illustrate that this was Christ's birthday. The issue? Who gets to blow out the candle? Two five-year-old students solved the problem by taking the cake to the open door and letting the breeze blow out the candle. No one had to pretend to be the birthday child. The teacher was quoted: "The culture of the children was held up to me like a mirror with which to check myself. I learned among other things that I didn't nearly have the faith and respect in the metaphysical that they and their community have. Although I always considered myself an environmentalist, my fundamental view was that you do something to the environment to affect it, to harm it, to protect it, or to harness it. I never thought of it as having inherent spiritual power, as these children did."

Summary and Reflections

Providing for the education of Native American students enrolled in state-funded public schools in New Mexico is the responsibility of the state through its constitution and statutes. The federal government, through the many treaties and laws signed over the years, shares responsibility for providing quality education for Indian students through Bureau of Indian Affairs schools, special funding, and regulations. Local districts carry out all federal, state, and local board policies to provide education to Native American students enrolled in district schools. Some funding is provided to the state public schools through federal funding and regulations. Many factors must be addressed, such as providing equitable access, increasing educational opportunities, improving and enhancing programs, closing the gap in student achievement, and preventing dropouts. Teachers and administrators must utilize cultural sensitivity and become competent in addressing diversity. Joseph Suina writes of the helplessness created in Native American students who are often left in a state of conflict because teachers, who start with good intentions, create confusion because they (the teachers) do not relate to the different cultures.

Textbooks, teaching, and teaching materials must be historically accurate and must reflect cultural awareness; supplementary materials must be developed and made available. Gregory Cajete's efforts to "represent a new, creative, and sophisticated effort to build intellectual bridges between two entirely different systems of knowing the world" provide a stimulating opportunity to learn.

In 1912 when New Mexico became a state, Native American students began to enroll in public schools; however, enrollment was slow because Bureau of Indian Affairs schools were available. In 1951 the New Mexico Department of Education began receiving increased funds for the education of Indian children; enrollment increased, and in 1975 a Division of Indian Education within the State Department of Education was established. Failure to adequately tap Native American leadership in developing educational programs and processes was, in hindsight, a major loss to education in New Mexico; this collaboration could have assisted in providing a better understanding of the Native American culture and improved instruction because of that interaction.

More recently, the state has worked to improve the quality of education provided Native American students and to ensure their academic success. The State Department of Education completed research on what was to become the Indian Education Act of 2003 passed by the New Mexico State Legislature. The achievement gap between Native American students and the rest of the student population that has been recognized and made public has hastened these positive steps. Darva Chino's cogent commentary that "We must not forget that Native Americans are the first Americans; we must now put their needs first" is compelling. The legislature, the secretary of public education, the Public Education Department, the Public Education Commission, and local administrators, teachers, and boards of education are working to develop a more collaborative relationship with Native Americans to provide the most successful opportunities for students. Tribal leaders have shown that they are ready to develop and continue more formal relationships.

Implementation of New Mexico's Indian Education Act continues with dedication of resources and development of preparation programs. Vision, effort, and more resources are being expended to stimulate and enhance the education process for Native American students. Gregory Cajete's research can stimulate the process of developing and integrating philosophical and cultural perspectives within the Common School curriculum.

This discussion has been designed to allow the reader to review some of the history and to encourage the reader to become involved in the development of educational programs appropriate for Native American students. There continue to be challenges, but recent efforts at the highest level of tribal and state governments bring hope for success.

"The battle for Indian children will be won in the classroom, not on the streets or on horses. The students of today are our warriors of tomorrow."
—Eddie Box, Southern Ute, 1958

Chapter 3 Questions and Related Materials

Discuss the policy of the Catholic Church in New Mexico regarding the education of the Native American population during the Spanish and the Mexican periods.

During the American territorial and the early statehood periods, what was the New Mexico education approach to Indian education?

How effective do you believe present-day New Mexico educational policies and programs have been for the education of Native American students?

Prepare a presentation on your beliefs about why Native American students are underachieving in our public schools, when their scores are compared with the achievement levels of Hispanic and other students. What does research reflect?

With other students in your class, research the role of the boarding school system of Indian education. Why did this concept not succeed? Were there successes and why?

Bandelier, Adolph (1871)
Beers, C. David (1989)
Cajete, Gregory (1994)
Kitchens, Richard (1998)
New Mexico First: American Indian Education (1998)
Sando, Joe (1971)
Smith, Anne (1968)
Status Report on Indian Education (1998–1999–2001)

CHAPTER 4

⟶

Education as a Profession

W hen asked about someone who impacted our lives, who inspired, encouraged, and worked with us, most people will immediately mention a parent and a teacher. The teacher who modeled care and commitment is recalled when there is talk about school careers. Some students may not have felt they were blessed with such memories; an implied part of the goal of professionalism must be to ensure that students have positive school experiences.

The study of teaching, teachers, and the educational profession reveals the tremendous impact of formal education on individual students and on society. It may appear that teachers bear the major responsibility for the education of young people because of frequent classroom contacts and because of the high visibility and expectations of the classroom and school experience. Perhaps this perception of teacher responsibility is created by the concept of formal instruction while the impact of others may be perceived as informal involvement. It is the responsibility of parents, administrators, business leaders, school board members, legislators, and other community members and leaders to support and provide resources for teachers as they go about the formal business of education.

In New Mexico, teaching as a profession grew from a desire to Christianize Native American students to a need to prepare students academically and socially to become part of an educated citizenry. As the numbers of schools, teachers, and formal teacher preparation programs grew in New Mexico, so grew the expectations of parents and community. From increasing numbers of teachers who recognized a need for sharing, for "political" influence, and for influence on their own profession came the development of a formalized and institutionalized professional structure. That growth is reflected as one reviews the state of education in New Mexico and the growth of the profession during each historical period.

83

History and Background

Early Native American Education

The inhabitants of the many Pueblos and villages of the Rio Grande Valley and in other parts of New Mexico had a system of teaching their youth which included modeling and instruction in survival and cultural areas such as hunting, constructing shelter, making weapons, and worshiping their deities. This teaching also included language skill development; language was transmitted in an oral and pictorial fashion. Parents and elders assumed the role of teachers of Native American children. Their methods included storytelling, practicing daily living, and learning to survive in their environments.

The Spanish Colonial Period (1540–1821)

The system of the family and the elders educating the youth was in place until the Spaniards came in the 1500s, with their major goals of conquest and religious conversion.

Early Spanish teaching efforts concentrated on the indigenous population. Colonists' families did their own tutoring and teaching of their children, and some families joined together to pay a teacher to teach the basics of reading and writing. Some families could afford to send their students to Mexico or to the United States for further education. Poverty, distance, privilege, and the lack of teaching other than by families or the elders were to be precursors of some of the issues that exist today. In 1721, public schools were to be established under the direction of the friars in the Pueblos and villages by decree of the king of Spain. The means to support these public schools were left to the individual communities; consequently, only a few schools were established.

The Mexican Territorial Period (1821–1846)

When Mexico gained independence from Spain, few schools had been established. One year later, in 1822, the Mexican government mandated that public schools be established; however, teachers and schools were to be financed by the individual parents in the different communities, with the method of pay varying by community. Because of the economics of different communities, the system was neither systematic nor adequate; poverty and privilege continued. By 1827, there were nineteen schools in the province (Nanninga 1942, 5).

The American Occupation and Territorial Period (1846–1912)

The Catholic Church, under the direction of Bishop Lamy, provided religious teachers to several schools including Loretto Academy, Saint Michael's College in Santa Fe, and other schools in Las Vegas, Mora, Las Cruces, and Bernalillo. Bishop Lamy began a primary school for boys, which was operated by Loretto Sisters he had brought to New Mexico (De Aragon 1978, 67). For many years, Catholic sisters and the friars were the only teachers available for the schools. Little is known about their qualifications as teachers except that they were religious and knew the English language. Their teaching preserved the religion, and students were learning the English language (which, in effect, was part of the plan for becoming a state.) The history of education in New Mexico and the Catholic Church have been connected since the early days of the Spanish colonial period.

Protestant churches provided many teachers to the educational system after New Mexico became a territory of the United States. Churches involved in the process included Presbyterian, Methodist, Congregationalist, Baptist, and others. The Presbyterian Church had a school and teachers in the Albuquerque area and in other communities, primarily in the northern part of the state. "Some missionary wives who were childless enjoyed distinguished careers as teachers, Emily Harwood, for example" (Foote 1990, 47).

GENTLEMEN'S AGREEMENT?

There almost appears to have been a gentlemen's agreement about churches and the schools. South of Albuquerque, there were no Spanish Presbyterian Churches; and north of Albuquerque, there were no Spanish Methodist Churches.

The impact of these schools and of these teachers has been great in the development of the state. Schools provided a degree of economic and physical stability for their communities, and they produced students who became educators, lawyers, scientists, and outstanding leaders in the civic life of their communities (Walker 1991).

FRONTIER SPIRIT

Harriet Bidwell Shaw, wife of Baptist Missionary
John Milton Shaw, was one of those exceptional missionary wives who taught in the various short-lived
primary schools that the Protestants opened from
1849 through the Civil War period. She is unique in
missionary history for several reasons. Her letters
home to New York and Vermont reveal a deep dis-
like for territorial New Mexico. She called it in one
of her letters "a wicked land." Nonetheless, she was
a courageous partner to her husband in missionary
work and gave birth to four children on the frontier,
from Ft. Defiance (AZ) to Socorro (NM). The most
startling aspect of this story is that she gave birth to
those four children with the use of a frontier medical
text, Dr. Gunn's Medical Book, and the services of a
midwife. Imagine, if only one copy of that book
could be found! By the way, one of Harriet's children
became Socorro County School Superintendent in
the 1880s.

The first attempt by the territorial government to establish a
public school system in the territory came in 1855. Laws were
very specific and included attendance laws, provision for teachers' salaries, and the establishment of a board of education in
each county. There appears to be nothing in the law about
professional preparation of teachers. These laws were in effect
that year but were repealed in 1856. Failure of the state to provide funding and perhaps leadership in some areas was to continue. The people of the state were against the concept of paying
for education.

The School Code of 1860 specified who could teach and
required that the teacher be able to read and write; this was the
beginning of a licensure procedure. Governor Bradford Prince
established a more formalized system for licensure in 1891,
with the support of the Territorial Education Association.

Go West, Young Man

Teacher recruitment has always been an important and kind of exciting part of the educational scene—new faces, new starts, new adventures, all that sort of thing. In the 1880s, Socorro County School Superintendent George Shaw advertised for teachers in the New York Times. The ad played up the colorful "West" as a place to go and begin a great adventure. Reports failed to show how many Easterners took up the challenge in Socorro County.

Growth of the teaching profession is evidenced by the increasing numbers of teachers: in 1898, there were 846 teachers; by 1901, there were 1,046; and, by 1910, there were 1,474 teachers.

Superintendent Qualifications?

Another major factor attributing to the growth of the educational system was Governor Prince's appointment of Amado Chaves as Territorial Superintendent. Mr. Chaves's qualifications for Territorial Superintendent? He was a Catholic; he was of Spanish descent; and the people trusted him. There were no legal licensure qualifications to be met. Mr. Chaves was a lawyer by profession; he had also served in the Union Army; and he had an abiding interest in education.

The Statehood Period (1912–)

Teachers took on a more prominent role as professionals after New Mexico became a state. With education a major component of the state constitution, professional organizations grew as teacher legal status improved and as interest in public education grew. The number of teachers increased, and their training improved. Numbers increased from 1,474 in 1910, to 4,379 in 1940, to the present 20,000 +. Salaries of teachers have increased from an average annual salary of $600 in 1918 to the present $34,000 average. Legislation passed in 2003 was designed to

increase those salaries. The number of days taught by public
school teachers has increased from 168 in 1921 to the present
180 days as there has been a gradual decrease in the agrarian
nature of the economy and a rise in the amount of revenue to
pay for more instructional days. The 180-day school year per-
sists today, perhaps because of lack of funding.

~

TEACHER QUALIFICATIONS?

An example of the improvement in the teaching profession comes from one of our New Mexico authors,
Fabiola Cabeza de Baca, who states "I had a normal
school education and that was more than few had in
the whole country. The school was governed by three
school directors, and one resented my appointment as
the teacher for his school; what my qualifications
might have been did not concern him since he has a
compadre" (Cabeza de Baca 1954).

~

Increasing numbers and increasing requirements for teacher
licensure created the need for organizations designed to enhance
the professionalism of teachers and to improve their working
conditions.

Professional Organizations

Professional organizations grew as groups of teachers and other
educators came together for a common purpose and advocated
for improved salaries and benefits for employees and for
improved education for students.

~

PROFESSIONALISM

Professionalism in the fledgling years of education in
New Mexico was marked by innovative and unique
creativity of both teachers and principals. One enterprising principal in Bernalillo County, before the
merging of county and municipal districts took place
in 1949, submitted annually and often a request for
desks for his county elementary school. To the surprise

of superiors, many years later it was discovered that very few desks were needed at this school; he had sent desks on to other elementary schools in nearby school districts. No hint of chicanery or fraud, just neighborliness or professional goodwill among fellow principals. This footnote to history was reported in the centennial celebration of that particular elementary school, and with pictures, to boot!

⟵

The two major national professional teachers' organizations in the country and in New Mexico are the National Education Association (NEA) and the American Federation of Teachers (AFT). Both of these organizations represent teachers at all levels: preschool, elementary, secondary, and college and university levels.

National Education Association

The National Education Association is the largest organization committed to advancing the cause of teachers involved in public education. NEA was founded in 1857 in Philadelphia and is headquartered in Washington. The organization has approximately two million members who work at every level from preschool to university graduate education level. NEA has an affiliate in every state and in over 13,000 communities across the United States. The organization and its affiliates lobby state boards of education, legislatures, and Congress at the national level and work for improved education for students, for higher achievement standards for students, and for improved working conditions for educators. A major initiative is to provide improved compensation and better working conditions for all certified personnel in the schools. The establishment of the NEA represented the beginning of the growth of the modern-day formal professional organizational structure that brings teachers and other certified personnel together for their personal common welfare and for the improvement of instruction and education.

The National Education Association–New Mexico (NEA-NM) began as the Territorial Education Association (TEA) in 1886, and the membership included teachers and administrators. NEA-NM now represents over 8,000 members. The TEA exerted leadership in creating the structure for the New Mexico public school system.

↩

Beginnings — TEA

The territorial legislature failed to pass a law establishing a public school system in 1876, 1878, and 1880. In the fall of 1886, Professor Ellis Whipple, Superintendent of the Santa Fe Indian School, joined Professor C. E. Hodgin and Principal F. E. Whitmore in calling for the creation of a professional organization. On November 26, 1886, a group of mostly Santa Fe educators met and drafted a resolution calling for a convention to establish the "Territorial Education Association" (TEA). On December 28, 1886, the first state convention was held in Las Vegas, New Mexico.

↩

At the first state convention, the TEA elected Professor R. W. Bryan of the Albuquerque Indian School as its first president. (After statehood, the Territorial Education Association became the New Mexico Education Association [NMEA] and is now NEA-New Mexico.) At this convention, TEA called for the establishment of the office of territorial superintendent of public education, a normal school to prepare teachers, and women's suffrage in school affairs on equal terms with men. In 1888, the legislature narrowly defeated a comprehensive school system bill. The bill was reintroduced in 1891, based upon strong recommendations from TEA, and passed. This bill created the office of the State Superintendent, the State Board of Education, normal schools, (specifically the University of New Mexico), and women's suffrage in New Mexico. The TEA continued its push to establish professional and educational standards, including the licensure of teachers and the adoption of a statewide curriculum with textbook selections.

In 1903, based upon strong recommendations of TEA, the legislature created two normal schools for teacher education in Las Vegas and Silver City. In 1904, TEA lobbied for a strong policy-making process and specifically called for removal of political elections for county superintendents, statewide standards for teacher training, licensure of teachers, increased funding for schools, and better pay for teachers (NEA-NM 1996). In 1909, the legislature established Northern New Mexico Normal

School in El Rito for the purpose of preparing Spanish-speaking teachers for the schools in the northern part of the state. Teachers and administrators were designing a system that remains the structure for today's schools.

~

CHALKBOARD POWER?

In a small elementary school in central New Mexico, a giant of a man sought to instill in his student charges the best of reading, writing, and arithmetic. His name? Adolfo (Tiny) Chavez, a man who went on to become a county superintendent and to make his presence felt in legislative and educational circles, including a tour of duty as president of the NMEA. Chavez was a force in the classroom as well, and his students, Elsie Adeline and Gloria B., were two of the most talented who went on to their own careers, including that of becoming homemakers. The significance of Tiny Chavez and these two very bright students was that from his family and their subsequent families came generations of teachers, several of whom are still in classrooms in New Mexico. That "dream" of service, of mission, of commitment to public service makes our profession so very special. Their legacy continues.

~

Until the 1960s, administrators were members of the NEA-NM. Historically, administrators, primarily superintendents, were elected as representatives or delegates to NMEA and dominated the policy making of the association. The 1960s saw the end of this domination as teachers began exercising their power by sheer numbers. A few administrators stayed on as life members of the association.

~

THE LAST OF THE SUPERS

Dr. Noah Turpen of Albuquerque Public Schools claimed to be the last superintendent to hold membership in the NMEA. The story goes that Dr. Turpen was a lifetime member of the NEA-NM, and he intended to fulfill that obligation. He believed with considerable passion that he was first and last a teacher, an educator, not only an administrator. Notwithstanding the separation of teachers and school administrators, many of the old-time superintendents felt as did Noah Turpen.

$\longleftarrow$

In recent years, NEA-NM has collaborated closely with the American Federation of Educational Employees. This conjoining of organizations may have happened because of the need to avoid "divide-and-conquer" entrapment; survival and success in achieving common goals and in placing pressure at the local and national levels depended upon mutual efforts. The groups have common goals, and they have the need to become a national force. NEA-NM, AFT, and other professional groups have impacted education in New Mexico; legislators and the State Board of Education call upon the expertise of professional organizations as education issues arise.

American Federation of Teachers

The national organization of the AFT was founded in 1916 in Washington and is a recent, but forceful, addition to the educational community in New Mexico. The organization was established with the basic philosophy of enhancing and protecting democracy in education, for protection of teachers' rights, and for political involvement of teachers in issues impacting education. In 1962, some teachers from Albuquerque contacted the AFT in Washington and asked for help in forming an AFT chapter in New Mexico. (They had been influenced by publicity in New York City, where future AFT President Albert Shanker had led a successful strike.) The New Mexico AFT was chartered in 1962 with three local unions: Albuquerque, Taos, and Los Lunas-Belen (interview with Elmer Jackson, former AFT official).

The AFT believed that teachers were being treated as second-class citizens and in an unprofessional manner by administrators and the boards of education. The AFT very clearly and deliberately associated itself with other labor worker groups such as the Teamsters and other labor unions. The AFT philosophy would emphasize and attempt to correct the low salaries of teachers, the working conditions, and the authoritarian practices of administrators (Holder 1969).

Some of the major goals of AFT in the 1960s included (1) establishment of a strong independent union of teachers; (2) substantial economic improvement for teachers; (3) great improvement of working conditions; (4) establishment of a grievance procedure; (5) academic freedom; and (6) freedom of teachers to participate in all aspects of community life, including social and political life (AFT 1963a). The basic goals and philosophy were based on those of the national organization. They included (1) collective bargaining for teachers; (2) passage of a "right-to-eat" guarantee, granting a duty-free lunch period of at least 45 minutes; (3) uniform salary schedule for all teachers, commencing with a base of $5,000 per year; (4) tenure based on a teacher internship program of a year's duration; (5) support for an increase in vocational and technical training; (6) and a sabbatical leave of nine months every seventh year, with half pay or a sabbatical leave every 14 years with full pay (AFT 1963b).

The Albuquerque Public Schools AFT Chapter adopted these goals and added a few which included (1) definite hours of work for teachers in a regular work day; (2) higher academic standards that would apply to all students; (3) promotion based on training, length of service, and competitive examination; (4) the right of all teachers to inspect their personnel records; (5) free required physical examinations; (6) tuition for required in-service training; (7) dues check off; (8) nine-week examination periods in high school; and (9) centralized ordering and cataloging of books (AFT 1963b).

One of the first major accomplishments of the state AFT was gaining the right of teachers to serve on the State Board of Education. In 1962, AFT publicly endorsed Jack Campbell for governor of New Mexico. Another issue AFT undertook was the goal of dividing school districts into board of education districts based upon population. The beginnings of AFT were not well received by school administrators and boards of education. However, their impact was significant in that the organization was forceful and provided action on issues such as supporting political candidates. A major accomplishment that took many years to achieve was passage of a collective bargaining law.

Collective Bargaining: NEA-NM, AFT

During the early years, there was strong opposition toward AFT by the NEA-NM; NEA-NM was assumed to be a professional organization, while AFT was considered a labor organization. The State Board of Education supported this perception. An examination of the history of the two organizations in New Mexico shows that NEA-NM adopted many of the strategies that AFT utilized, i.e., collective bargaining and exiting administrators from the teachers' organization. (Collective bargaining involves a group of employees bargaining with their employer, in this case, the board of education, for improved compensation and conditions of employment. This includes salaries, benefits, length of contract, and other conditions of employment. In the recent past, collective bargaining has included professional development and shared decision making.)

Collective What?

Professionalism has wended its way from the ragged edges to the twenty-first century human resources model. One of these ragged events took place in an urban school district when the superintendent summarily dismissed overnight (fired, that is) a school administrator whose behavior was suspect because of a possible sexual indiscretion. That same year, a teacher who was considered a master teacher was terminated for being too free with his slapping hand in disciplining students. These cases suggest that administrative action was quick and final before collective bargaining and human resources development were well established in New Mexico. Stories abound about the malefactors being ushered out of town before sun up!

The story of the beginnings of AFT in the Albuquerque Public Schools can be found in newspaper articles describing the confrontations between the AFT and the local board of education on many projects that AFT ultimately achieved.

Through board policy in 1970, the Albuquerque Public Schools recognized the local NEA-NM affiliate, the Albuquerque

Classroom Teachers Association (ACTA), as the first collective bargaining organization after a major crisis: the first and only teachers' strike in the history of New Mexico. The striking tactic is one that AFT favored; many would say AFT had influenced the work stoppage by ACTA.

⟶

TO STRIKE OR NOT TO STRIKE?

Meetings were attended in Albuquerque to discuss the possibility of a strike and to hear about the issues; much individual thought went into making such a decision because education of those students was uppermost in the minds of teachers. Being paid a better salary, having improved working conditions, and being involved in decisions that impacted those conditions were significant, too. In the end, most teachers did strike. Some could not, in all good conscience, walk out; they went to schools, as usual. It was depressing to find many more students at school than teachers for them. There continued to be so much respect among the faculties that, even though there might be disagreement on this issue, faculties quickly melded; professionalism and friendship remained strong.

⟶

In 1979 AFT challenged NEA-NM and ACTA in an election for the right to bargain collectively with the Albuquerque Public Schools Board of Education. The AFT won and has maintained that right ever since. Since 1979, there has been a statewide increase in the membership of AFT. Many of the organization's goals were accomplished through a negotiated agreement with the Albuquerque board. This pattern continued in other districts; in 2003, the AFT had negotiated agreements with approximately thirty of the eighty-nine school districts in New Mexico.

In the middle 1960s, the State Board of Education passed a resolution that was interpreted to mean that school districts were encouraged to enter into collective bargaining with their employees. This meant that the professional organization could bargain for compensation and benefits for teachers; administrators were not to be included in this process. This resolution precipitated the formation of an administrators' association. In 1992, the

Employee Bargaining Act was passed by the legislature with the
strong lobbying of NEA-NM and AFT. The act had a sunset
clause, which meant it had to be voted on again in 2001. The act
was allowed to sunset in 2001; this represented a setback for the
teaching profession since a majority of the school districts had
entered into or were in the process of entering into bargaining
agreements with their teachers and other employees.

NEA-NM and AFT have worked together in many efforts for
improvement of the teaching profession in the recent past. In
2002 the legislature voted for a new collective bargaining law,
but the governor vetoed it. Collective bargaining no longer
existed. A new collective bargaining law was passed and signed
in 2003. Both organizations, NEA-NM and AFT, lobbied collectively for passage of the law. Key persons in this effort have
been Paul Broome, Christine Trujillo, and Ellen Bernstein, AFT;
Charles Boyer, Eduardo Holguin, and Mary Lou Cameron,
NEA; and Mel Bernstein, Ramon Huerta, Elmer Jackson, Jim
Murdock, and Irwin Nolan, who have worked diligently for
teachers' rights through their leadership roles in the professional
organizations. In the recent past, the two unions have worked to
influence the legislature to pass a comprehensive education
reform bill which includes a three-tiered licensing process and
improved salaries (Education Reform Bill 2003).

There has been a national movement for the two organizations to merge, but both national organizations agreed to leave
this merger as an individual state issue. In New Mexico, there
has been greater cooperation between the two organizations.
One school district, Rio Rancho Public Schools, was the only district in 2003 in which both organizations worked together to represent the teachers and other certified staff.

A major step taken by AFT has been to include other educational employees such as teacher assistants, custodians, and bus
drivers in their membership. This has also brought the organization closer in concept to AFL-CIO labor organizations at the
state level.

A Tree Grows in New Mexico

The great influence that teachers and principals have
with children and young people has been voiced many,
many times for generations. Ralph Bunche of United

Nations fame gave a classic and majestic example of this when he credited his fourth grade teacher at Fourth Ward Elementary School in Albuquerque (now Lew Wallace Elementary) for having been the "telling influence" in his life. There are countless stories that swirl in our educational history, offering proof of this influence that teachers possess. M. Elise, a teacher in our live-wire metropolis, recalls that in elementary school, two teachers made her a lifelong learner, and secondary teachers nailed down her resolve to become a teacher. Her experience has not been without travail, but the seed of "teaching" was planted and continues to bloom, thanks to those long-ago mentors who made the art and the craft of teaching so exciting and promising. The state of New Mexico and the nation owe teachers like these a debt of gratitude and support for building even better schools for everyone. Education is the mother of all professions, and giving birth to more teachers for our schools is a signal responsibility for all New Mexicans.

School Administrators

Educational administrators from the K–12 public schools and universities and private schools influenced the development of the state public school system. The beginning of the Territorial Education Association involved several administrators, including leaders such as C. E. Hodgin, Ellis Whipple, and R. W. Bryan. Hiram Hadley, who became the state superintendent in 1905, was another administrator and leader of the TEA. There was a department for educational administrators within NEA-NM until the late 1960s, when teacher leaders recognized that administrators were absorbing leadership positions and were influencing the major decisions of the organization. NEA-NM members voted to limit membership in the organization to teachers and to exclude administrators.

The Keys to the Kingdom

The evolution of the superintendency in America is an interesting journey; the story of superintendents in

New Mexico is filled with fun and is quite instructive. The relations between the early boards of education and their chief executive officers remain to be told, but Phillip Gonzales, educational leader and superintendent of schools in various communities in New Mexico, recounts his exciting introduction to school power politics in Pecos, NM. As a new superintendent, he quickly realized the need for changing from wood fuel for heating the schools he supervised to coal fuel for economic reasons. Proceeding to make the change, he found out quickly what it meant to meet the "real power in the community." It turned out that the chairman of his local school board was the owner and distributor of the wood used by the schools; in brief, the chairman of the board had the wood concession. Mr. Gonzales, in his book, *Barefoot Boy from Pecos*, tells us about the superintendency in a real way (Gonzales 2000).

In the late 1960s, administrators started promoting the establishment of an umbrella professional organization for all administrators to include superintendents, principals, directors, and other administrators. In 1967 a committee under the leadership of Mr. Earl Nunn designed an organization for all administrators. Discussion and study continued between 1967 and 1971, when the New Mexico School Administrators Association (NMSAA) was actually established. The organization received a grant for $6,000 from the American Association of School Administrators (AASA), the parent group, to start the organization. A constitution was adopted by the superintendents' section of the NMSAA, and by-laws were developed, including principals, superintendents, business officials, directors, and administrators in the project.

Viva la Difference!

In 1968, an ad hoc task force of people in educational administrative positions met in Tucumcari to put together an "umbrella" organization format to present to the NMSAA. The document reports that, although the interests of teachers, administrators, and school board members are congruous in relationship to children, there are substantial differences concerning procedures, lines of responsibility, and matters related to the administrative and policy-making functions. The umbrella group desired to continue a professional relationship with the NMEA and the NEA. However, "present forces and trends in the profession placed this affiliation and relationship in peril."

⟶

Since 1971 when the NMSAA was established, the group has been actively involved in making recommendations to the legislature and to the State Board of Education. Of major importance has been the close working relationship that has developed between the organization and the state superintendent of instruction. The organization works closely on lobbying efforts with the New Mexico School Boards Association (NMSBA).

⟶

GREATNESS COMES IN SMALL PACKAGES

Tom Wiley wrote about the "power of urban school leaders." In fact, the laws of New Mexico in the early statehood period favored municipal school districts over rural districts. One of the giants among school superintendents of the time was a diminutive man named John Milne. He came to New Mexico in the early 1900s by way of Scotland. An extremely able educator with a flair for business, he dominated New Mexican school life for over forty years as a superintendent, educational lobbyist, and leading citizen. A small man in size, he possessed a long bony forefinger, which he used to great advantage in both debates and lectures. He was a watchdog over school funds and school lands and could be called "Mr. Prudential," so assiduously did he monitor school monies.

⟶

Membership in the NMSAA has increased significantly; dues for the administrator organizations are paid by the school districts. The membership now includes eighteen administrator organizations; prominent among those organizations are the

New Mexico School Superintendents Association (NMSSA), the New Mexico Association of Secondary School Principals (NMASSP), the New Mexico Association of Elementary School Principals (NMAESP), the New Mexico Association of School Business Officials (NMASBO), and others. Membership and active participation in New Mexico's administrators' educational associations have, at various times, waned. Each of the distinct organizations has its own mission and goals.

⌐

ALL FOR ONE?

The New Mexico Association of Elementary School Principals has been one of the most independent of the administrative groups, sometimes articulating positions not necessarily inimical to NMSAA, but attempting to establish and maintain a clear identity of its own. Veteran elementary school leaders have fostered this independent spirit because of their feeling of being ignored by the superintendents' organization. Generally, however, the subunits of NMSAA have meshed with each other to form a cohesive voice for school administrators and for taking positions on policy and legislation that coincide with those of the teachers' organizations and other interest groups to bring improvements to New Mexico education. A rotating chairmanship of the NMSAA that includes the member organizations, i.e., secondary and elementary, has proven effective in promoting a unified approach.

⌐

School and district level administrators have had to develop skills in collective bargaining and contract negotiation processes. One of the major issues administrators must address is the proper and adequate handling of formal grievances filed by employees.

Some of the most noteworthy issues supported by school administrators have been those dealing with school finance and changes to the funding formulas. Other administrative themes have involved accountability issues, the role and extent of testing, capital outlay legislation, and professional licensure requirements. Less visible, but equally vital, have been curricular or instructional changes proposed by the associations for state department level or legislative initiatives. Assessing positions held by administrators is sometimes difficult since administrators, like other educators and citizens, vary in their opinions of what constitutes an effective reform. However, administrators as well as teachers give voice to their first concern: the welfare and well being of children and youth. Whatever their affiliation, (Democrat, Republican, or other; rural or urban) administrators have brought their professionalism and their basic concern for the education of students to the forefront (Ball, et al. 2001).

RECENT HEROES IN EDUCATION IN NEW MEXICO

The history of education in New Mexico is filled with the names and efforts of many school administrators, schoolmasters, and other leaders. Among those heroes, we find names like Earl Nunn, Phillip Gonzales, Mildred Fitzpatrick, Cal Taulbee, Ed Gaussion, Placido Garcia Sr., Travis Stovall, Georgia Lusk, Tom Wiley, Jim Green, Clara Hummel, Harold Goff, Alan Morgan, Henry Pasqual, Leonard DeLayo, Sue Cleveland, Harry Wugalter, Mary Ann Binford, Jo Thomason, Susie Rayos Marmon, Jim Miller Sr., Jane Blumenfeld, Michael Davis, Joe Otero, John Milne, Glenn Ream, A. C. Woodburn, Barney Caton, Wesley Laine, Pat Murphy, Luciano Baca, Veronica Garcia, J. Placido Garcia Jr., and Lura Bennett, Charles Spain, Ed Marinsek, Fred Pomeroy, Jack Bobroff, Ralph Dixon, Robert Montoya, Frank Sanchez, Margaret Peggy Dike, and Chon LaBrier.

Historically, administrators have sought allies among other community organizations. In the '60s and '70s, administrative/community teams traveled to other urban communities in New Mexico, seeking support for an upcoming legislative session. Officials of local chambers of commerce and other business leaders often took the initiative in these efforts. The goal was to seek support for additional funding for urban problems not found in rural districts.

～

OVERLOAD?

One particular year, such an event focused on what urban legislators and superintendents called "urban overload." They were attempting to build a case for supporting urban schools, which faced special problems of transportation, juvenile delinquency, an influx of special needs or challenged children, crime, and other urban factors. Sometimes, rural and urban superintendents, as well as their respective principals and other administrator groups, have found themselves at odds over legislative proposals. This rivalry has a colorful history in the legendary clashes between Albuquerque's Superintendent John Milne and Raymond Huff of Clayton—not the original rural/urban clash, but one of the most notable. Noah Turpen, APS superintendent, squared off verbally with several legislators at the Robin Hood Inn in Albuquerque, defending the merits of urban school districts requesting special consideration for urban circumstances. No blows, but Noah was vindicated when the legislature responded to some of his arguments.

～

Professional Licensure Framework System

A significant issue ignored in the early years of education in New Mexico was a formal method for determining qualifications for teachers, administrators, and other personnel involved in the public schools. Teacher and administrator professional organizations have worked with the State Board of Education, the state superintendent, and the legislature to devise a system for formal licensure of all professional educators.

Any person teaching, counseling, providing special instructional services, or supervising an instructional program in a public school or state agency and any person administering a program in a public school must hold a valid license authorizing that person to perform that function. In 1981, the New Mexico State Board of Education adopted a requirement that students enrolled in university teacher preparation programs demonstrate adequate skills by passing a basic skills test. The State Board of Education also required that a written test of general knowledge, communication skills, and teaching practices (The National Teachers Examination) be passed by all applicants for teaching and administrative licensure. In 1983 and 1984, the state board adopted essential job competencies for principals and teachers and required that they be evaluated based on those required job competencies. A basic requirement is a baccalaureate degree from an accredited four-year institution of higher learning. New licensure requirements were passed by the 2003 Legislature and approved by the governor (New Mexico State Legislature 2003, 64–77).

There Have Always Been "Superstars"

Notwithstanding the brickbats hurled at public education nationally or in New Mexico, fairness and historical truth must prevail. There have always been great teachers; such a teacher was Prospero Jaramillo, who taught in several New Mexican communities, closing his illustrious teaching career in the Albuquerque Public Schools. A "born" teacher, he impacted the lives of literally thousands of children. He made his classroom come alive, whether it was social studies, mathematics, or science. Every school remembers his "harmonica bands," his woodworking classes, his sports activities. Prospero Jaramillo was a master teacher, and he left a legacy few teachers can rival. A challenge for those who follow?

New Mexico Licensure System

Licensing of teachers and administrators has been in place since the organized or structured beginning of the profession in New Mexico. Dr. Nanninga states in his book *The New Mexico School System*, "Before a teacher can get a regular certificate from the state board in addition to meeting all other requirements *she* must earn at least six semester hours or nine term hours of satisfactory work in an institution of higher learning of college or university ranks" (Nanninga 1942, 171). Teachers were able to get a waiver of licensing, even then.

Formal authority for licensing was placed under the direction
of the state board by the legislature in 1929. Requirements have
changed over time as preparation programs have developed in
universities and colleges. Recent changes in teacher and administrator licensing were enacted in the Education Reform Bill of
2003 and are included in New Mexico School Code 22-10A-
7–22-10A-11.

The Reform Bill of 2003 created a three-level license for teachers, starting with Level I, in which the teacher is considered
"Provisional." A teacher in Level I must be properly certified,
have a Bachelor's degree, and must be mentored and appropriately assigned. To proceed to Level II, the teacher must be evaluated annually by the principal; that evaluation must be verified
by the superintendent. The state department will assign two
experienced professionals to evaluate the teacher's dossier and
the evaluations of the principal and the superintendent. If those
professionals agree with the evaluations, the teacher proceeds to
Level II. If the teacher is not approved for Level II, the license is
discontinued after three years. The time frame between Level I
and Level II is three years.

Level II is called the "Professional" level. The teacher again
is evaluated annually by the principal, with that evaluation
verified by the superintendent. Teachers can remain at this level
for all their careers, or they may request to move to Level III.
After the initial three-year period at Level II, teachers may
request movement to Level III. A teacher must have a Master's
degree or must have earned the National Board of Professional
Teaching Standards certificate.

Teachers may prefer to stay at Level II for their entire careers.
They continue to be evaluated by the principal based upon seven
identified competencies. The next level is Level IIIA and Level
IIIB. Level IIIA is the "Master" teacher level in which the teacher
takes on additional responsibilities. This is a nine-year license
and is granted to a teacher who annually demonstrates instructional leadership competencies.

Level IIIB is a nine-year license granted to school administrators who meet the qualifications for that level. License for an
administrator will be granted to an individual who has been at
Level IIIA for one year and who has satisfactorily completed
State Board of Education–approved courses in administrative
and instructional leadership competencies. Those requirements

must be verified by the local superintendent through a highly objective and uniform statewide evaluation standard.

The legislation also provides for salaries commensurate with each level: Level I will have a base salary of $30,000; Level II will have a salary between $35,000 in 2004–2005 and $40,000 in 2005–2006; Level IIIA will have a beginning salary range between $45,000 and $50,000 in 2006–2007. Level IIIB for administrators will range between $58,000 and $68,000, depending upon student enrollment in their assigned schools.

Procedures have been adopted under Title 6, Chapters 60–69 of regulations dated August 31, 2003, to begin the process of implementation of the three-tiered licensure legislation. This organized, structured, and monitored progression for licensure is commensurate with salaries. Professional educators have struggled to develop professional standards and processes which ultimately are designed to improve education for each student and to promote professional competencies and conditions of work for educational staffs.

THE POWER OF THE PROFESSION

Success in school comes in many forms. Our schools in New Mexico have, as elsewhere, adopted and fostered policies and practices that celebrate and nourish the multiple talents to be found in all children. One prominent businessman, T. Askew, remembers his odyssey through school, especially high school, and how one very brilliant physics teacher, Manuel Olguin (a former school superintendent), impacted his life. From the military to university sciences to successful mercantile and real estate careers, the legacy of teacher Olguin and other great teachers makes itself known.

Summary and Reflections

The education profession in New Mexico has changed since its beginnings as a Native American legacy and then as a Spanish, Mexican, and American model. It has accelerated incredibly in recent years through a variety of initiatives, including those of the professional organizations, the legislature, the State Board of

Education, and the higher education institutions. Each "governing" entity is involved in assessing and enhancing education and the education profession on a continuing basis. Involvement of community and community agencies has been growing, and their continuing interest and involvement have made a difference because of increased knowledge and their willingness to get involved in support of a better educational system for New Mexico youth.

A strong initiative undertaken by the State Board of Education and the Commission on Higher Education (the higher education coordinating body) provided a collaborative push to improve teaching and to enhance support for teachers. New Mexico is recognized as having a sound standards and benchmarks program (*Education Week* 2002, 71–84). The accountability system is developing into a statewide system for assessing progress of students, individual schools, and school districts. Another productive initiative, the Partners in Education, started in 1998 by Superintendent of Public Instruction Michael Davis, brings together leaders from different organizations such as the Parent Teachers Association (PTA), AFT, NEA, New Mexico School Boards Association, New Mexico Coalition of School Administrators, the League of Women Voters, New Mexico Retired Teachers Association, New Mexico Research and Study Council, and others to advise and reach consensus on educational issues to present to the legislature.

Major challenges exist. The state is not attracting an adequate supply of strong candidates into teaching and, specifically, not enough candidates from minority populations. Many teachers who graduate from state colleges and universities leave New Mexico for other states that pay higher salaries; the average teacher's pay in New Mexico in 2002 ranked 47th in the nation. The goals of professional organizations must be more clearly identified; their efforts must support the common goal of improved education for students of the state; and they must be able to identify leaders who can enhance opportunities for both the students and the citizens of the state.

New Mexico must elevate the status of teachers and principals with better incentives such as improved salaries and support systems of mentoring and professional development. The state must encourage respect and support for teachers in the schools, in our communities, and in our school districts. As we look to continued support for the education profession, we must not forget the need for strong school principal and district superintendent leadership. These two professional positions support classroom teachers by providing instructional leadership as well as financial, material, and other resources.

A review of the growth of education as a profession reflects concentration on further education, licensure, improvement of working conditions, improved and adequate salaries, involving concerned citizens outside the field of education, and assurances that this profession chosen by committed and dedicated individuals continues to grow as a respected profession.

Chapter 4 Questions and Related Materials

Identify ways professional organizations of teachers and administrators might work more closely together to achieve educational change and improvement.

From your research and readings, what has been the benefit of teachers' organizations such as the two major organizations in New Mexico? Has the concept of teachers' organizations been a hindrance or a help to the development of education for students?

How effective are administrator organizations in influencing education in New Mexico? How might these organizations work more effectively with boards of education to improve education for students?

The legislature in 2003 approved a new collective bargaining law. Identify the major components of that law. How do you relate to the bargaining process?

Ball, Sharon; Volckmar, Andrea; Flynn, Nancy (2001)
De Baca, Fabiola Cabeza (1954)
Getz, Lynne Marie (1997)
Jenkins, Myra Ellen (1974)
Nanninga, S. P. (1942)

CHAPTER 5

Curriculum

A New Mexican Perspective

Pero no únicamente instruían los franciscanos á sus neófitos en la doctrina, sino también les enseñaron artes y oficios, propagaban la cría de ovejas y el cultivo de la uva, eran ellos en realidad los verdaderos padres de los indios. Llevaben á sus misiones caballos, ganados vacuno y lanar, credos: inducían a los naturales a la cría y cuidado de los animales domésticos mejoraron sus telares de hilar y tejer, establecieron escuelas donde se enseñaba á los niños leer, escribir y contar: les daban instrucciones de música vocal, y les enseñaron a tocar algun instrumento: fundaron talleres de carpintería, herrería, aprendiendo en ellos sus catecumenes el manejo de los herraminentos; salían de sus manos, indios que era buenos oficiales de albañileria, cantería y hasta escultores. Prestaban gran auxilio á la agricultura introduciendo mejor beneficio de cultivo y muchas semillas y granos nuevos. Fueron bien-hechores de la humanidad (Builders of Humanity).

—De Thoma, Francisco,
Historia Popular de Nuevo Mexico, (1896)

A brief, not literal, translation: De Thoma captures the genius and the practicality of the earliest curriculum developed by the Franciscan fathers. Catholic doctrine may have been the guiding tenet; but Native American children were actually taught the practical arts of sheepherding, the cultivation of grapes, and the care of animals. Imagine all this, and reading, writing, counting, vocal music, and learning to play musical instruments. As if that curriculum were not enough, the

Franciscans, who were more like parents of the Native American children, also taught them carpentry, masonry, and even sculpting.

The legacy of the priests, preachers, and pioneer teachers of New Mexico speaks volumes about educators, the educational profession, and curriculum. If the language that describes their early efforts is at times overly dramatic, it does manage to convey the kinds of dedication, devotion, talent, and vision that were offered to the pupils. The legacy of those early educators was created with a basic and practical curriculum born of the land and its people and was suffused with religious doctrine. That early "curriculum" was based upon family, community, culture, and survival.

As we look at the institutional entities involved with curriculum in the state of New Mexico, we can consider Beauchamp's use of the term *curriculum* as a *curriculum system* (Beauchamp 1968, 6). Curriculum development is increasingly a process with systemic concerns. Beauchamp's notion of curriculum as a system is, for our purposes, a useful tool for describing curriculum developments in New Mexico and its 89 school districts. This enables us to think about a curriculum system in the schools: what it is, how it is developed, and how it is implemented in individual schools, in school districts, and at the state level. Crucial to our understanding of curriculum development in New Mexico is an examination of the sources of curriculum.

Sources of Curriculum

A broad definition of curriculum, in our judgment, is well suited for New Mexico and its vast landscape of people and topography. New Mexico's land, its peoples, and its history suggest a curriculum system that should be, first, firmly grounded in the diversity of its population (Native American, Hispanic, Anglo American, African American, Asian American, and others). Second, curriculum should be cognizant of that population's long and distinguished history; third, it should take full advantage of the "frontier" nature of the state (distances, developmental stages, location). Fourth, it should be forward-looking, even futuristic, in its reach because of the major impact of science and technology in its midst. Los Alamos and Sandia National Laboratories, White Sands Missile Range, Holloman, Kirtland, and Cannon Air Force Bases, and private businesses and national corporations involved with research and technology encourage growth and change in the curriculum system in New Mexico. It must be recognized that these four elements involved in the curriculum system will be affected by political realities which also reflect the land and the peoples.

Poets and artists of New Mexico have developed and will continue to evoke strong and beautiful visual images of the state, its landscape, and its people. This suggests to those who develop and teach the curricula that another source of curriculum may be found in the natural "picturesqueness" of New Mexico. Charles Lummis in his lyrical *The Land of Poco Tiempo* writes of "a universality in the New Mexico deserts and mountain . . . every landscape is characteristic and even beautiful—with a weird, unearthly beauty." He continues "most of New Mexico, most of the year, is an indescribable harmony in browns and grays over which the enchanted light of its blue skies casts an eternal spell" (Lummis 1952, 4). It would appear difficult for geography, literature, reading, science, and history teachers to ignore the nature of the landscape and the peoples while teaching in New Mexico. As farfetched as this source for curriculum may appear, Lummis reminds us that New Mexico came to be a part of the nation only at the beginning of the twentieth century; however, it is a century older in European (Spanish) civilization than other states and many centuries older in its Native American origins.

When we think of New Mexico's sage and sky, we may wonder about the state's apparent tranquility and its people's pioneering a new educational system starting in 1540. That blaze of exploration continues unabated in the field of education and curriculum today; that exploration is both exciting and complex in scope and nature. These sources of curriculum, *the history, the peoples, and the land*, intertwine with *professional sources* to design the curriculum system to be used as the basis for the formal education system in New Mexico. The organized knowledge (the disciplines: mathematics, history, science, language arts, and the arts) must meld with knowledge of children's growth to create that system. We find in our appraisal of curriculum in New Mexico that throughout the various historical periods, Spanish, Mexican, and territorial, even statehood, contending forces, internal and external, sought to influence educational developments. Some historic or traditional characteristics of the curriculum are compromised by each new interest. Some

efforts, in hindsight, may have been designed to suppress or
ignore the peoples and cultures which were indigenous to New
Mexico; some efforts enriched and led to new insights.

State and federal influences are reflected in curriculum and its
development, but regional and local interests and liberties in curriculum continue. Rural influences may demand areas in the curriculum which are not significant in the mind of the urban
dweller. Regional interests representing Native American culture
(northwestern New Mexico: Farmington, Kirtland, Aztec,
Gallup) may have differing concerns. Southwestern New Mexico
(Silver City, Cobre, districts with Southern Apache culture) with
mining interests and history involve that history in meeting the
needs of those communities. Central New Mexico, with its
smaller communities, farms, businesses, local fairs, and fiestas,
will add a different flavor to traditional disciplines. Northern
New Mexico and its *acequia* life in the northern villages, historic
Spanish and Native American traditions celebrated in schools,
churches, fiestas, literature, history, and family life may provide
a more personal touch to the accepted or required curriculum.
Border schools (Las Cruces, Gadsden, Jal, Deming) are touched
by continuing Mexican immigration and culture—rich traditions
that have been established and which continue to blend. These
are significant issues, as are the realities of language and finance.
The broad rangelands (Roswell, Carrizozo, Magdalena) and
other areas where ranching and farming dominate lifestyles with
rodeos and fairs incorporate special flavors into the curriculum.
This local and often rural influence, combined with state and
national government elements, complements our democratic
institution and way of life. The extent of local, state, and federal
interaction is perhaps captured best in a brief historical treatment
of curriculum development in New Mexico.

Curriculum: Early Native American

Teaching and learning for the indigenous peoples before the
Spanish incursion of the sixteenth century was a family- and com-
munity-based process. Young people learned of their culture and
conditions for survival, community building, and pleasure from
modeling and instruction by their elders. Another book would be
necessary to present even portions of that magnificent period.
However, there was a program, part formal, part informal, which
met the needs of the young people. Respect for, awareness of, and

involvement with aspects of that early curriculum can only add flavor and substance to New Mexico's curriculum.

Curriculum: The Spanish Period

The period from 1581 to 1680 was marked by the establishment of the Franciscan missions. De Thoma, Palm, and Salpointe, among other historians, have described the earliest curriculum as "not only centers for religious training, but also as places of instruction in reading, writing, singing and the manual arts" (Palm 1930, 33–34). There are early references to industrial subjects as well as applications of learning to the agricultural economy of the time (De Thoma 1896, 87). It is significant to note that at the time of the Pueblo Revolt led by Popé in 1680, efforts were being made to eliminate religious festivals and practices of the indigenous population. The strong presence of the Catholic Church was a major influence in education, and the curriculum of those early centers of instruction was that imposed by the conquerors.

Some evidence of formal education has been noted by Bernardo P. Gallegos (1992, 21–43) in the post–Pueblo Revolt period. Fray Antonio de Acevedo established a school in Santa Fe in which learning to read was the principal mandate, along with religious instruction. In 1776, Father Anastacio Dominguez described the pedagogy of some of the Native American Pueblos and as described by Gallegos "he observed the young *doctrinarios* reading and even teaching others" (1992, 24). It should also be noted that the "language of instruction in the missions was not Spanish, but Latin" (Gallegos 1992, 26). An interesting aspect of the reports of Dominguez and others is that it appears that a school in Santa Fe in the 1780s had enrolled students from the surrounding Indian nations (Ute, Comanche, Navajo, and Apache). The curriculum of these early schooling efforts remained essentially the same during this period; although in 1800, there is some marked interest in education and increased educational activity both "in relation to policy and in the establishment of schools" (Gallegos 1992, 29). Gallegos notes one particular report from a Nemesio Salcedo of Chihuahua, Mexico, which called for "instruction to occur in the mornings and afternoons and the teacher should be very careful to teach the Christian doctrine, reading, writing and counting" (1992, 29).

⟵

La Llorona Bridges History and Cultures

Instructional materials used in New Mexican schools
did not always celebrate our wondrous quadra-cul-
tural history. The curricula represented mostly traditional "American" history with scant references to the
rich medley of New Mexicans who forged this state's
history. Since the 1960s, we have observed the inclusion of some fascinating material, not the least of
which has been the story of "La Llorona," the Wailing
Woman, whose travails have been used to alert children, parents, and communities to the dangers of the
ditches of New Mexico. Convoluted as the story may
be about how La Llorona met her demise, it is classic
folklore in New Mexico, Cuba, Central America, and
South America. A heralded version is that of New
Mexican author Ray de Aragon, whose book *La
Llorona* offers an intriguing story of star-crossed
lovers and peasants versus patrones (upper class families) which leads to the death of the woman's two children by her own hand and her subsequent death and
burning at the stake as demanded by the authorities.
A stage play based on the book is currently making the
New Mexican theater circuit. New Mexico's schools
at all levels can today mine a rich trove of indigenous
curricular materials.

⟵

The beginning of the nineteenth century witnessed concerted
efforts to expand educational opportunities. Most telling was the
effort of Pedro Bautista de Pino as revealed in his famous report
of 1812 calling for the establishment of a seminary college of
higher education in New Mexico. There was also the option of
sending children to school in Mexico (Jenkins 1977, 5).
Curriculum offered to them at a Mexican school called the *Royal
Cantabrico Seminary* mentions, in addition to religion, the best
in physical education, current political education, and literary
education, and, more significantly, for primary education using
the methodology of Pestalozzi (Gallegos 1992, 41).

⟵➤

"WHAT WAS PESTALOZZI DOING
ON THE FRONTIER?"

Several New Mexican writers have indicated that in the territory's early years, primary education included the methodology of Pestalozzi. Like real life detectives, some of our colleagues found in Kane's History of Education a most interesting biography of Johann Heinrich Pestalozzi which stated, among other things, that there "is a whole library of books about him" (1954, 328). Calling him an educator who was "ridiculously inefficient" and a cumbersome writer, not a scholar, not a clear thinker, yet to be remembered in educational history because "he was a promoter." As a promoter of "democracy in education" and "with an enthusiasm for elementary education," Pestalozzi's methodology appears to have been centered on "a psychological method of teaching based upon sense perception through a curiously forced analysis of all perceptions into number, form, and language" (Kane 1954, 335). There appears to be an effort in the Pestalozzi methodology to champion industrial education. The fruits of the method in New Mexico's early schools remain, at best, a case for further research.

⟵➤

Curriculum: Mexican and Territorial Periods

Following the independence of Mexico from Spain in 1820 and the arrival of the Americans to the territory of New Mexico in 1846, the curricula of the existing New Mexican frontier schools shifted ever so slightly; but reading, counting, and writing remained central to the program; religious education was diminished. Jenkins reported that a Lancastrian School in Santa Fe offered a curriculum that included grammar, philosophy, and ethics; the Lancastrian model was purported to be a tutoring arrangement where instruction was "one on one." Also of note on the frontier was "instruction in military drill" along with academic subjects. The children of the more wealthy Hispanic families were sent to Missouri, and there are indications that some children traveled to Mexico for further education (Salaz 1999,

189). One historian suggests that some children were sent as far east as New York. Those who wanted only a Spanish education with religious instruction were sent to Durango, the headquarters of the Catholic Church in the Mexican Southwest.

After the American occupation of New Mexico and the establishment of civil government under General Stephen Kearney, some private schools were established. Mrs. Howe, wife of an officer in the United States Army, opened English schools in Santa Fe. Around 1853, the Loretto Academy, known then as the "Academy of Our Lady of Light," was founded by the Catholic Sisters of Loretto in Santa Fe; similar schools were opened in Mora in 1864 and in Las Vegas in 1869. Among the first Protestant schools to be opened was a Santa Fe Academy established by Reverend Hiram Read, a Baptist Missionary; the curriculum included "AP Cology [sic], Farley's Geography, with the sublime mysteries of simple subtraction" (Salaz 1999, 25).

A school called the Joseph Institute in Taos listed the following subjects: reading, writing, and arithmetic for boys; needlework, embroidery, and guitar for girls (Salaz 1999, 267). In 1859, it appears that *El Colegio de San Miguel*, later to be known as St. Michael's College, was the leading institution of Catholic education in the territory. Its curriculum was imposing, offering courses in French, German, Spanish, phonology and writing, mineralogy, elementary English, business English, and instrumental music. Some students were admitted free of charge because they showed academic promise.

Descriptions of curricula in these schools are scant, but they suggest that religious doctrine, reading, writing, and arithmetic were the core teachings. Instruction in English carried a premium in some schools because the teacher who could teach in English could earn a higher salary (Anderson 1907, 248). Quality of instruction was judged by the availability of education for children in both English and Spanish.

References to curricula in legislative documents of the American territorial period are limited. In fact, one historian depicts that, up until 1891, the school code itself was "worse than unsatisfactory. It was vicious" (Getz 1997, 17). Getz, writing about territorial education, cites the struggle over control of schools, especially laws regarding the language of instruction; laws were being interpreted as mandating English-only instruction or calling for bilingual instruction. In 1891, Amado Chaves, the distinguished first territorial school superintendent, issued an administrative ruling that only English should be used in the schools (Getz 1997, 20). However, he also championed bilingual instruction in a plea before the legislature. In 1907, the New Mexico State Board of Education approved the adoption of English-only textbooks. This attempt to foster English-only instruction was often accompanied by statements from educators and political figures of the period that they hoped Spanish Americans would not lose their Spanish language in gaining the English language. The primary objective, writes Getz, was English literacy; Spanish literacy was a "secondary concern" (1997, 20–21). Even prior to statehood, the curriculum itself was used to further English literacy. For example, English instruction was strengthened while instructing in health education.

In the 1891 to 1912 period, there were also efforts at furthering a vocational curriculum; educators argued that not all students could be expected to go to college, that some would benefit from vocational training. Regrettably, some New Mexico educators believed that Hispanic children needed only vocational education because they would not be expected to go to college or achieve any kind of advanced education (Getz 1997, 23). Perhaps this attitude represented the early issue of a desire to suppress or contain certain populations.

No Life for a Lady

Education on the frontier had its rewards, albeit slight. Agnes Morley Cleveland, in her classic New Mexico book, recounts the following: "Although I distinctly felt that in Philadelphia (where she had been sent for schooling), there was a lot of overemphasis on nonessentials, the severity of the discipline which circumstances had forced upon me on the ranch equipped me for the discipline of the schoolroom. I overheard one of my teachers say to a colleague, 'If the educational system could begin with a few years on a New Mexico cattle ranch, I think children might make better progress in school.'"

Curriculum: The Statehood Period

The arrival of statehood in 1912 and the Constitution of the State of New Mexico brought new curriculum requirements. Of special and historic interest was Article XII, Section 8, which reads: "The legislature shall provide for the training of teachers proficient in both the English and Spanish languages, to qualify them to teach English speaking pupils." Accompanying the new constitutional provisions for education was a new strong framework for education and a more standardized school curriculum. The 1912 legislative session witnessed the provision of laws that mandated a number of curriculum studies never before so clearly identified; among them, the study of domestic science, agricultural education, commercial science, the ever-popular manual training and (shades of the 1960s) teaching about the effects of narcotics and alcohol (Wiley 1965, 32). The New Mexico education laws of 1912–1913 instituted industrial education.

Wiley says that between 1923 and 1930, the first school curriculum standards for instruction set by the State Board of Education were: reading, writing, language, grammar, New Mexico history, U.S. history, geography, Spanish, spelling, and arithmetic. Few, if any, changes to these basic curricula were made until the 1940s, when laws required new social science studies, especially a course in humane education. Nanninga's history identifies the rationale for this particular course as "teaching pupils in the humane treatment of dumb animals and to develop in the pupils a spirit of kindness, humanity and tolerance" (1942, 169).

THEORY TO PRACTICE?

Nanninga himself may have had a special affinity for a course that meant teaching pupils about humane treatment of animals and that developed in students a spirit of kindness, humanity, and tolerance towards others. He has been described as "a farmer at heart," and it is even reported that when he died, he was irrigating the land; his pet dog guarded him when others tried to minister to him.

Curriculum: Informal and Formal

The development of curriculum across the United States and in New Mexico during the 1920s and 1930s reflected the emergence of the United States as a world economic power. Following the Spanish-American War, World War I, and the Great Depression, the curriculum fostered vocational studies, economics, and business as central to the mission of the school. Even religious books highlighted the "business" concept. Following that period and just prior to World War II, the New Mexico educational scene in some areas celebrated the 1940 Coronado Centennial and the Spanish arrival in New Mexico. Long before political correctness was a major consideration in our society, the celebration of the Centennial with its emphasis on Spanish history, music, and dance, and Don Francisco Coronado's journey through New Mexico became a part of the informal curricula in some schools. (Even Menaul School featured this celebration in the 1940 Yearbook. Recently, a statue of a conquistador in a small New Mexico community was desecrated, indicating that negative feelings toward the conquistadores/conquerors exist today.) This informal curriculum was followed by other symbolic celebrations during and after World War II, as the stories of defeat and victory became part of our history curriculum.

More significantly, perhaps, was the impact of this war and post-war period on the teaching of mathematics and science in our schools, particularly at the secondary level. Courses like the famous Dawn Patrol class of Dr. E. R. Harrington of Albuquerque High School produced science students (physics majors and chemistry scholars) who went on to enjoy distinguished careers (Harrington 1963).

TEACHER AS LEGEND

Dr. E. R. Harrington was a legendary educator whose career with the Albuquerque Public Schools spanned over fifty years. He was the holder of several master's degrees and two doctorates. A master science teacher at Albuquerque High School, he later served as the first director of secondary instruction for APS. Teachers, school principals, and students welcomed his visits at all the high schools and junior high schools. He would

often arrive with a roar on his Harley-Davidson motor-
cycle, his coat pockets filled with fruit and candy bars
which he shared with everyone he could. Dr.
Harrington was a superb teacher and influenced hun-
dreds of students and guided them in their choice of sci-
ence-related fields. Beloved as a person and as an
educator, he was from an era of education that many
today feel no longer exists.

⟶

The post–World War II period witnessed even stronger pressures for the teaching of science and mathematics. The Russians
launched Sputnik, and the race for space was on. In the schools,
according to Wiley, traditional areas of art and music and even
vocational training were put on hold or pushed aside to make
room for more science and more mathematics. Physical education in the curriculum at the secondary level was promoted by
events of World War II. Examination of State Department of
Education curriculum manuals shows that minimal requirements included the fine arts, health, language arts, mathematics,
science, social studies, physical education, and exploratory vocational programs. Vocational programs in New Mexico schools
did not achieve the sophistication of secondary vocational programs in other cities and states where industry and commerce
were much more prevalent; vocational classes most often
included woodworking, metals, home economics, and business.
It was to take another twenty years for vocational education of
a more advanced nature to mature in New Mexico schools.

Secondary programs in New Mexico high schools have been
enhanced by the establishment of technical vocational institutions like the Career Enrichment Center in Albuquerque, the
Luna Community College in Las Vegas, Northern New Mexico
Community College in El Rito, and the Albuquerque Technical
Vocational Institute. Concurrent enrollment in colleges and universities while still in high school, advanced placement classes,
and technology have impacted curriculum in the public schools
of New Mexico. Proximity to institutions of higher education
has complemented high school programs and provided expanded
opportunities for students. Rural school students, through technological advances and distance education, can have access to
such programs.

Conflict and Curriculum

The 1960s brought protests against U.S. involvement in war in Vietnam and social unrest among minority and other groups. From kindergarten through university level education, the curricula in New Mexico began to reflect the new concerns, the new agenda. Topics of discrimination, racial prejudice, poverty, student rights and responsibilities, and other issues made their way into the classrooms, not always without controversy. Social science curriculum (history, government, economics) included issues more in keeping with the current concerns of the general society. Multicultural education flourished both nationally and in New Mexico. School administrators and boards of education found themselves confronting issues of instruction that had not been part of their deliberations in the past. Some issues, such as the place for Chicano Studies in the curriculum, were not handled comfortably when they were initiated; some have now become accepted as part of the curriculum.

THE CHILDREN OF SANCHEZ

Always hoping and seeking to understand cultural differences in New Mexico classrooms remains a priority for educators, administrators, and teachers alike. School districts, in the aftermath of the 1960s, offered in-service education for teachers and principals on multicultural education. Still, there were surprises. One Albuquerque principal remembered a wonderful visit with Erna Fergusson, famed New Mexico writer, who told him that the characters in a novel called Stephana were not the Spanish people she knew along the Rio Grande Valley. Her "friends" were not, as depicted in the novel, "typical teenagers of the '50s and '60s who participated in the mainstream of Albuquerque youth activities, the same dress, the same sports, the same teenage idols of Anglo youth." She was recalling an earlier time in New Mexico; so the principal invited her to visit the school classrooms, to lecture, and to see for herself this new generation of Spanish-speaking children.

The national debate over bilingual education made itself known in New Mexico schools where it had been a sleeping giant since territorial days and the Constitution of 1912. There were advocates for different forms of bilingual instruction (total immersion program, English as a Second Language, and others); and practitioners of different bilingual approaches made themselves heard in local districts and in the executive and legislative halls of Santa Fe, some testifying before education committees in Washington. It was a heady time for language instruction, as well as for mathematics and science. Federal funding created by Public Law 874 was shared by New Mexico schools, and dollars for language laboratories, science equipment, and instructional materials flowed into the schools. The expenditure of PL 874 funds and the success achieved in improving mathematics, science, and the teaching of languages ushered in an era of technology that continues unabated in the twenty-first century.

Critics of the American educational scene, including those in New Mexico, have insisted that the school curriculum and its implementation have not kept pace with the times and that the "factory model" of instruction and curriculum has not changed. The dropout dilemma which continues to face secondary schools was impacted by perceived lack of growth and change in the educational institutions. Urban schools appear to have been more the focus of these criticisms than were rural schools. The breadth of the curriculum in rural settings also has come under attack; computer-based instructional programs have moved to counterbalance some of this urban/rural inequity. Improved teacher preparation programs, shared theories of learning, professional development, improved teaching strategies, growth in effective use of technology, and enhanced parental involvement are in place in most school districts and should address concerns about change.

Curriculum content issues continue to be addressed by New Mexico schools. Issues such as the place of ethnic studies, bilingual instruction and its various applications, the rise and fall of music and art education, education versus the smorgasbord curricula, core curriculum versus choice of subjects, the role of educational technology, programs for special needs children, and the introduction of reading skills versus social adjustment of children first—all continue to be discussed. Early childhood programs, including Head Start and other programs, have been implemented as a part of school and legislative goals. The implications of early education programs for stimulating learning will, no doubt, make tremendous differences in the success of New Mexican students. Early childhood programs also present the opportunity to involve more parents in developing educational programs.

Other Crucial Curriculum Influences

In attempting to provide the best education for students, New Mexico's schools contended with a myriad of influences, some very crucial to our history. Preserving the natural ingredients of the New Mexico curriculum—geographical, historical, social, economic, and religious—has not been without difficulty and compromise. From the Spanish and Mexican periods through the territorial and statehood periods, New Mexico's traditional cultural and social values have been often limited and ignored. There was often a failure to incorporate the cultural riches of the peoples and their land into the curriculum and instructional program; the curriculum did not adequately reflect or incorporate the potential and the presence of the state's people and their environment. Our history of curriculum and its sources identifies a number of educators and leaders who sought to preserve our heritage and highlight that heritage in school curricula.

THE LAND OF ENCHANTMENT

There are no excuses for failing to acknowledge and celebrate the cultural wealth of New Mexico in the school curriculum. A treasure trove of primary and secondary materials is there for the asking. Lansing Bloom's pioneer history of New Mexico from the 1940s with its distinctive graphics is a historical gem. Ruben Salaz' multi-history of New Mexico is an education in itself. Novels, histories, short stories, memoirs, and a host of nonfiction books tell the story of this "land of enchantment."

In the twentieth century, other critical external forces or influences made their presence felt in the curriculum at both the state and district levels. Textbook companies, seeking to serve a national constituency, failed to address regional and local concerns and needs. The rich indigenous setting of New Mexico was ignored or slighted. National testing programs have impacted curriculum in a similar fashion. Driven by the demands of a national agenda for testing and standardization, local and state testing and programs have been influenced. Higher education admission requirements have impacted the academic and curriculum content at the local school district level. With the best of intentions, many national and even international forces and programs have made it necessary to modify or change curriculum. Because some of these external programs have financial or regulatory implications, local interests or needs have been compromised.

School administrators and teachers, past and present, have sought to balance external and local demands. Administrators and teachers clearly have a special responsibility to incorporate the cultural and educational legacy of New Mexico into the school curriculum.

School Districts and Curriculum

Significant issues impact the area of curriculum content: (a) the processes by which local school districts and educational leaders determine what curriculum is to be offered and (b) the players in this process (school board members, superintendents, principals, curriculum specialists, teachers, state leaders, specialists, and parents) make for interesting and complex educational drama. Debates in New Mexico on evolution and creationism in the science curriculum are illustrative, not only of content battles, but of the curriculum development process. Questions of governance loom large in these matters. Jurisdictional interests are confronted as local schools and local school districts attempt to make curriculum decisions. The Public Education Department has requirements and mandates, some emanating nationally and some from the legislature, which must be met. Parental and community involvement in program planning is encouraged as schools work to develop, modify, or implement improved and updated curricula. Legislative mandates in the 1980s, 1990s, and 2003 required parent and community involvement. In the schools, site-based committees have been successful in involving teachers, parents, and administrators in working together. The role of school administrators who actually become educational and instructional leaders has tremendous implication for the improvement of schools and educational program.

⟵

Pie, Anyone?

Just think about how we might integrate "Pie Town" into the schools! The Pie Town Festival is celebrated annually in July in Pie Town, New Mexico, halfway between Magdalena and Datil, and the story goes that every conceivable kind of pie may be found there, even peanut butter pie!

⟵

Among the most active participants in decisions about curriculum are our teachers and their professional organizations, a most crucial component in the process of curriculum development. Many professional organizations from the Association of Supervision and Curriculum Development to the individual subject matter organizations at the local, state, and national level impact the curriculum development process. Community organizations seek a voice in the process of building programs. Religious communities, chambers of commerce, historical societies, and others make their presence felt in these deliberations. Institutions of higher education have long played a significant role in the decisions about curriculum and content in the public schools; there has been an unmistakable influence because of the resources the universities represent to local school districts and to the state. Historically, the marriage of "town and gown" (interaction between school communities and universities) has not always been consistent or constant in every community or region, but institutions of higher education have represented talent, promise, and leadership to local decision makers.

Decisions about curriculum implementation traditionally have been left to the local school district, with minimum standards and direction from the state. As accountability and assessment at the state and federal levels has been demanded through legislation and through the No Child Left Behind Act, pressures on curriculum areas have increased. Examples of what should be or might be presented in the various social science and science courses are legion. A prime example of the complexity of teaching history and incorporating new and challenging materials offered by ethnic studies was to be found in the case of the

Vaughn, New Mexico, schools. The local board found itself at
odds with two teachers over content in the classroom. A more
recent case involving the use of controversial materials in the
classroom has presented staff issues and social issues for some
Albuquerque high schools. School districts throughout the state
face these curriculum issues often, sometimes quietly, sometimes
quite publicly. These issues create educational interest, controversy, publicity, and sometimes change; and the results become
part of the history of education in New Mexico.

⟶

IF CHILDREN COULD DECIDE
ON CURRICULUM . . .

New Mexicans, like other Americans, want to honor
their local heroes. Choosing heroes can be rewarding,
but also sensitive and controversial. So it has been with
the great Indian leader Popé of 1680, the conquistador
Juan de Oñate, and even Billy the Kid. This does not
appear to be the case with Elfego Baca, New Mexican
lawman and politician. He is the stuff of legend; own-
ership is claimed by many. At Los Padillas Elementary
School in Albuquerque's South Valley, Elfego Baca and
his exploits were the subject of a fourth grade classroom discussion. Alexandria Noelle asked her grandfather about Sheriff Baca because a student with the
Baca surname was making strong claims about being
a close relative—Alexandria needed family history to
justify a claim because she wanted "bragging rights."
Grandfather confirmed those rights, even though
Alexandria was "coyote" (part Anglo). She raced to
school the next day to announce that her great, great,
great grandfather was a first cousin to the famous
Sheriff. The connection and the curriculum in the classroom came alive for little Alexandria Noelle.

⟶

Traditional disciplines have survived; and, although constantly
being restructured because of new research or technology or new
social demands, they survive as a curriculum foundation.

New Mexico Standards-Based Curriculum

The state and the schools have responded to new challenges for a standard-based education as a result of national, state, and local efforts to improve public schools. Curriculum content, instructional guides, and assessment measures are the focus of these standards. *The Standards Primer: A Guide to Standards-Based Education in New Mexico* includes New Mexico content standards and benchmarks. These standards are designed to improve schools and to "provide equitable opportunities for all students to reach high standards" (New Mexico State Department of Education 1999). Nationwide standards as well as those standards developed in New Mexico attempt to examine and assess what students are expected to know and what they must be able to do.

↤

STANDARD: RANCHO RABBIT

Setting educational standards has always been a crucial responsibility, albeit imprecise or not as technically proficient as we find it to be in the twenty-first century. School performance standards have, of course, always been a legitimate concern of school principals and classroom teachers. In one Bernalillo County elementary school, the task of establishing performance standards was taken seriously, although with a touch of humor, "New Mexico style." It seems the physical education teacher/coach, in reporting running times or speed requirements for his charges in the PE program defined a standard: "All Rancho students will compete against the Rancho Rabbit's running time." It seems a certain Beatriz Dawnelle had posted a phenomenal speed and was to be known forever after as the "Rancho Rabbit." That mark may still be standing!

↤

Standards-based education in New Mexico is comprised of content standards and benchmarks that identify major, specific expectations for New Mexico students and includes three parts: curriculum, instruction, and assessment. Content standards are "descriptions of knowledge and skills students should acquire in a particular subject area." Benchmarks are statements "of what all students should know and be able to do in a content area by the end of a designated grade or level." Current groupings for New Mexico benchmarks are K–4, 5–8, and 9–12. Future benchmarks may be more specifically grouped as K–2, 3, 4, 5, 6, 7, 8, and 9–12.

New Mexico Standards for Excellence are examples of demonstrations of knowledge and skills framed by the content standards and benchmarks and were adopted as state regulation for career readiness, health education, language arts, mathematics, physical education, science, and social studies. Benchmarks were adopted as regulation for arts education and modern, classical, and Native languages; however, the benchmarks were recommended as guides for curricular development. In keeping with the statewide plan, the 89 school districts are following through "by aligning curriculum, instruction, and assessment with the standards" (New Mexico State Department of Education 1999). Assessment, testing, and accountability in New Mexico include (1) assessment at the classroom level, (2) school/district level accountability, (3) state level accountability, and (4) national accountability.

Perhaps the most significant feature of this new accountability era in New Mexico is the continued leadership role of parents, principals, classroom teachers, and content area specialists in identifying these new content and performance standards. *The Standards Primer* is a detailed and informative treatment of the curriculum and learning standards adapted by the New Mexico schools in 1999.

Summary and Reflections

The curriculum of early New Mexico schools has moved along a traditional curriculum development line of "reading, writing, and 'rithmetic" to a comprehensive curriculum that attempts to incorporate most subject matter disciplines as well as the instructional methodologies that accompany them. Early New Mexico education, like early Native American education, included religious study. The Spanish, Mexican, and American territorial periods in New Mexico included the basic subjects, along with a surprising array of vocational courses of study that reflected the needs and demands of community life. The curriculum of subsequent years through the statehood period, the years of the Great Depression, World War II, and the last half of the twentieth century, bears the influence of those historic times and events. The American territorial period witnessed the initial secularization of the curriculum when issues of the separation of church and state were raised. Major historical events from the beginning of the twentieth century through Sputnik affected the curriculum nationwide and in New Mexico; some of those events and curriculum changes were "close to home" and almost local in application.

Curriculum development in New Mexico not only includes the historical events described here; it also calls for an understanding of the mechanics of the curriculum development process in New Mexico. Viewed both as a state function with standards and curriculum guides and as a very strong local prerogative in the 89 school districts, the curriculum development process is complex. In addition to the requirements of the Public Education Department, there are also legislative mandates. Curriculum specialists at the state level in concert with district-level specialists, teachers, principals, and parents are all part of the curriculum development process. Increasingly, parents have been encouraged to take part in this curriculum development undertaking by statute and through state and school district efforts.

The curriculum development process is further complicated and enriched because each subject matter or content area has its advocates. In addition, national, state, and local curriculum organizations weigh in with their expertise and agenda. In this enterprise of curriculum development, the traditional disciplines have survived; and, although constantly being restructured because of new research, knowledge, technology, and increased social demands, those traditional disciplines continue to serve as the curriculum foundation.

An examination of New Mexico's curriculum, past and present, reveals some highlights that bear a New Mexico style. These would include strong efforts in bilingual education, Southwest history, and the fine arts. The New Mexico style also would have to include the exciting and demanding activities in the fields of science and mathematics. Since Sputnik and the National Defense Act of 1968, we have witnessed outstanding science fairs and curriculum innovations in most schools. A New Mexico–style curriculum suggests even more in terms of celebrating both state and local community events. The integration of historical events with the celebrations and local events within the curriculum provide informal paths for the history of New Mexico's schools to be "on stage" in the schools.

Reflecting on how curriculum is created, maintained, and changed in New Mexico challenges us to be cognizant of the rich resources at our disposal; most precious of all those resources are the people of New Mexico. We must also be mindful of several demanding professional concerns: first, that as we have developed scores of programs, we must strive to improve methods of evaluating those programs; second, as we contemplate the future of education in New Mexico at the outset of the twenty-first century, we must raise some caution flags about the assessment and testing program and its impact on the individual learner. Is it valid to suggest that sometimes our schools, wherever they are located, may be victims of a kind of state and national curriculum tyranny that does not allow latitude for location, community, economics, or history? We believe New Mexico schools have shown a capacity for incorporating the best of the national and state curriculum requisites, while still building and creating a curriculum that celebrates New Mexico and its communities. The history of curriculum and curriculum development in New Mexico continues to expand and will require significant research at the state and local levels. The role of the student in developing curriculum is often ignored, and the appropriate role for student participation in developing curriculum has not been determined. How often do we take time to discuss programs with students (appropriately, at the appropriate age) other than to say you will thank us someday or you will need to know this someday? Further, how do we recognize and value each entity and each individual who contributes in some way to the decisions made about content and curriculum in the public schools in New Mexico?

The journey of curriculum building in New Mexico schools from the roots of the earliest Native American learning environments to the highly complex technological operations in many of our schools is interesting, informative, and challenging to follow. We have traveled from the less formal curriculum to a standards-based curriculum. Still, in many ways, curriculum in this state is very distinctly New Mexican. Every teacher, school administrator, student, parent, and citizen can contribute and learn from this journey.

Chapter 5 Questions and Related Materials

Identify some of the most significant trends in curriculum development in New Mexico. How do those trends correspond with national movements and trends?

As a principal, what recommendations might you make about the current curriculum development process and content in your school district?

In your judgment, who should participate in the curriculum development process? Why? Offer a rationale.

Standards-based curriculum is now required by both federal and by state law. In what ways is this concept a limiting factor in what children might learn? In what ways is this concept a support for the education of students? Why are standards-based teaching and curriculum receiving such strong emphasis?

Define at least five major sources of curriculum in the public schools in the state of New Mexico.

Gallegos, Bernardo (1992)
Harrington, E. R. (1963)
Mondragón, John (1970)
New Mexico State Standards (2001)
New Mexico State Board of Education Strategic Plan (1999)

CHAPTER 6

⟶

Financing Schools in New Mexico

Financing of schools is basic to the process of education; without money, there will be no public schools. The commitment of the state of New Mexico to its youth and to its future is reflected in the financing of its schools and is a direct factor in the economic development of the state. Commitment to financing education in New Mexico is required by the state constitution. Article XII, Section 1 of the New Mexico Constitution states: "A uniform system of free public schools for the education of, and open to, all the children of school age in the state shall be established and maintained."

The constitution also created the Permanent School Fund, which consists of

> The proceeds of sales of Sections 2, 16, 32, and 36 in each Township in the state, or the lands selected in lieu thereof; the proceeds of sales of all lands that have been or may hereafter be granted to the state not otherwise appropriated by the terms and conditions of the grant; such portion of the proceeds of sales of land of the United States within the state as has been or may be granted by congress; all earnings, including interest, dividends and capital gains from investment of the permanent school fund; also all other grants, gifts and devises made to the state, the purpose of which is not otherwise specified.

The state invests this permanent fund, and the interest is devoted to education. Current value of the Permanent School Fund is approximately 6.8 billion dollars.

The history of financing education, the funding formula, and possible future direction of the financing of education in New

Mexico reflect complex issues. It is important for citizens to be knowledgeable about school finance, and it is crucial that educators have in-depth knowledge of the financing of schools and the managing of resources that support the education process.

Colonial Period

Support for education in New Mexico prior to territorial times was a local community enterprise. Most of the teachers were Catholic nuns and priests. There were no preparation programs for teachers. In 1792, public schools were established under the direction of Franciscan friars by decree of the Spanish king. Each Pueblo and settlement was to "cultivate a field" for the remuneration of the teacher. One school building was built in Santa Fe around 1777, but it was never opened because of lack of funds (Nanninga 1942, 4). A few private schools were opened around 1800, but they lacked organization and continuity. The best-known private school was located in Taos and was under the direction of Padre Martinez, who printed the first books in New Mexico (Nanninga 1942, 4).

Mexico took control of the territory in 1821. One of the first acts in 1822 by the *Deputacion Provincial* was to approve the first school law, which provided that the town council "complete the formation of primary schools." By law, each town council was notified to complete the formation of primary schools according to the circumstances of the community; however, the results were almost negligible. A second law in 1823 established secondary education. By 1827, there were nineteen schools in the province (Nanninga 1942, 5). Lack of revenue made successful establishment and operation of schools a difficult task.

Territorial Period

Except for the role the United States government took in establishing schools for Native American children after the Treaty of Guadalupe Hidalgo in 1846 (at the end of the Mexican-American War), education was left entirely to residents of the New Mexico Territory. Public education, as we define it today, was almost nonexistent during early territorial times, although a few schools were established in communities where sufficient interest was found. There were no territorial appropriations for

education, and public education was given little financial support locally. While there were some laws establishing components of a public school system enacted by the territorial
legislature, no real effort was made to enforce these laws.

Pressure for the education of their children grew among newly
arrived settlers along with their numbers during this early period,
but those new settlers from the East and other supporters of
public education were no match for the forces against an educational system. The most powerful of these forces emanated
from native Spanish-speaking people and from big business interests. The former feared their traditions and beliefs would be
affected by the public schools; the latter, represented most promi-
nently by mining, oil and gas, and railroad interests, were determined to keep taxes at the lowest possible level.

Even in the face of such resistance, there was discussion as
early as 1850 of the creation of a public school system in the territory of New Mexico. American authorities, newly arrived in
what had been first a province of the Kingdom of Spain and later
a territory of the Republic of Mexico, were concerned that most
residents did not speak, read, or write English. The vast majority of the residents of the new American territory could neither
read nor write their native Spanish. Most of the Native American
residents spoke only their native languages.

When the first territorial board of education was created by
the legislature in 1869, Catholic Bishop Jean Baptiste Lamy of
New Mexico was appointed as a member. Bishop Lamy brought
the Sisters of Loretto to establish an academy for girls in Santa
Fe. He later brought members of the Christian Brothers, a French
teaching order, to open St. Michael's College for boys; both of
these schools were authorized by the territorial legislature in
1874. The Catholic Church supported both of these schools.
After the American Civil War, Protestant church groups began to
establish schools in the new territory. The most active of these
were the Presbyterians, the Methodists, the Evangelical United
Brethren, and the Baptists. Some of these schools still exist today;
McCurdy School in Española and Menaul School in Albuquerque
are two of those. It is noteworthy that by 1895 both the Catholic
and Protestant churches were strong supporters of public schools.

Most of the educational activity in early territorial days was
by religious educators. By the late 1880s, there were some efforts
to establish a public school system; however, the property tax base

was so low that most school districts could not support much of a school year. Two exceptions were in Las Vegas and Albuquerque, where the railroad contributed sufficient taxes to support schools. During the 1880s, the legislature took steps to create a public school system, authorizing county school boards and creating local districts with directors and elected county superintendents. In 1891, the legislature created another Territorial Board of Education. (The first board authorized in 1869 never was established.) During the early years, county schools were actually operated by directors of the local districts, who had the power to hire teachers and advise the county superintendent about tax rates needed to meet the budget. This system endured.

⟵⟶

VICTORY OVER VICIOUS

According to the census returns in 1880, the number of public schools in the territory was 162; however, the facilities or buildings to house the children numbered only forty-six Attendance at the schools was sparse at best, and it was reported that over 60 percent of the people in New Mexico who were over ten years of age were unable to read. Critics blamed the local populations for defeating legislative measures for improving and financing the schools. The School Code, up to that point, was considered "vicious" by one historian; however, it was also reported that W. S. Burke, a superintendent for the Bernalillo County Schools, praised the local citizens, especially the "native people" for supporting the schools and for not working against the teaching of the English language. Burke wrote "No better evidence of this could be given than is to be found in the fact that district directors are always willing to pay a higher price to a teacher who is able to instruct the children in English than one who understands Spanish only." Shades of the future of finance and governance, capital outlay, and bilingual education!

⟵⟶

During the early days of the developing educational system, property owners were resistant to levying ad valorem taxes to pay for schools; therefore, only a few of the school districts had enough taxes to pay for a full nine-month term for schools. A major impetus in the creation of a school system was that the U.S. Congress was reluctant to grant statehood to a population that was largely illiterate and unable to speak English. When he appointed highly respected Amado Chaves as state superintendent, Governor Bradford Prince provided credibility for the establishment of an educational system. Dr. Tom Wiley, historian and former State Superintendent of Public Instruction, in his 1968 book, *Politics and Purse Strings in New Mexico*, states: "The entire process can be described as one in which the controlling forces were unalterably opposed to a tax supported system of education; therefore in actuality, a public school system did not exist" (1968, 2). Great effort was made in developing the concept of tax-supported schools, but lack of financial support prevented the establishment of a sound public school system.

WE WANT A SCHOOL!

There's a story that the citizens of Silver City, the largest town in Grant County, wanted to tax themselves to build and operate a public school and that they tried for several sessions of the New Mexico territorial legislature to get this authority. Finally, in 1877, the legislature passed such a bill. The residents were happy at this final victory, but after they got home, they discovered that they now had the authority to impose taxes, but no authority to collect them. They had been fooled once again by the "Santa Fe Ring." They then called a town meeting and voted to secede from the territory of New Mexico and to join the territory of Arizona. (A connection between Grant County and Arizona already existed as miners and businessmen from the Silver City area were first to develop the rich silver and copper mines of the eastern counties of Arizona. The ores from Arizona were generally shipped to Silver City smelters; and there was extensive trade and travel between southwestern New Mexico and southeastern Arizona.)

Of course, the citizens of Arizona were overwhelmingly in favor of annexing this prosperous county. Governor Safford of Arizona recommended that the

Arizona Legislature memorialize Congress; this was passed by only one vote. The Arizona delegate in Congress introduced House Resolution 795 on October 29, 1877. After two readings, it was referred to the Committee on Territories, where the resolution died.

The New Mexico legislature got the message and unanimously passed a charter for the incorporation of Silver City on February 15, 1878, which gave Silver City broad authority to impose and collect taxes and included building and operating a public school. Silver City followed through and, by some accounts, built the first "substantial" public school building in the Territory. (Nagle 1968, 225–40).

⤙

Statehood Period

In 1910, Congress passed the Enabling Act for the New Mexico Territory to become a state. The people adopted a constitution, and Congress passed the act admitting New Mexico to statehood. President William Howard Taft proclaimed New Mexico as the 47th state of the Union in 1912. Statehood brought rapid changes benefiting public education. Provisions in the state constitution, developed according to strict guidelines imposed by the U.S. Congress, would establish the state's permanent school fund and an extensive system of public lands for school support. These funds would become the first major source of nonlocal tax money providing revenue for the common schools. "From this time forward, state level government was a force in public education, largely because of its financial subsidies to the local districts from these revenues" (Wiley 1968, 44–45).

From Statehood to World War II

Several powerful advocacy groups emerged representing the interests of educators, major taxpayer groups, and parents. The New Mexico Education Association, the New Mexico Taxpayers Association, and the Parent Teacher Association played a major role in determining the philosophy and character of the New Mexico public school system.

There were several other events during this period that affected the future of education. The School Budget Office was established in 1923 with a director to be appointed by the governor; this office later came under the Department of Finance and Administration created in 1957. By constitutional amendment in 1986, the Department of Finance and Administration became part of the State Department of Education. The Legislative Act in 1923 created the Public School Code, which included the creation of a statewide 20-mill property tax. (A mill is $1 per $1,000 of assessed property evaluation.) This provision, in effect, limited the amount of taxes that could be assessed for education. Earmarking funds (identifying the sources for which the funds could be spent) for education became the norm; for example, gross receipts taxes became earmarked funds.

In 1923 the legislature passed a law that limited the tax levy against property to 40.5 mills for all purposes. This was passed under the influence of the Taxpayers Association which existed from 1916 to 1971. This 1923 legislation provided 18.0 mills for county school tax and 5.0 for school district tax. The Great Depression brought hard times to New Mexico schools. In 1933, the state voters approved a constitutional amendment that would limit to 20 mills (down from 23) the maximum levy that could be imposed on property for schools except for voter-approved bonded indebtedness. This mill limitation caused major financial problems for schools. In 1934, Governor Andrew W. Hockenhull called a special session of the legislature, and a gross receipts tax was created; this gross receipts tax included a 2 percent tax on almost any retail enterprise, including gas, oil, and potash mining.

The Governor's Citizens Taxpayers Committee was appointed in 1940 to address the distribution of financial resources for all state government needs. The committee recommended laws separating the school transportation budget from operating monies distributed to school districts determined by an equalization formula, which was based on average daily attendance (ADA). From the 1940s to the 1960s, the formula for distributing school funds remained essentially static: the state distributed monies based on ADA to school districts; those funds were used for daily operations; the school district levied local property taxes for capital outlay (building and equipment) projects. Major discrepancies resulting from varying property values developed over the years in school districts across the state.

From World War II to Sputnik (1957)

No major financing changes occurred between 1945 and 1957, despite major discussion and controversies about local control and state restrictions and disputes about distribution of funds between rural and urban areas. Several studies of educational organizations and administrative matters were mandated by the legislatures. The first study by the Education Survey Board of the State of New Mexico produced *Public Education in New Mexico* in 1948 (New Mexico State Board of Education: A Report prepared by George Peabody College). This was the most extensive study of education ever conducted in New Mexico; however, with the exception of a provision that provided for legislative support for operational reserves to be used for the construction of classrooms and capital outlay emergencies, no change came about as a result of this study.

A second study authorized by the legislature was undertaken in 1951–52. This study came to be known as the "Little Hoover Commission Report" (Wiley 1968, 103). While the report made several recommendations that affected public school funding (creation of the Department of Finance and Administration, the abolition of earmarked funds, the reorganization of the State Board of Education, and the creation of a weighting formula for distribution of funds), these recommendations were not implemented until the late 1950s and 1960s.

A major event during this time was a court case (*Zeller v. Huff*) referred to as the "Dixon Case," which questioned the practice of Catholic nuns teaching in the public schools. The case became moot when Archbishop Edwin O. Byrne withdrew the nuns from teaching in public schools. This case had a financial impact because it forced school districts and the state to train and hire regular teaching staff. This event also necessitated a more involved compensation system for public school teachers; regular teaching staff required higher salaries than those paid to nuns who were partially supported by the Catholic Church.

The Late '50s and the Turbulent '60s

New Mexico and the rest of the country reacted with calls for educational reform as the "Space Age" began. The decade after 1957 saw major legal changes in the organization and finance of state public schools. Reorganization began at the top, with different

procedures for selecting the state superintendent of public instruction and members of the State Board of Education. In 1958, the
people approved an amendment whereby the State Board of
Education, composed of one member from each judicial district,
would be elected; this board would have the power to appoint the
state superintendent. In 1959, the State Board of Education
named Tom Wiley, who previously had been elected to the position, as New Mexico's first appointed state superintendent of
public instruction. This action brought the state a step closer to
having the programmatic as well as the financial function of
schools under the State Board of Education, the constitutional
agency responsible for education in the state.

Several obstacles, some of which exist today, hampered
attempts to improve public education during the late 1950s and
early 1960s. Teacher salaries were low, resulting in loss of quality teachers to other states or to other careers. New Mexico had
the second highest ratio in the nation of school-age children to
the general population, producing overcrowded classrooms.
Sources of earmarked revenues dropped because of poor economic conditions, leaving too little money to meet current needs.
A new retirement system established in 1957 was costing the
state three times the cost of the previous plan. Each of these
obstacles was aggravated by lack of financial resources.

In 1960, Governor John Burroughs named a Commission on
Educational Finance to study the financial situation and report
before the legislative session; however, with a change in governor that year, these recommendations went nowhere. In 1961,
Dr. Paul Mort of Columbia University Teacher's College completed a study commissioned by the State Board of Education
(*Toward a More Dynamic Fiscal Policy for New Mexico
Schools*). This study contributed to legislation that reduced educational resources, because the total tax impact on the citizen
had to be considered and the resources of the school district
reduced to offset municipal government costs.

⟶

AND THE WINNER IS?

Warfare of a benign nature was always the rule in
describing the relations between the Governor's Finance
Office and the State Superintendent of Schools. Whether
budget auditors or later finance chiefs, there existed a

definite rivalry, with skirmishes over budget and pro-gram. The unification of these functions under the State Department of Education brought that era to a close.

⤙

Several efforts at comprehensive studies of public school finance were undertaken and reports issued during this period. The Educational Research Committee (funded by the legislature), the State Department of Education (with the cooperation of the Legislative School Study Committee), and the New Mexico Education Association (with the assistance of the National Education Association and the Albuquerque Public Schools) col-laborated in efforts to study public school finance in New Mexico.

Public School Finance Since 1969

By the end of the 1960s, several studies determined that great inequities existed in the amount of money that school districts had to budget for their schools. At that time, the basic approach was for the state to provide a basic foundation or minimum fund-ing for each school district; the districts were then free to sup-plement with their own resources, primarily property taxes. The use of property taxes was inequitable because of the differing property values in each district; in 1973, for example, the amount by which districts could supplement the state minimum ranged from $50 to $700 per child.

⤙

SEND IN THE MARINES! AND AGAIN!

State Superintendent Leonard DeLayo was a strong and outstanding educational spokesman in New Mexico's schools; and his positions were often challenged by an equally powerful voice in the Finance Office, that of Harry Wugalter, one of New Mexico's premier finance leaders. The story goes that Governor Jerry Apodaca's term of office was a tumultuous time because Governor Apodaca, Superintendent DeLayo, and Finance Chief Wugalter were all ex-Marines. It was like fighting a World War II battle all over again. These men, even with their rivalry, made significant contributions to the advancement of education in New Mexico. The Marines, again! A story goes that in the early 1980s,

the University of New Mexico's Department of
Educational Administration invited Finance Chief Al
Clemmons to address a small forum of university and
public school administrators on the issue of public
schools, finance, and other matters at a luncheon meeting. State Superintendent DeLayo, on a visit to a neighboring school district, learned of the forum and invited
himself to join the discussion. Needless to say, radio,
TV, and newspapers practically outnumbered the participants. It turned out to be a "great debate."

⟶

   In the early 1970s, equity concerns became more compelling
as a result of nationwide attention to equal protection issues in
many social arenas created by two school finance cases, *Serrano
v. Priest* in California and *Rodriguez v. San Antonio* in Texas
(Colton and Mondragón 1998, 46). Both cases reaffirmed that
education is governed by the state, not the federal government.
Other factors and forces suggested the need for changes to equalize the tremendous differences in the ability of the individual
school districts to fund education. There was a national education finance project that provided a model for funding schools,
and a doctoral dissertation at the University of New Mexico utilizing a computer model for educational finance completed by
Dr. Larry Huxel showed that New Mexico had a system that contributed to this inequity (Huxel 1973). Legislators, the governor,
and the State Board of Education knew that the state would not
prevail if a lawsuit were filed; therefore, the legislature, which
had developed a coalition of Democrats and Republicans, was
ready to confront the issue.
   In early 1973, responding to widespread criticism of the
public school funding process, Governor Bruce King appointed
an advisory committee to study public school finance and to recommend improvements. The individuals and organizations on
the advisory committee included the chief of public school
finance, the state superintendent of public instruction, the representatives of the executive branch, the Legislative Education
Study Committee, the chair of the Senate Finance Committee,
the representatives of small and large school districts, and the
PTA representatives. Following the leadership of the chairman
of the Senate Finance Committee, the state superintendent of

public instruction, and the chief of public school finance, the committee recommended the State Equalization Guarantee, commonly known as the Public School Funding Formula.

⟿

POLITICAL TACTICS?

"Once the dimensions of the formula were firm, the question of sponsorship arose. LSSC membership . . . introduced the legislation and 'worked the floors' of both houses. Printed copies of the funding bill were unavailable during the first four days of the four-week session. Without printed copies, the opposition found it difficult to coalesce around verbal 'hearsay' and lists of weights.

"Where the bill entered the forum was strategic. It had been supposed that the chairman of the LSSC, a senator, would introduce the bill in the Senate Education Committee. However, the membership of that committee was split. Half of the membership resided in 'losing' districts. They were decidedly opposed to the bill. Therefore, it was resolved that the assistant chairman, a House member, would launch the bill in the House Education Committee where membership was favorable and where the bill would accrue verbal mileage, understanding, and support. Its reception there and later on the House floor was favorable.

"The bill then moved into the Senate Education Committee where its early demise had been sidestepped. One committee member favorable to the formula was, unfortunately, very ill. Another from a 'losing' district was politically unable to support the bill, but philosophically he favored equalization. This member was himself a sponsor of another bill to establish a park in his home area. Although he could not vote for the bill in committee, he might support a neutral motion if he saw subsequent support for his own park bill. A motion of 'no recommendation' would move the bill out of committee, while a 'do pass' motion would certainly be defeated. It was, therefore, moved that, in deference to their ill colleague known to favor the bill, the Senate Education Committee give

the bill a 'no recommendation.' The motion passed, as
did House Bill 85 later on the floor of the Senate."
(Krueger 1975, 86–95)

The Public School Funding Formula

The State Equalization Guarantee

The State Equalization Guarantee formula, rooted in the principle that each state public school student is entitled to equal educational opportunity despite differences in the wealth of local
school districts, was based on the National Finance Project
model developed in the late 1960s and 1970s. Three basic equalization features were recommended:

1. Funding through the formula all aspects of educational
   need, including special programs (i.e., bilingual education and special education) with a weighting system
   reflecting the different costs of various components of
   educational need;
2. Guaranteeing all districts the same amount of funds per
   unit of identified need; and
3. Taking the district's wealth into account before determining the amount of state funds for which the district is
   eligible.

Goals: The goal of the State Equalization Guarantee, based
on the 1974 Public School Finance Act (22-8-17 through 25
New Mexico Statutes Annotated [NMSA]), is to equalize
financial opportunity at the highest possible revenue level and
to guarantee each New Mexico public school student equal
access to programs and services appropriate to his or her educational need, regardless of geographic location or local economic conditions. The formula also guarantees noncategorical
funding (school districts have latitude on how to use these
funds) so that school districts apply their allocation to meet
the needs of their particular school district.

Program Cost: The formula uses a cost differential to reflect
the costs associated with providing educational services to students with diverse needs (i.e., elementary, high school, special

education, bilingual). The program cost for each school district is determined by multiplying the student full-time equivalency in a particular grade and a program full-time equivalency by the respective cost differential to generate units. The membership is determined by the average of the 40th, 80th and 120th day enrollments. All of the program units are added, and the total of the program units is multiplied by the training and experience (T & E) of teachers index to produce the adjusted program unit. Other factors are added to the adjusted program unit:

- Units generated by students in nonprofit special education institutions,
- Units generated by various size adjustment factors in the formula for small and rural schools and districts,
- Units generated by growing districts,
- Units generated by newly created districts,
- Save-harmless units generated to protect very small districts from too rapid decline, and
- At-risk factors.

The grand total of all units is then multiplied by the unit value established by the legislature each year, resulting in a district's program cost, which is then adjusted to determine the district's State Equalization Guarantee. (See Figure 7 for the Operational Funding diagram.)

State Equalization Guarantee: Program cost is the amount of money assumed to be necessary for a given district with a particular configuration of students and educational programs. The district's State Equalization Guarantee is the amount of money the state of New Mexico "guarantees" to provide the district to defray most of the program cost. The exact amount is determined by

- **adding** first the revenue coming into the district as a result of a required half-mill property tax and second the revenue generated by PL 874 (Impact Aid), except that generated for special education and any revenue generated through Forest Reserve Funds;
- **multiplying** the result by 75 percent to determine the revenue for which the state takes credit; (the percentage was

OPERATIONAL FUNDING

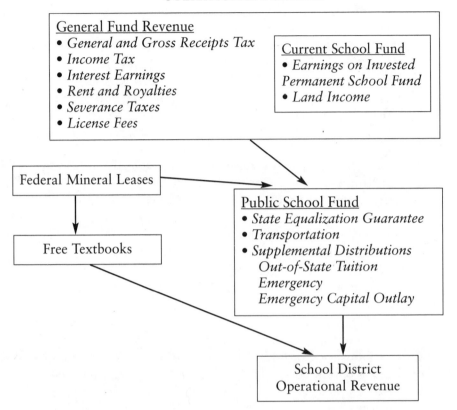

Figure 7. Nearly all state-level school district operational funds are distributed through the Public School Fund. Revenues are derived from the following sources: the General Fund, the Current School Fund, and the Federal Mineral Leasing revune. Only one significant state appropriation is not distributed through the Public School Fund, the Free Textbook appropriation, which is made from Federal Mineral Leasing revenue. The remainder of the Federal Mineral Leasing revenue is deposited to the Public School Fund. The Free Texbook allocation is made on the basis of the 40th day membership (22-15-9 NMSA 1978).

originally 95 percent; this has been changed due to litigation by some school districts in which the court ruled
a need to equitably address school district needs); and
- **subtracting** the credit amount from program cost. (See
  Appendix 4 for the Funding Formula design.)

Districts participating in the utility conservation (savings on
utilities) program will have an additional amount subtracted
from the program unit (New Mexico State Department of
Education 2001).

Ninety-five percent of all funds for operational purposes for
school districts are derived through the State Equalization
Guarantee formula, except for transportation and instructional
materials. (Table 1 presents a ten-year review of General Fund
appropriations.) While there have been some thirty adjustments
to the formula since its inception and a number of additional
adjustments have been suggested, the formula remains today
essentially the same as was enacted by the legislature in 1974.
In the legislative session of 1981, a bill coined the "Big Mac,"
introduced by State Representative Colin McMillan, reduced
the property taxes from $8.95 per $1,000 to $0.50 per $1,000.
One motivation for this bill was that the revenues for the state
had produced a large surplus primarily due to oil and gas taxes
on increased production stimulated by the oil crisis in the
Middle East.

Until the mid-1980s, significant gains were made in support
for education in the form of increased salaries for teachers and
for programs such as the arts, kindergarten, counseling, and
health services. Funds allocated for education increased to 51
percent of the state budget in 1988; that figure had decreased to
45 percent of the state budget by 1997. Reduced property tax
revenue and the declining surplus caused dramatic changes, and
the impact on the educational system was drastic. The 1986
Reform Act was designed to improve education, but with inadequate funding, it was not possible.

In 1994, a task force appointed by the legislature, the governor, and the State Board of Education completed a study of the
funding of schools, which concluded that the State Equalization
Guarantee funding formula was one of the most equitable in the
country. A major concern was identified about the amount of

money that the state was putting into the formula. The task force recommendation included putting an additional amount of approximately $55 million into the formula for 1996–97. The legislature in general agreed with the recommendation, and the governor signed the bill into law. The task force emphasized that while the financing for operations of the school was equitable, the financing and funding for capital outlay of school districts was inequitable.

THE GODFATHERS

Al Clemmons, one of New Mexico's outstanding finance chiefs, was part of a group of University of New Mexico doctoral candidates who researched the 1974 School Finance Formula. This group gained national recognition; participants included Dr. Larry Huxel, Dr. José Garcia, Dr. Placido Garcia Jr., and Dr. J. Patrick Garcia. Harry Wugalter was the author-creator-genius guiding the 1974 Finance Formula. These men, including some legislators, might be called the godfathers of the New Mexico State Funding Formula.

Capital Outlay Funding of Schools

State Supported Funding

The Public School Capital Outlay Act was enacted in 1975. This act is commonly known as the "Critical Capital Outlay Fund" because it addresses critical needs that local districts cannot finance. The legislature appropriates varying amounts from the General Fund to the Public School Capital Outlay Fund. (Until 2001, 60 percent of the funds from the New Mexico Lottery were included; currently, all lottery revenue goes for post-secondary student scholarships for qualified New Mexico students.) The Public School Capital Outlay Council (PSCOC) allocates capital outlay funds to qualifying districts.

The PSCOC membership includes the secretary of the Department of Finance and Administration, the secretary of public education, the governor, the president of the New Mexico School Boards Association, the director of the Construction Industries Division, the president of the Public Education

Commission, the director of the Legislative Education Study Committee, the director of the Legislative Finance Committee, and the director of the Legislative Council Service. Legislative appropriations have varied from $36 million in 1996 to $0 in 1997 and $33 million in 1998. This variation in the amount of dollars allocated reflects the influence exercised by the New Mexico State Legislature.

To be eligible for PSCOC funding, a district must meet two financial qualifications: (1) the district must be bonded to at least 65 percent of its constitutional bonding capacity; and (2) the district must have the Public School Capital Improvements Act (NM SB 9) two-mill levy in place. (As indicated in the chapters on governance and the judicial system, this part of the financing of schools has changed to make the system more equitable.)

Local Financial Support

Before capital outlay revisions in 2001, approximately 90 percent of the Critical Capital Outlay funding for improvements for schools came from the local districts. The practice had been that public school capital outlay funding was primarily a local responsibility and was based on the property wealth of individual school districts. Methods that districts used to finance their respective capital outlay needs included:

General Obligation Bonds: school districts could issue bonds for up to 6 percent of their assessed evaluation;
Public School Capital Improvement Act: a two-mill levy mechanism;
Public School Building Act: allowed districts to impose up to 10 mills for a maximum of five years on the net taxable value of property;
Education Technology Equipment Act: generated funds based on enrollment of the school district; amount established annually by the legislature.

Some of these methods for capital outlay revenues are currently used, and some modifications to these methods were made in 2001, 2002, and 2003. There is also a fund in the general state budget from which the secretary of public education can allocate funds to school districts experiencing emergency needs.

Litigation Impacting Capital Outlay

In 1998, three school districts filed a lawsuit against the state proclaiming that because a large amount of property in their districts belonged to Indian tribes, the tax base was not sufficient for district capital outlay needs. These districts and others that qualify for federal assistance under PL 874 (impact aid) claim that because 95 percent of this impact aid money goes into the state equalization formula, a mere 5 percent of the aid is left for their capital outlay needs. Assigning PL 874 to the State Equalization Guarantee formula was allowed by federal definition. The suit claimed, however, that this was against the state constitution; and that the state was not providing a free and equitable education with adequate funding for students. The court found in favor of the school districts. However, the ruling provided the opportunity for the state to develop a system to address this inequity; and the judge allowed the legislature and the State Department of Education to appoint a task force to study the issue and devise a plan to correct these inequities. Legislation has been enacted to recognize these changes.

Revisions to Capital Outlay Funding of Schools

The 2001 legislature made revisions to the Capital Outlay Act. The State Board of Education through the State Department of Education added new procedures to address the capital outlay program for school districts. These new regulations include the following:

> *Deficiency Corrections for Health and Safety:* A new section of the law was developed that allows the PSCOC to award funds for correction of health and safety–related deficiencies in public school facilities for all school districts. The PSCOC was required to develop guidelines by September 2001, consistent with the Construction Industry Licensing Act, to identify serious code deficiencies in public schools and charter schools. Needs identified are earmarked, and a method of allocating funds to correct deficiencies is developed and implemented. School districts qualify for deficiency correction regardless of their bonded indebtedness.
>
> School districts have identified deficiencies, and the state is required to provide funding. Funding of $200 million from

the general funds and bonds will be provided. There is a fund of $1.1 million provided to establish a deficiency correction unit within the PSCOC to oversee this component.

The Public School Capital Outlay Act (PSCOA): This act was designed so that a school district must lower its bond indebtedness by September 2003 to 65 percent (down from 75 percent) to qualify for critical capital outlay funds. Districts are required to include charter schools and full-day kindergartens and must have a five-year plan to include a "current" preventative building maintenance plan for each school in the district. The revised PSCOA also called for all school districts to be eligible to apply regardless of their bonded indebtedness.

Funding priorities are to be established statewide based on adequacy standards. A distribution formula will be implemented that considers the ability of the school district to levy taxes and the relative wealth of the district when compared to the state average. The Public School Capital Outlay Council requires that districts follow guidelines to ensure that a five-year plan is followed and that funds are utilized in a prudent manner and are based on state standards.

The Public School Capital Improvement Act (PSCIA): Under this act, the state guarantee for capital improvement projects is increased from $35 to $50 per student membership unit for fiscal year 2002 to fiscal year 2004 and thereafter as certified by the secretary of public education. The Public School Capital Outlay Council was required to determine the amount required by June 1, 2004, and June 1 thereafter for the next fiscal year.

Severance Tax Bonding Act (STBA): This act authorizes the State Board of Finance to sell State Severance Tax Bonds (SSTB) when the Public School Capital Outlay Council certifies that SSTB are needed for public school capital outlay projects as authorized under the Public School Capital Outlay Act. Starting in the fiscal year 2002, the proceeds from the School Improvement Act and the Public School Capital Improvement Act are deposited in the Public School Capital Outlay Improvement Fund, with the remaining funds deposited in the Public School Capital Fund (except in the fiscal year 2001 when $50 million was deposited in the Public School Capital Outlay Fund for the correction of outstanding capital outlay deficiencies).

This Public School Capital Outlay plan continues to be assessed by the judge under the auspices of a special Master of the Court. The legislature has also continued to have a capital outlay task force continue to study and make recommendations for improvements to the formula. One of the major changes included the reduction of the amount of local funds that go into the State Equalization Funding Formula from 95 to 75 percent for the 2001 fiscal year, increasing the amount of property school districts could tax for their capital outlay needs. It is possible that limited financial resources will create an emphasis on adequacy in capital outlay funding rather than equity in funding.

⌐

GOVERNMENT LEADERS AND DETERMINED CITIZEN HEROES

Public education and New Mexico's children depend upon government leaders, legislators, and determined citizens for support and leadership. Analysis, assessment, vision, ingenuity, imagination, integrity, political finesse, and just plain old hard work in response to challenges might typify some of our heroes. Without the support of these leaders and other citizen leaders, New Mexico financially might still be "planting a field of corn" or looking for reform for each new generation: Aubrey Dunn, Eleanor Ortiz, Toney Anaya, Lenton Malry, David Salmon, Catherine Smith, Jack Campbell, Mimi Stewart, Bruce King, Cynthia Nava, Jerry Apodaca, Leonard Tsosie, Bill Richardson, Flora Sanchez, Millie Pogna, Rick Miera, Bill Warren, Joe Fidel, Manny Aragon, Jeanette Stromberg, Hank Willis, Sam Vigil, Virginia Trujillo, Richard Romero, S. Y. Jackson, Joe Carraro, and a host of others. The list goes on and on and on . . .

⌐

Summary and Reflections

Equitable financing of New Mexico public schools is the ultimate goal of the state legislature and the secretary of public education, and the process for assuring equity has been changing and improving over the years. Increasingly, adequacy has become a major issue, which means there are inadequate financial resources to meet all school district needs in an equitable manner.

New Mexico began supporting schools by planting a field of corn and has progressed to the present equitable financial support system. It is the intent of the legislature, the governor, and the state to be in compliance with the constitutional mandate for providing efficient and effective public schools for every eligible student in the state, including the capital outlay funding for schools. New Mexico citizens have been recognized for their high per capita level of contribution to schools. Studies have shown that the state has developed one of the most equitable finance formula distribution systems in the nation; however, adequate financial support is still lacking. There are not enough resources—taxes and permanent school fund revenues—to appropriately and completely meet the commitment to each student in the state.

Providing resources for public schools is becoming increasingly complex as the space age and global issues impacting education are assessed, such as technological, environmental, economic, cultural, and health. Lack of a substantial tax base in many of the school districts in New Mexico means that there must be sharing of resources if the state is to continue to be faithful to its concepts of equality, equity, excellence, and accountability. School buildings and equipment must be replaced; funding must be provided on an equitable basis so that those districts with a low tax base have adequate facilities for the education of all children.

While financing of the public schools in New Mexico has been studied, analyzed, and improved over the years, it is absolutely essential that the strength of the funding formula developed and utilized by the state of New Mexico continue to be utilized, even as changes in governance and guidelines are made. Some changes continue to develop. The 2003 legislature proposed a constitutional amendment and the voters approved the amendment to increase the annual amount of interest that may be taken from the permanent school fund from 4.7 to 5.5 percent. This would generate approximately 75 million additional dollars for the public schools per year for five years. This is just an example of how the elected state representatives are willing to improve funding for public schools. Another major change created by the 2003 legislature (NM HB 212) was a comprehensive educational reform bill that provides for a strong compensation system for teachers; the beginning salary for a teacher will range from $30,000 to $50,000, in a phase-in plan over the next five years. This will help retain excellent teachers. It will also draw teachers from other states, rather than losing them to other states.

As we reflect on finance, we must begin to review the roles of local, state, and federal involvement in providing a sound education for all students. To compete with the rest of the country for highly qualified teachers and administrators, New Mexico and other states at the lower end of the financial spectrum may require assistance from the federal government. Demands and expectations from the community, the state, and recent federal legislation call for greater support for the public schools. Are the federal and state government entities willing to increase financial support? Support for education in New Mexico is approximately 95 percent from the state, 3 percent from the federal government (this percentage does not include direct federal appropriations to school districts, i.e., Title I, Title VII), and 2 percent from the local district. Will the state continue to increase its contribution? Is the federal government willing to increase its contribution? Local level support is limited because of the needs of other government entities, a premise that might also be said for state support. What would the implications for education be if focus shifted from a concept of equity to a concept of adequacy? We cannot emphasize one over the other; both equity and adequacy are important.

Citizens of New Mexico expect an effective and productive education to be provided for their children; this effort will be enhanced with improved economic development of the state. It is important that every citizen become aware of the economics surrounding the education profession and of the increased economic implications that accompany each child's achieving an appropriate education.

Chapter 6 Questions and Related Materials

Analyzing New Mexico school finance from a historical view, what would you consider to be the most important or crucial changes that occurred?

Why is the New Mexico school finance system considered a national model?

Describe the concepts of *equity and equality* as they apply to educational finance in New Mexico.

Will or should the federal government consider equalizing educational funding across the country as New Mexico has equalized education across the local school districts?

Describe the New Mexico Public School Permanent Fund that is provided in the New Mexico Constitution.

Ball, Sharon (2002)
Colton, David; Mondragón, John (1998)
Hain, Paul; Garcia, F. Chris; St. Clair, Gilbert (1994)
Huxel, Larry (1973)
Krueger, Jo Ann (1975)
Mort, Paul (1961)
New Mexico State Department of Education:
    How New Mexico Schools Are Funded (1976)
Wiley, Tom (1968)

CHAPTER 7

School Improvements and Educational Reform

The history of the New Mexico education system reflects changes not always known as educational reform. Some of these changes have been based on need, while some have been created by the political climate. Other changes have been the result of demands by local, state, or national agencies or interest groups, and some have been created by individuals. Change may indicate efforts to comply with the wishes of one or more groups; it may indicate efforts to modify or improve that which is already in existence.

Major players in school improvements and change in New Mexico have been legislators, state boards of education, state superintendents, governors, teachers' unions, school administrators, and other interest groups concerned with specific issues. Special interest groups have been involved with organizers from outside New Mexico, and some have begun at the local school level with issues involving their students only. Other reforms or changes may have been caused by economic, urban/rural needs, or by immigration issues. Federal initiatives and financial incentives have also created change in education in New Mexico.

While change may have been generated on a formal, legal, or organized basis or on an informal action such as a meeting or a walk-out, the term *reform* in education has come to mean deliberate and specific efforts to create planned changes in specific areas of the educational program. These changes may be in program, in finance, or in organizational operations. Tyack and Cuban define educational reform as "planned efforts to change schools in order to correct perceived social and educational problems" (Tyack and Cuban 1995, 4). The ultimate goal of educational change or reform, regardless in what area of the system, is to improve the quality of education; some reforms have had more positive effects than others. An inherent property of reform may result in loss of control, loss of funding, even loss of power. Local and state reforms have been impacted by changes and reforms at the national level, a phenomenon of interest because public education is the responsibility of state government. There is no mention of education as a national responsibility in the U.S. Constitution.

What's New?

Educational reform can be contagious; suddenly there are many players who sincerely want to be part of change. In the middle 1980s, the various institutions of higher education in New Mexico received a request from a school superintendent in one of the school districts asking for a list of innovative programs and practices that were currently in vogue (!) and that the universities and colleges could recommend. The superintendent meant well, but ignored the most basic of considerations: what were the needs of the students in that school district?

However, a review of the major reforms at the national level serves as a backdrop to reforms at the state level. Historical realities peculiar to New Mexico have influenced educational reform, particularly in its financial and economic forces. The multicultural nature of New Mexico has most emphatically affected educational reform. Major themes that are reflected by both national and state reforms include equity, equality, excellence, and accountability. Equity is providing financial support according to needs, i.e., special education, bilingual education, students at risk; equality means providing equal support—the same amount of financial support per child, regardless of need. A growing issue, in light of financial resources in New Mexico, is that of adequacy.

National School Reform

An early major purpose of public education was to change the indigenous peoples, to educate immigrants, and to bring cohesion to the nation. A later major purpose of public education was to inculcate democratic principles spelled out by the founding fathers in the Declaration of Independence and in the Constitution. Conflicts were created when needs were ignored or were deliberately approached in ways that did not parallel the basic principles of a democratic society.

A major fallacy was the attitude toward education of the Native American population and the general policy pertaining to Native Americans. Much might be written about similar attitudes that existed about other minority populations, such as physically challenged children, female students, and those students who were educationally challenged. Developing an appropriate educational environment that met the principles of equity, equality, excellence, and accountability for all students only gradually grew to be a part of the concept of public education for all students.

Another major group that was deliberately treated inequitably from the general population was the African American students. African American children were to be educated in "separate but equal" schools. Mexican American students represented another group left out of the system in many communities. These students, too, were not part of the mainstream of the educational system because of language, culture, and bias. Disabled students often were not included in the public school system and were either kept at home or placed in institutions away from their families and communities. Another group that was somewhat excluded, although included to some degree, was female students. Female students were in the system, but their participation was sometimes restricted in such programs as science, mathematics, vocational education, sports, and athletics.

While state changes and reforms did not always address issues in a timely manner, national events that occurred after World War II encouraged major groups to begin to demand equity. Veterans returning from World War II and the Korean conflict went on to higher education on the GI Bill, which led to better jobs and increased expectations of opportunity and equality. The civil rights and women's rights movements contributed to the desire for social equity. Education was at the top of the list of demands. Education and schools are fairly common life experiences to all. When issues that may have remained dormant in New Mexico were brought to the forefront by national demands for reform, the people of New Mexico and its education system responded. Major national changes and reforms took place that had tremendous impact on the educational system in New Mexico.

Brown v. The Board of Education 1954

The African American population became dissatisfied with the education offered their children. The "separate but equal" system had been established by a ruling of the U.S. Supreme Court that stated that as long as education was equal it could be separate (*Plessy v. Ferguson*, 1896). In 1954, in *Brown v. The Board of Education*, the U.S. Supreme Court ruled that the "separate but equal" system of education was in conflict with the 14th Amendment to the U.S. Constitution. The Court ordered that involuntary segregation cease within a reasonable time (Pullian and Van Paten 2002, 241). This ruling was received by some states with opposition and resistance.

The Civil Rights Act of 1964

Resistance to integration in other areas besides public schools led to the passage of the Civil Rights Act of 1964. This act specified that no person could be discriminated against on the basis of race, color, sex, or national origin in any program that received federal assistance. This meant, in effect, that federal funding could be withheld from school districts that failed to adopt reasonable and acceptable plans for integration. Access to federal funding had become by 1964 a small percentage of the total school budgets, but that funding provided significant impetus for development of school programs.

The Elementary and Secondary Education Act 1965

Federal aid to education took a giant step with the passage of the Elementary and Secondary Education Act (ESEA) of 1965. This act provided funds for textbooks, materials, and services; however, the major purpose was to ensure that children from low-income families had access to an appropriate education. One of the programs was Title I, which provided funding specifically for reading and math programs for students determined to be in the greatest need. This act has been renewed every four years. The latest ESEA version was approved in 2002 and is known as the Leave No Child Behind Act. Added in this new version is a strong accountability component that includes provisions for qualified teachers and a strong student and school testing program based on identified standards.

Multicultural and Bilingual Education 1968

The composition of the national population became more diverse with the arrival of new immigrants; minority populations became the majority in many cities and states. Global economic and political changes fostered rapid growth in urban areas. Provision for bilingual education was created by the passage of the Bilingual Education Act of 1968, which allocated funds intended to provide an appropriate education to students with a language other than English as their first language. In a U.S. Supreme Court case known as *Lau v. Nichols,* it was ruled under the Civil Rights Act that Asian students were denied an appropriate education because they were taught in English, which they did not understand. This case strengthened the Bilingual Education Act of 1968. The act addresses the many language minorities, including Hispanic and Native American students.

Education of the Exceptional Child 1974

Public Law 94-142 was passed by Congress and signed by the President in 1974. At that time, it was estimated that 1.74 million students were not in school because of a disability and that another 4.0 million were not receiving an appropriate education. Parents brought such pressure that the law was passed by Congress with a great majority. The law requires that students with disabilities must be educated in the least restrictive environment for the individual child. The law was amended in 1997 and is now known as Individuals with Disabilities Education Act (IDEA). This legislation and its improvements have been supported financially by both state and federal governments.

⤚

Taking a Chance?

Career Education loomed large as an educational reform at the national level in the 1970s under the leadership of U.S. Commissioner of Education Simon Marland. At the state level, and even more so at the local level, it took some strange turns. The most bizarre was that of an enterprising teacher and principal team that saw "gambling in New Mexico's future" and sought to provide instruction in the maintenance of one-armed bandits, an apt description of slot machines. Although today casinos are in full evidence in New Mexico, this instructional tale is missing from official reports.

⟶

Title IX of the Education Act of 1972

Title IX addressed inequities related to gender-based treatment of female and male students. Until Title IX was passed in 1971, female students did not have access to the same educational opportunities available to males. Major areas that were often subtly denied to female students were in science, mathematics, engineering, and vocational courses. Another important area denied or offered to female students in limited ways was organized competitive sports; in New Mexico, athletic programs were, in general, offered only on an intramural or a club basis. A significant issue also addressed in Title IX was sexual harassment of female students and employees in the educational system. It also sought to increase employment and pay of female educators.

Nation at Risk Report 1983

National gains in equity and equality accrued during the 1950s, 1960s, and 1970s continued to influence efforts supporting school reform. The focus changed in the early 1980s. During the term of President Ronald Reagan, emphasis was on the impact that education had on the economics of the country, especially as the country became more competitive with other industrial countries. The President directed Secretary of Education T. H. Bell to conduct an evaluation of the education system. The secretary appointed a commission made up of business leaders, educators, and political leaders from across the country. This commission produced a report in 1983 known as *A Nation At Risk: The Imperative for Educational Reform*. The report warned that the "education foundations of our society are presently being eroded by a rising tide of mediocrity that threatens our very future as a nation and a people" (1983, 3). The commission found major shortcomings in the nation's educational system; and it made several recommendations involving curriculum, performance of students, time in school, the relationship between K–12 and colleges of education, and citizen involvement. This report was a strong statement on the state of education in the country and generated vigorous debate. Dozens of reports followed the publication of the *Nation At Risk* report, involving governors, legislators, state boards of education, state departments of education, educators, business groups, and other interest groups.

Goals 2000

After 1983, state governors became very much involved with education, perhaps because of the national reform movements and because of the *Nation At Risk* report specifically. In 1989 a Coalition of Governors conference was called, in which governors and major business corporations participated. The governors developed plans that became known as Goals 2000, setting goals that would be accomplished by the year 2000. The goals included the following:

1. All children will start to school ready to learn.
2. The high school graduation rate will increase to at least 90 percent.
3. Students completing grades 4, 8, and 12 will have competency in academic subject matter, including English, mathematics, science, history, and geography.
4. Students will be first in the world in math and science.
5. Every child will be free of drugs and violence.
6. Schools will offer an environment conducive to learning.
7. Schools will promote partnership and parental involvement.
8. The nation's teaching force will have access to professional development.
9. Every adult American will be literate and possess knowledge to compete in the world economy.

Congress appropriated and made funding available through the Educate America Act of 1994 to address these goals on a nationwide basis, based upon the recommendations of this special interest group. With reauthorization of ESEA (No Child Left Behind) in 2002, funding for Goals 2000 was eliminated. Some of the goals developed by the governors' conference were accomplished, but to varying degrees.

Other National Reforms

With the passage of ESEA and its reenacting through the years since 1965, the federal government became an influential force in educational reform. The federal government contributes only about 7 percent of the total budget support for public education, and its major emphasis has been to provide an equal opportunity to students in greatest need.

Other reforms and changes that have impacted the states and their education systems include magnet schools authorized by the Emergency Assistance Act of 1970 (the magnet concept was not implemented widely) and charter schools, which were created under the 1994 ESEA reauthorization. These schools provide options supporting choice, offering equal educational opportunity, and promoting integration. The U.S. Supreme Court decision of 2002 on vouchers may have great impact on school choice and privatization of public education and the future of educational systems.

⌒

THEY COME AND GO

Educational reforms come and go. There is a certain faddishness to educational reform. In Albuquerque, in the 1970s, the heyday after the 1960s, a "child-centered, open classroom" school was dedicated with great fanfare. Modeled after an English blueprint, it was the latest and the greatest. An outstanding principal and faculty were assigned to guide the new educational entity. A few years following the fanfare of this reform, a most simple incident triggered the demise of the open school concept in Albuquerque. A student—with teacher permission—had been investigating an anthill close to the school; parents came looking for their child, but an alarmed faculty could not locate him. Town meetings followed town meetings; and the classrooms that were open began to be changed as walls were built to assure accountability of children, with assignment of the children to specific teachers. The concept died slowly. Remnants of open, multigroup instruction survive, but the educational reform of the open school died aborning.

⌒

These national reforms are but a few that have had direct influence on educational reform, educational equity, equality, excellence, and accountability at the state level. New Mexico must be sensitive to the needs of its students, its communities, and its relationship to the national education scene.

Reform at the State Level

Educational reform at the national level encompasses changes in educational activities including curriculum, governance, finance, and increased educational options. The needs and pressures brought about by national level reform varied from program needs to economics, politics, and governance. Reform in states followed many of the national trends, addressing the issues of equity and excellence, and a careful balance of these two concepts has been addressed in reforms in the New Mexico education system and in the option of choice of educational opportunities.

The 1923 School Code of New Mexico

Dr. Tom Wiley in his book, *Politics and Purse Strings*, stresses that the financial controls placed on the educational system provided little opportunity or ability for the system to change. Pulling together all the laws involving education under the School Code of 1923 showed that the state had taken leadership in the organization of school laws and statutes, a first step in comprehensive reform. The laws dating back to the New Mexico territorial period were organized under the 1923 School Code to give direction and stability to New Mexico's school system. The School Code is now updated every time a new statute is adopted by the state legislature.

The San Jose/Nambé Reform Project

Special projects and legislative action have directly affected equality and excellence in programs for special needs in New Mexico. One of the first real reform efforts in program and curriculum in New Mexico was known as the San Jose/Nambé Project. The name comes from the schools and the communities where the project was conducted. This program was implemented in collaboration with the University of New Mexico, the State Department of Education, the Albuquerque Public Schools (East San Jose Elementary School), and the community of Nambé. In the 1930s, Dr. Lloyd Tireman from the University of New Mexico organized two experiments in cross-cultural education (Bachelor

1991). Funding for the project came from a grant and from the state. The purpose was two-fold: (1) to provide a more meaningful curriculum for Spanish-speaking students, and (2) to train teachers to serve schools throughout the state with an emphasis on rural communities. The Nambé Project utilized the student's first language and included an extensive community component. The project proved very successful and served as the first bilingual multicultural program in the state. Unfortunately this project was discontinued because of lack of resources.

MEMORIES OF A CADET TEACHER— SEVENTY YEARS LATER

Lincoln County Superintendent Ola Jones took an interest in my teaching after only one year of formal training (1933), and when she heard that UNM was offering a teacher training program, my name was submitted to become a cadet teacher in the East San Jose program. I was one of five teachers from Lincoln County who participated in the project. Dr. Tireman was in England, so we did not get to meet the director of the training program, but his professors and teachers followed the methods outlined in his textbook. The children were mostly poor and Hispanic; if they spoke English, it was limited, and in many cases, they knew no English. The main focus was on vocabulary in grades K–2. Three new words were introduced each day to the kindergarten students on Monday through Thursday, with oral testing on Friday. I spent a month in each grade observing the mentor teachers; one week of that month was spent observing teaching methods. After that time, the cadets took over the classes, developing lesson plans and materials. At the end of each day, the mentor teacher and sometimes the professor would critique our lessons and give us guidance and valuable ideas for improvement. Reading, writing, spelling, grammar, conversation, and math skills were included in the units taught. I do remember that the mentor teachers were very kind and affectionate with the children.—Nellie Miranda Trujillo, 2003

State Constitutional Amendments of 1958, 1988, 2003

A major political and governance reform that was to affect education in the state occurred in 1958 when a constitutional amendment was approved by the citizens creating an elected ten-member State Board of Education with representation from throughout the state. This elected board of education was to then appoint a state superintendent of public instruction. Prior to this time, the board of education was appointed by the governor and the superintendent was elected on a partisan ticket. This meant that the State Board of Education could now carry out its constitutional responsibility for operating the public schools more effectively by selecting a superintendent to manage the State Department of Education and to oversee the public school system.

Another constitutional amendment that brought about management change in education was approved by the voters in 1988 and involved the position of Chief of Public School Finance. The position changed from appointment by the governor to being a staff member in the State Department of Education under the authority of the state superintendent of public instruction. The amendment also approved increasing the membership of the State Board of Education from ten to fifteen. Ten members were elected by voters in the districts, and five were appointed by the governor. This change brought about more unity and balance between program decisions and financial decisions. Several other states have this same organizational arrangement.

An amendment to the constitution in 2003 resulted in a significant change. The amendment provided for the governor to appoint a secretary of public education who would become a member of the governor's cabinet and for an elected ten-member public education commission.

New Mexico Consolidation of School Districts

A recurring issue in New Mexico was the concern about the number and size of school districts. Proponents for reducing the number of small school districts argued that such reorganization was necessary to improve education in the state. This issue emanated directly from the concern of urban school districts about the costs of maintaining the many smaller school districts. Tom Wiley wrote: "Certain legislators became concerned about the cost of small administrative and attendance school units.

Most of these legislators, of course, were from the larger population centers" (1974, 106). The state house of representatives and the senate addressed legislation for school district reorganization; although the senate failed to support the bill, the house passed a bill during the 1962 legislature which directed the State Board of Education to proceed with plans for merging small districts. It also mandated that county school systems having fewer than 1,500 pupils were to be terminated (Wiley 1974, 106). (A summary of New Mexico consolidation laws can be found in Tom Wiley's *An Appraisal of New Mexico School District Consolidation in Bernalillo County, New Mexico*, 48–50.)

The reorganization effort was a tug of war between local districts and the state agency responsible for education. The state had a legal responsibility to deal with ineffective organizational units. Wiley quoted one authority as saying: "Excessive costs, inadequate education service, and inefficient management will continue to be characteristic of the public schools in many areas as long as the multitude of school districts is retained" (1974, 129). School consolidations were part of the long-term struggle between rural and urban districts. Rural problems centered on issues of bonding capacity, transportation, accessibility, demographic changes, and staffing. The focus of urban problems was on growth, municipal overload, special needs, bonding capacity, and management issues.

HUFF AND PUFF?

The struggle for and against consolidation of rural school districts is reflected in the confrontations between Raymond Huff of the Clayton school district and John Milne of the Albuquerque school district. Each rural and urban "baron" argued for his school situation and for improvement of schools in his respective domain.

What emerged from the entire consolidation process was the reduction in the number of school districts in New Mexico. By 1964, progress had been made in reorganization. In 1941, there were 930 school districts; in 2004, there were 89. School officials, legislators, and citizens recognized that reorganization was important for an efficient school system. Issues between rural and urban New Mexico continue. "The real issue relates to the quality of their educational offerings" (Wiley 1974, 130).

~~

Visit School Districts?

Prior to 1945, if you took a ride up the Rio Grande in Bernalillo County, starting at Isleta Pueblo, you could enjoy visiting some wonderful and special school communities: Los Padillas, Pajarito, Armijo, Atrisco, Albuquerque, Old Town, Duranes, Candelaria, Griegos, Alameda, and Corrales. If you required mountain air as a respite from the valley, you could find more exotic school communities in Yssarri, Chilili, Escobosa, Tijeras, and San Antonito. You could pass through seventeen school communities in that short ride.

~~

Public School Finance Act of 1974

One of the most significant educational reforms occurred when the legislature approved the Public School Finance Act of 1974. (Details of this act are found in Chapter 6.) The formula equalized educational funding for all of the state's students regardless of their geographical location. The Public School Finance Act resulted from court cases being pursued across the country. Two of the better known cases dealing with equalized educational funding are *Serrano v. Priest* (in California) and *Rodriguez v. San Antonio* (in Texas). The Serrano case was filed because the plaintiffs claimed that the educational finance system was unconstitutional. The Rodriguez case went to the U.S. Supreme Court but was returned with the ruling that the state legislature was responsible for funding education.

The Public School Finance Act of 1974 sought to correct years of funding and educational disparities among state schools. This 1974 reform is recognized as one of the most equitable funding formulas in the country. There have been some changes and adjustments designed to better serve all the students of the state. This formula made it possible for all school districts to plan programs for their unique student populations with the legislature, the governor, and the State Board of Education taking responsibility for financial support. Even though there were intense debates and negotiations, "the rich and the poor" school districts worked together for the benefit of all the students in the state. Poverty and privilege were no longer the norm as they had been in the very early days of education in New Mexico when those communities that could "plant a cornfield" could have teachers.

The 1964 U.S. Civil Rights Act and New Mexico
Bilingual Education

The bilingual education program in New Mexico resulted from a court case known as the Serna v. Portales Municipal School District in 1974. Parents of students in the Portales School District claimed that their children were not receiving an appropriate education because their first language was not English; and that as a result, the children were being discriminated against. This case is similar to the *Lau v. Nichols* case (children taught in a language they did not understand) in California; and, most importantly, it is based on the Civil Rights Act of 1964. The Portales parents won the case, and the state legislature enacted the Bilingual Education Act. This decision brought major reform to the instructional program for a large number of students. The state legislature adjusted the funding formula to provide finances for bilingual programs. Some school districts have increased needs over other districts; the funding formula balances those needs.

Special Education

A major reform in New Mexico to address the needs of students with disabilities was instituted in 1980. Until 1980, the state had refused for more than fourteen years to accept federal funding even after the federal legislation was approved; the state claimed that it did not need federal involvement in program to address the needs of the disabled student. However, the majority of special needs students were not in school; and those who were attending class were taught in self-contained, segregated schools. In 1980, a case was filed in district court by parents and by the New Mexico Association for Retarded Citizens on behalf of students who were not in school because of their disabilities. The plaintiffs won the case based upon the U.S. Civil Rights Act of 1964. New Mexico was mandated to provide a "least restrictive environment" program for a large number of students. Again, the state funding formula was adjusted to provide for the special

education needs of these students; and the state began accepting
federal funding.

⌣

TAKE IT OR LEAVE IT?
It is said that State Superintendent Leonard DeLayo
and APS Superintendent John Milne opposed the controls that accompanied the reform movement for special education; Dr. Milne believed that such programs
would tend to segregate students.

⌣

These two examples of educational reforms in bilingual education and in special education resulted from federal legislation
and were more readily implemented with federal financial categorical assistance. Special programs and reforms have been
developed in bilingual education and in the education of special
needs students in schools across the state. These categorical
monies addressed the needs of specific populations that were not
being appropriately served. Since that time, the state funding formula has contained a factor to support these students.

High School Proficiency Exam 1979
In 1979, the State Board of Education approved the High School
Proficiency Exam that included a performance-based writing
assessment. This marked the beginning of criterion-referenced
testing in New Mexico. The High School Proficiency Exam
identified certain basic skills that all students must possess in
order to receive a high school diploma.

Teacher Preparation and Licensure 1981, 2003
In 1981, the State Board of Education adopted a requirement that
university students enrolled in a teacher preparation program
must demonstrate adequate teaching skills and pass a nationally
endorsed basic skills test. A written test of general knowledge,
communication skills, and teaching practices must be passed by
all applicants for teaching or administration licensure.

In 1983–84, the State Board of Education adopted essential
job competencies for school administrators and teachers and
required that they be evaluated based upon the required competencies. School districts have designed various instruments to be

used for assessment and evaluation of all administrative and teaching personnel.

In 2003, the legislature created a three-tier licensing program in NM HB 212. This law was to be implemented beginning in July 2004.

Student Competencies 1983

In April 1983, the State Board of Education approved a plan requiring school districts to include student competencies of critical thinking and problem solving in all courses. Students were to demonstrate proficiency in the specific competencies of required subjects before they graduated from high school, beginning with the class of 1986–87. This reform has been modified, improved, and evaluated on an ongoing basis since its implementation.

Graduation Requirements 1983, 2003

In April 1983, the State Board of Education adopted new high school graduation requirements, increasing the number of required credits from 18 to 23. Required courses in math and science were doubled, and computer literacy was added. These changes were almost identical to recommendations found in the *Nation At Risk* report in 1983. Graduation requirements have been the focus of both legislative and local district actions; and, in the 2003 legislature, laws were presented, passed, and signed by the governor to increase and modify graduation requirements.

Public School Reform Act of 1986

The New Mexico Public School Reform Act of 1986, which in many ways mirrored the recommendations of the *Nation At Risk* report, was enacted by the legislature. It was the legislature, not the State Board of Education nor the governor, that took the lead in developing this reform act. A coalition of legislators gained enough votes to pass this law. A Reform Commission appointed by the legislature and the governor included representation from the Republican and Democratic parties, educators (public and higher education), and State Board of Education members.

The Public School Reform Act contains a comprehensive package including (1) developing a schedule for reducing class size, (2) releasing teachers from noninstructional duties, (3) setting teacher licensure requirements, (4) establishing student

learning competencies, (5) improving school attendance requirements, (6) expanding testing and graduation requirements, (7)
establishing the number of hours of schooling by grade levels,
(8) testing students, and (9) requiring the recitation of the Pledge
of Allegiance daily. It established standards for student participation in extracurricular activities and had other requirements.
These provisions were to be phased in over a period of five years.
However, many of the requirements in the Public School Reform
Act of 1986 had to be rescinded because of lack of resources
and/or practicality. This lack of resources echoes the historical
plight of education in New Mexico. A significant requirement in
that act that has been implemented is the reduction in class size.

The Reform Act of 1986 represented a political struggle of
liberal, conservative, and centrist or coalition interests. What
emerged was a centrist view of educational reform that succeeded
to the extent that resources allowed and which mirrored national
trends. Coincidentally, history shows that the financial picture
also changed with the passage of the so-called "Big Mac" legislation (named after State Representative Colin McMillan, the
author of the bill), which reduced property taxes from $8.95 per
$1,000 to $0.50 per $1,000. The problem of adequacy would
not go away. In 2003, with approval by the citizens of
Constitutional Amendment Number 2, which will generate
sufficient amounts of revenues ($62–$80 million) to improve
education significantly, the Reform Act of 2003 will bring the
state back to the pre-"Big Mac" days. (See Appendix 5 for a summary of the 1986 Reform Act.)

⟶

REFORM?

The reform movement following the Nation At Risk
report was both contagious and productive. The engine
of reform was driven by state governors and state legislators. In New Mexico, the 1985 Reform Commission,
appointed by Governor Toney Anaya, was appointed
with a bipartisan membership and included professional educators as well as lay persons. The commission
had an ambitious agenda; and, in retrospect, much of
the agenda was adopted into legislation, although the
timelines and funding proved significant obstacles to
implementation of the entire reform bill. Of major

interest was the political or ideological battle waged among commission members for the heart of the bill. Conservatives and liberals vied for power and acceptance of their pet ideas. One glaring and painful exchange occurred when a very conservative state legislator on the commission suggested that a partial answer to school dropout problems could be found by lowering the school "exit" age to thirteen or fourteen, thus eliminating children who were not going to make it anyway! The implication had economic and ethnic overtones, and the commission in a most bipartisan manner attacked the concept. It was never voiced again! In fact, a centrist view emerged among the commission members and even extreme liberal and conservative members realized the merit of such an approach in the 1985 legislation. Idealogues lost that battle. Educational reform was advanced in New Mexico.

The Effective Schools Research

Research in Michigan and New York by Dr. Ron Edmonds significantly influenced educational reform in New Mexico. Dr. Edmonds's research showed that schools with a heavy population of poor and minority students could be effective schools. This research was a response to studies that claimed that the most powerful and perhaps the only influence for the success of students was the home and parents. Edmonds showed that there are indeed schools from poor and minority populations in which students can succeed when certain factors or characteristics are present. According to Edmonds's study, the characteristics of effective schools included the following:

1. A safe and orderly environment exists.
2. There is a climate of high expectations for success.
3. There is strong instructional leadership.
4. There is a clear and focused mission.
5. There is frequent monitoring of student progress.
6. There is a strong home-school relations program.

These effective school characteristics were incorporated into the New Mexico state educational standards (Edmonds 1983).

Site-Based Management

A number of national reports recommended that one effective way to reform schools was to empower the local school faculty, principal, and parents to provide an appropriate educational environment and curriculum for that particular school site. This empowerment reform was provided in many schools in New Mexico in the mid-1980s when local school boards, encouraged by the State Board of Education and the legislature, implemented site-based management, which, in many cases, included site-based budgeting. This concept and practice was supported by the teachers' organizations, and some districts included these practices in the negotiated agreements. Management councils, which included teachers, parents, and other staff, were instituted. These councils were successful to the extent that leadership and support were provided by the district and local school administration. One ingredient basic to the success of site-based management was a strong in-service program for administrators, parents, and teachers provided in a collaborative environment. Site-based management is required by NM HB 212 passed in 2003.

Year-Round Schools

The year-round school reform started in the mid-1980s and had as its foundation the concept that the instructional program could be spread throughout the calendar year. It was also viewed as an excellent way to save on the capital outlay budget and to utilize the savings for the instructional program. According to California research, student achievement was enhanced by the year-round school concept. This major reform effort in New Mexico was implemented in the Albuquerque Public Schools with about thirty schools involved on a voluntary basis; the program continued in six schools 20 years later. A major problem was faced by the district when it attempted to mandate implementation of year-round programs. Parents in K–12 communities saw many disadvantages in this reform effort, including scheduling for parents with children at more than one level (elementary, middle, and high school) and perhaps, most importantly, because of athletic programs.

Technology

Reform involving technology in education escalated with the influence of federal legislation. In New Mexico, the reform was of particular significance because of the large numbers of technological industries in the state. The state legislature enacted the Technology Act in 1994, which provided categorical funds from the legislature based on student population and provided for the establishment of a Technology Advisory Council composed of representatives from across the state. The council provides advice and annual reports for the legislature and for the State Board of Education.

This reform has created an emphasis on technology instruction at the local school level. Boards of education have made commitments to purchase equipment and to access the Internet at individual school sites. The legislature provided funding for the establishment of a "virtual high school" that was operated out of the State Department of Education and that was accessible to high school students throughout the state. Funding cuts briefly curtailed this special technological program. In this program, students in schools all over the state can be involved in global education in a very real way, because computers provide access to that which had only existed in books and in the minds of teachers.

Charter Schools

Charter schools have been in existence in New Mexico since 1993 when the legislature enacted the Charter School Act that authorized creation of charter schools by local school boards of education. This legislation was based on the Improving America Schools Act of 1994. The charter school concept carries site-based management to a higher level with increased parental involvement and participation. The program in New Mexico started with six converted schools, each with a local council or board created to manage the business of education for students in the local chartered school. Early charter schools continued to be affiliated with the local school district in management and finance areas, but they had more power in the area of curriculum and staffing. In 1999, a new law was passed by the legislature giving charter schools more autonomy from the local board of education and increased connection to the State Board of Education. The Public Education Department is responsible for evaluating the charter schools and assessing the achievement of students enrolled in charter schools.

Home Schooling

The original schooling in New Mexico may be considered examples of home schooling; public school education took away some of the original concept of parents teaching children in their homes. Home schooling in New Mexico is permitted by law. A qualified person who must register with the local board of education is required to do the teaching. Students are tested with the regular state mandated testing program, and instructional materials may be obtained from local school districts. Approximately 6,000 students were home schooled in New Mexico in 2003. Some districts have programs at the school site where home school students may participate on a part-time basis.

HOME SCHOOLING OR PUBLIC EDUCATION?

The school year 1933–34 was my first teaching position. I was assigned to teach in a one-room school at Los Alamos Canyon in Lincoln County. The Salcido family, large landowners in the area, raised angora goats on the ranch. The grandparents, Faustino and Maria, were the parents of seven sons and one daughter; the sons were all married and had enough children for a one-room school. It was the first school in that community; and all materials were new, including desks, tables, chairs, and blackboards. My mother helped me assemble the furniture and set up the classroom. I lived with the Salcido family; the classroom was one room in their home. (I had attended New Mexico Highlands University for only one year in preparation for teaching.)—Nellie Miranda Trujillo

State Standards

New Mexico state standards in all curriculum areas were developed under the direction of the State Board of Education. Under the Educate America Act of 1994, states were to develop standards in all curriculum areas. New Mexico content standards and benchmarks were developed by committees that included teachers, administrators, and community members, and have been adopted by the State Board of Education. The Public Education

Department utilized national curriculum organizations such as the National Council of Mathematics to help develop standards. The ultimate goal was to develop a criterion-referenced test based on these standards. By 2003, New Mexico schools had criterion-referenced tests in science and math for grades 4 and 8. The process continues, and all norm-referenced tests will be replaced. This effort began in the fall of 2002 with monies provided under new Elementary and Secondary Education Act (NCLB) legislation.

Building Reform?

It can be said of St. Michaels College, Loretta Academy, Menaul School, and Harwood School that they graduated many future lawyers, teachers, priests, business men and women, and homemakers who made their mark on New Mexico's communities. Perhaps less well known, but equally important at the turn of the century was the Rio Grande Industrial School in Albuquerque's South Valley. A Congregational Church–sponsored school, it, too, saw its graduates become teachers and leaders in the community. The odyssey of the Rio Grande Industrial school site is an interesting one. In the 1940s, the school was reopened as the Lourdes Catholic School and included a sanctuary where Catholics from the area worshipped. In the 1960s and 1970s, the site was transformed into the DARE Drug Addiction Treatment Center and was known throughout the state. In the twenty-first century, this same site and some of its buildings have become Joy Junction, an institution known for its humanitarian enterprise in Albuquerque. Those early Congregational teaching pioneers must be happy in knowing that their school has been through some reforms and still exists, although in a different form.

Accountability

Accountability became a significant subject of educational discussion in the 1960s and 1970s. Leon Lessinger and Ralph Tyler were leading analysts of accountability in education, albeit patterned on industrial models of accountability, which were considered inappropriate for education (Lessinger and Tyler 1971). Concepts of educational accountability were sought and adapted. One of the chief implications of accountability in education is that citizens increasingly demanded to know how their children were learning, what they were learning, and why they were being taught whatever they were being taught. Clearly accountability is one of the important and critical functions of the state educational system.

Accountability in New Mexico schools is based upon the outcomes of education identified in the *Nation At Risk* report of 1983. The *Nation At Risk* report recommended standardized testing at major transition points from one level of schooling to another, particularly from high school to college or to work. The purpose of these tests would be to (a) certify each student's credentials, (b) identify need or remedial intervention, and (c) identify the opportunity for advanced or accelerated work. The intent was to have states pursue these outcomes without a federal educational policy; the goal is excellence in education. Interestingly enough, the New Mexico Reform Act of 1986 addressed almost every educational component in the national report; but it failed to address outcomes. However, in 1989, legislation was passed to correct this oversight. The legislation also identified a requirement that school districts were to publish an annual report that would include standardized achievement test results.

In 1999, an amendment to this law required the "high stakes" testing that is part of the New Mexico accountability process. This amendment carried with it monetary incentives and recognition for high performing schools and sanctions in the form of intervention and corrective actions for low performing schools. Five indices mandated by the statute for accountability are assessments for (1) student achievement using a standardized test, (2) school safety, (3) dropout rate, (4) attendance, and (5) parent and community involvement. Schools are rated based on these indices with ratings that include (1) exemplary, (2) exceeds standards, (3) meets standards, and (4) probationary. If a school is on probationary status for three years, the state superintendent takes over operation of the school; and corrective actions take place. Possible corrective actions include the following: (1) the state takes over with a monitor to oversee the school; (2) the state contracts with a private agency to take over the operation of the school; or (3) the district can provide a corrective plan.

Finally, the state superintendent enforced this accountability action in 2002 by taking over fifteen schools that fell under the provisions of the law. Schools were allowed to develop their own improvement plans.

This accountability program has been in place in the state since 1999, and it mirrors the program mandated in the 2002 reauthorization of the Elementary and Secondary Education Act. Success with the concept of sanctions has yet to be determined other than that no school or district wants to be in danger of being "taken over" by the state. One of the major parts of the new accountability procedure is the requirement to disaggregate test scores by ethnic and economic levels of the students; this has presented some additional challenges for schools and school districts. Those schools that achieve at a high level receive financial incentives; perhaps more important than the money is the pride in being recognized for excellence.

Education Reform Act of 2003

The Education Reform Act of 2003 passed by the New Mexico State Legislature may have had its roots in the report issued by the 22nd New Mexico Town Hall in 1999. The Town Hall sponsored by New Mexico First included 143 representatives from across the state; the representatives included educators, legislators, business people, school board members, teachers, administrators, tribal leaders, State Department of Education staff, and university personnel (New Mexico First 1999). The report, while not an official state report, was distributed widely to legislators and the governor and to public officials and educators throughout the state. The report stated in its introduction:

> The Twenty-Second New Mexico Town Hall convened in Taos on June 3, 1999, to explore the educational system in New Mexico and identify potential reforms to establish a world class educational system for the children of the state. The focus of the discussion was the public school system. Based on the focus of children being our first priority, the Town Hall states unequivocally that our public education system is inadequate (1999, 1).

The report continued with several recommendations on various aspects of the educational system.

Legislative Session of 2001
After much deliberation and discussion during the 2001 legislative session, a task force was appointed by the legislature. The task force had sixty-five members and was composed of legislators, educators, business officials, teachers, administrators, and school board members. The task force was cochaired by David Townsend and I. B. Hoover, two respected citizens. Their charge was to devise a comprehensive education reform bill for the 2002 legislative session. The task force worked diligently for months and prepared a comprehensive report for the legislature. After much debate, the legislature passed a bill in 2002 that addressed major reforms. However, the governor vetoed the legislation, stating that it was too costly.

Legislative Session 2003
The task force continued working with the Legislative Education Study Committee and had an updated report for the 2003 legislative session. With strong support from the newly elected governor, the legislation sponsored by State Representative Mimi Stewart and State Senator Cynthia Nava, NM HB 212, was signed into law. Some of the major components of NM HB 212 included

1. Revision of major portions of the New Mexico School Code;
2. Updating of the accountability law to be in compliance with the federal law, which included an annual report on student achievement;
3. A three-tiered licensure structure with commensurate salary and performance measures for teachers and administrators;
4. Major change in the local governance, which shifted major personnel, instructional, and financial responsibilities from the local board of education to the district superintendent and the school principal;
5. Legislation calling for an elected school council at each school to be involved in the operation of the school; and

6. Notification of parents of teacher, educational assistant, and principal qualifications. (See Figure 8 for HB 212 synopsis.)

Major pieces of reform legislation in 2003 included two constitutional amendments. One amendment impacting the governance of public education created a cabinet position for a secretary of public education appointed by the governor, a Public Education Department, and an elected Public Education Commission. The second amendment increased from 4.7 to 5.5 percent the amount of interest revenue (used for public education) to be withdrawn annually for five years from the School Permanent Fund.

Impact of Reforms and Changes

The reforms and changes mentioned here, and others, deserve to be reviewed to determine their impact on public education in New Mexico. Clearly the inherent problems of providing for the costs of major reform and technological change as well as the jurisdictional problems are multifaceted. The funding cycle and legislative appropriations battles, agreements or disagreements on the scope of the reform, timing and coordination with federal agencies, and the pace (how soon, how fast) must be organized. Agreements on the trial period, agreements on accountability measures, and overcoming the "inertia" that often confronts reform or school improvement proposals are all challenging.

Fiscal reforms from 1923 to the present, have, in general, satisfied one of the fundamental goals of public education in New Mexico—the continuing effort to provide equity and equality in the distribution of public funds. Increasingly, there is a concern for adequacy as the state attempts to fund education. From the 1923 School Code enactment through the highly praised 1974 School Funding Formula, reform measures and current reform actions address the mission of the national No Child Left Behind goals. Accountability measures proposed at the national and state levels, although controversial, in part addressed concern for the individual student. Fiscal reforms of the past seventy-five years have been redressing the historic neglect of public schools in New Mexico. Reform measures directed at student populations with

House Bill 212
State of New Mexico

46th Legislature—First Session, 2003
Introduced by Mimi Stewart
New Mexico House of Representatives

AN ACT RELATING TO PUBLIC EDUCATION:
Providing public school reforms

Enacting the Assessment and Accountability Act
Creating an assessment and accountability system based on
challenging academic content and performance standards
and rigorous testing against those standards to determine
annual yearly progress of students, public schools, school
districts, and the state department of public education

Providing for sanctions and rewards
Providing for improvement indicators in addition to the assessment and accountability system

Providing for more stringent competency requirements for
teachers and school principals
Providing for licensure of certain school employees

Changing certain governance structures

Providing for School Councils
Providing powers and duties

Enacting the Family and Youth Resource Act

Amending, Repealing, Enacting and *Recompiling* Sections of
the NMSA 1978.

Making appropriations

Declaring an emergency

Figure 8. New Mexico House Bill 212.

special needs (special education, bilingual education, vocational education, alternative schools) are in keeping with the spirit of providing education for all students. They also go beyond merely supporting a fiscal principle of providing finance formulas because they acknowledge the cultural and social gaps and the need for some kind of parity in those domains. Reform acts of a more comprehensive nature have sought to make improvements in governance structures, teacher preparation programs, graduation requirements, and parental and community involvement. Sometimes challenged, sometimes supported, these changes have, in general, been positive forces.

Reform measures have not been without controversy. At issue is whether efforts for reform are exclusionary or inclusionary in scope. Community and other groups seek to have their voices heard, depending on the issue. Always challenging for New Mexico and for educational leaders have been the responsibilities involved in following national trends and fulfilling federal mandates. Insufficient or recurring funding, confusing guidelines, changes in political leadership, and lukewarm leadership all contribute to the challenge of carrying out reform mandates.

A review of New Mexico's reform scene would not be complete without acknowledging that, while there have been sins of commission (reforms attempted, not properly designed, funded, or completed), there are also sins of omission. There have been long periods of neglect and indifference to Native American student education needs.

Strong accountability measures are, in general, viewed as positive developments, and reform requisites are viewed as a means of restoring confidence in the public school system. There has been the search to improve the quality of education. Some reforms and changes have had the hue of fads, but reforms dealing with finance, governance, teacher preparation, curriculum, and community issues could be referred to as "bread and butter reforms."

Always present, notwithstanding territorial and political differences, has been evidence of a growing maturity and professionalism among legislators, educators, and citizens as these reform and change efforts have changed public education in New Mexico.

Summary and Reflections

Educational reform in New Mexico may be observed as following or being influenced directly or indirectly by developments at
the national level. In general, education appears to be influenced
strongly by the economics of the country and by the globalization of the economy, environment, and culture. This can be a positive set of forces, but we must be aware that curriculum can be
so narrowed that certain critical areas of need for youth can be
neglected because teachers are under pressure to improve test
scores in the basic areas of reading, math, and science to ensure
that schools are not sanctioned. In the process, fundamental
teaching and learning principles can be compromised. Reform
measures must be cognizant of historical factors that are unique
to New Mexico, including the multicultural values and the history that enrich the lives of students, schools, and communities.

Educational reform in the state often follows national trends;
some national reforms are of a more durable nature, others are
short-lived. Other reforms stem from regional, state, and even
local sources. In New Mexico, reform activities have often been
identified with the need for statewide financial reform. The
state's education and legislation history is dotted with a series of
major finance reform studies or reports, followed by legislative
enactment of many of the recommendations.

Individuals who have made a direct or indirect impact on
reform and education in New Mexico are numerous. Those governors, superintendents, principals and other administrators, legislators, teachers, parents, business people, and support staff for
all areas of education have helped to shape education in this state.
Equally significant have been the research and legislative reports
of legislative committees, especially the Legislative School Study
Committee, staffed successfully for many years by Dr. Placido
Garcia Jr., and Dr. Pauline Rendoni. Led by State Representative
Rick Miera and State Senator Cynthia Nava, many others have
been heroes of public education in New Mexico. Political impetus is a major force in determining the outcome of many of the
reform measures. There are, of course, other reform efforts that
revolve around governance issues, curriculum designs, accountability requirements, and professional development.

The reforms described are not totally inclusive, but those
indicated here make a statement that the New Mexico public

education system is strong and is constantly being assessed and improved to better serve students. Each of these reforms, however small, has contributed to an improved educational system. The New Mexico system is unique because its historical foundations are not duplicated in any other state in our country. Reforms have been implemented and are being implemented as the state has addressed its unique and diverse population. The people of the state ask that the New Mexico educational system continue to find answers to the changing issues and challenges to better serve all students. Support for change demands that administrators involve parents, community, government, and business in developing changes to produce the desired outcomes.

New Mexico has an equitable finance system for education; the system of governance is one that allows communities to participate and to be involved; the curriculum continues to be updated; more students are staying in school to complete their education; and students are achieving at higher levels. The New Mexico system of education continues to improve, but we must not forget the challenges that still exist. As it becomes more involved in developing and promoting the concepts of equity, equality, excellence, accountability, and accessibility, the public school system must continue to collaborate with the business community.

Educational reform requires that we understand our general educational history and acknowledge our financial and human resources as a state (both the bounty and the limitations of those finances and resources). It further demands that we study and master as much as we can of the processes of reform and change so that we might establish criteria for educational reform.

A continuing challenge in the face of the steady criticism of American education is that of crediting and acknowledging teachers, teacher coaches and mentors, principals, and other school-based personnel, parents, and community and political leaders for their efforts at school change and their involvement in educational reform. This must continue and be strengthened so that education in the state continues to improve, and our students gain in the process. In New Mexico, educational heroes have emerged and continue to emerge; they offer us educational reform "New Mexico style," denoting multicultural influences, political nuances, geography or topography factors, and historical influences peculiar to the Southwest.

Chapter 7 Questions and Related Materials

Identify and discuss at least five of the most significant educational reforms that have occurred in New Mexico since statehood.

A significant challenge for citizens and educators in New Mexico is to determine the success or failure of reforms or reform movements. Identify some of the criteria that should be utilized in assessing educational reforms.

Discuss three present practices that resulted from the *Nation At Risk* document.

What roles do student population, density, and diversity play in educational reform in New Mexico?

> Bachelor, David (1991)
> Edmonds, Ron (1983)
> Educate America Act (1994)
> Moyers, R. A. (1941)
> *A Nation At Risk* (1983)
> New Mexico First: K–12 Education in New Mexico (1999)
> Prather, Hugh (2001)
> Reform Act of 1986, 2003

CHAPTER 8

⌒➛

The Public Education and Higher Education Connection

The public school system in New Mexico consists of K–12 public education and higher education—education beyond high school. Public higher education institutions in New Mexico include six four-year universities and nineteen two-year colleges (includes branch and independent community colleges). Recently, there has been discussion of a K–16 system. This concept has been gaining support across the country, especially in light of declining resources for education. In New Mexico, approximately 70 percent of the entire state budget is allocated for public schools, including higher education.

The two systems, K–12 and higher education, are governed by two different types of policy-making bodies. The public school system is governed by the secretary of public education, and the higher education system is coordinated by the Commission on Higher Education. In addition, universities are governed by boards of regents and two-year colleges by boards similar to the public school boards of education; one exception is the Northern New Mexico Community College located in El Rito, which is governed by a board of regents appointed by the governor, as stated in the constitution.

History

The history of higher education in New Mexico dates to the territorial days. The New Mexico Territorial Education Association, established in the late 1800s, made recommendations for the public school system, including the establishment of a state board of education with a state superintendent of public schools and the creation of normal schools for the preparation of teachers. Legislators approved these recommendations; the governor signed them into law; and in 1889, the university system was established with boards of regents to govern each as they were created.

The University of New Mexico was created in 1889 and included a teacher preparation program. New Mexico State University (NMSU) began as a private college in 1888 and was created as a public agricultural college in 1889; it later also became a teacher preparation college (Hammond and Donnelly 1936, 141–42). In 1893, two normal schools, both for the preparation of teachers, were opened as New Mexico Normal School in Las Vegas and New Mexico Normal School in Silver City. In 1934, Eastern New Mexico College was established in Portales as a junior college and later became a teacher preparation college. New Mexico Institute of Mining and Technology, established in 1934, has recently added a science and math teacher preparation program. The ten two-year branch colleges were established as part of Eastern New Mexico University (ENMU), New Mexico State University, and the University of New Mexico. There are nine independent community colleges, including Northern New Mexico Community College in El Rito, which was established as the Spanish-American normal school. (See Appendix 6 for a list of the institutions of higher education in New Mexico.)

Town and Gown, Stage I

From the historic landscapes of England come many rich stories about the relationships between the university and the village in which it is located; some stories are even tinged with mystery. In our Land of Enchantment in the town of Socorro, the history of the college, New Mexico Tech, formerly the New Mexico School of Mines, has been witness to unusual relationships. For decades, the college was serenely aloof and went about its serious business of graduating top scholars in the fields of geology, physics, chemistry, engineering, and other fields. The county and city schools within shouting distance of the college campus also went about their business of schooling with little or no contact with the higher education entity in their midst. The politics that swirled in Socorro County was not the college's concern and except for local politicians and businessmen urging more funding for the

> college at the state legislature, there was no political
> agenda that the college and the public schools shared.
> The college had virtually no influence on the academic
> life of the public schools . . .

A constitutional amendment in 2003 designates a secretary of
public education appointed by the governor and an elected public
education commission. The secretary for public education will
be responsible for the operation and management of the K–12
public school system. The Commission on Higher Education is
composed of fifteen members appointed by the governor to coordinate the higher education system. These members include ten
selected from the ten districts that elect Public Education
Commission members, three members at-large selections, and
two students, who are appointed. Thirteen board members serve
four-year terms; student members serve one-year terms. The
Commission on Higher Education selects and appoints an executive director to coordinate the activities of the higher education
institutions.

The first higher education governance system was established
in 1951 by the legislature and was known as the Board of
Educational Finance (Budke 1977). The Commission on Higher
Education was established by the legislature in 1977 and has the
following responsibilities:

1. Budget review and funding recommendations for the
   public colleges and universities and the special schools
   (New Mexico School for the Deaf and New Mexico
   School for the Visually Handicapped), including operational and capital funding;
2. Planning and coordination for all sectors of higher education;
3. Approval of new associate degrees at vocational-techni-
   cal institutes and for new graduate programs at public
   universities;
4. Approval and licensure of private, proprietary vocational
   schools;
5. Administration of certain federal programs for higher
   education; and
6. General responsibility for

- Setting a state policy agenda and serving as an advocate for change,
- Special studies on issues such as tuition and fees, implications of technology for distance education, and student transfer and articulation,
- Academic program review,
- Student financial assistance programs, and
- Statewide higher education information system.

The Commission on Higher Education is unique because it provides regulation and services for both public and private institutions of higher education. The public universities and one of the two-year colleges are governed by boards of regents as provided in the constitution.

Traditional Relationships

Formal relationships between higher education and public education provide for collaboration of goals. There have been and continue to be less formal but important relationships over the many years of their existence. Some relationships are described as formal, with a variety of legal relationships between the two systems.

The Carnegie Unit

Historically, high schools in New Mexico and other states have been under the influence of the Carnegie Unit (the basic unit used to define the number of contact hours a student should have with a teacher to earn one unit of high school credit) used for student admission to colleges and universities. Four years of English and other requirements by discipline were staples in college and secondary school relationships. Reform movements have helped raise requirements, and universities have responded by raising academic and quantitative requirements and changing admission requirements to provide opportunities for students whose academic standing did not meet established criteria. This concept has been challenged, and higher education institutions are seeking to maintain higher academic admission requirements.

Orientation of Students

Recruiting, scholarship programs, college fairs, and other efforts at enrolling high school graduates are also points of contact with students for colleges and universities. Those higher education schools have made special and successful efforts at providing financial support or aid for many students. Programs such as the one pioneered by Dr. Dan Chavez at the University of New Mexico provided both financial support and educational counseling and guidance to many students over a four-year period (Chavez 1988). Similar support programs have been successful at other New Mexico universities. Efforts to attract and nurture high school students in the freshman year have been supported with special teams of university professionals visiting school districts throughout the state. Incoming freshmen are required to attend orientation sessions at some universities.

Councils and Committees

Another major informal contact in place is university and high school councils or committees. Representatives of the high schools and the universities have reviewed admission requirements and curriculum; they have addressed college requirements, standards, and activity programs and college campus life; and they have sought to provide transition information and assurance to parents and students. Special conferences have been held for high school representatives and university personnel to address issues involving public schools and the universities. The North Central Accreditation Association process, with its team of college and public school representatives visiting and evaluating high school programs for accreditation by the North Central Association of Colleges and Secondary Schools, provides another connection. Under the excellent administration and leadership of Dr. Bonner Crawford and Dr. Ignacio Cordova of the University of New Mexico, relations between the North Central Association and the public and private schools have been very productive and professional. This concept for accreditation for high schools was expanded a number of years ago to include accreditation of elementary and middle or junior high schools. The leadership of universities and colleges in New Mexico represents a most successful marriage of educational interests between higher education and K–12 programs.

Academic Departments

Another major contact is the formal and informal relationship that exists between university level academic departments and their counterparts in the secondary schools. Teachers of English in the public schools find common ground with university personnel who teach in the same area and who try to identify issues that may serve students more effectively. Clearly every major department (Engineering, Fine Arts, Health and Physical Education, Nursing, Medical School, College of Education, Student Services, and others) seeks to establish and present information to prospective students and to the community and schools at large. Scholarship and fundraising programs build upon the relationship with future students as well as with alumni of various universities.

New Mexico MESA

The New Mexico Mathematics and Engineering Achievement (MESA) Program started in the Albuquerque high schools in the early 1980s. The purpose was to identify students from underrepresented groups and encourage them to explore the fields of mathematics, science, and engineering. The first higher education program to help establish this concept was the College of Engineering at UNM. Centers for MESA are at UNM, NMSU, and Highlands University. Today, there are over 5,000 students across the state who have strong connections with five of the six state universities. These students come from thirty-seven of the state's eighty-nine public school districts.

Athletics, Activities, and Recognition Programs

A significant area of contact between the public schools and the universities is in the area of athletics and other activity programs. Proponents have enhanced the music programs for many years through such programs as the Albuquerque Youth Symphony, band and chorus festivals, and other activity programs. Science fairs are held at universities and colleges throughout New Mexico to stimulate interest in science among middle school and high school students.

Recognition by universities of the public and private school teachers and administrators who deserve to be honored for their work, leadership, and talent is provided by various community organizations that recognize teachers and administrators. One group is the New Mexico Research and Study Council, a cooperative consortium of school districts and the UNM College of Education. Through the Quality Education Awards Program, students and teachers are recognized for outstanding work in their respective schools. The Golden Apple Foundation, supported by the members of the business community and universities, provides professional development opportunities, scholarships, and other incentives to teachers selected by peers, students, and parents for outstanding performance. Golden Apple awards are made at the high school, middle school, and elementary school levels; and teachers from across the state have been honored and acknowledged as Golden Apple Scholars.

Improved relationships have been developing between public schools and higher education, which will improve the quality of education for New Mexico students.

Interactions with Other Entities

Both the public schools and the universities and colleges have a vested interest in maintaining connections with other state and community groups. For example, there are business and economic forums that have educational agendas, not the least of which is the Chamber of Commerce in most communities. The New Mexico Taxpayers Association has had an impact on schools and school funding in the past and some of that historical interest may now be represented by other groups. Community groups that represent social, environmental, art, music, and vocational interests have a vital connection in both public schools and universities and colleges. Political associations constitute a significant connection and source of influence, and other professionally related entities are important in terms of research, projects, and support for educators. The connections and interactions between K–12 public schools and the institutions of higher education across the state provide opportunities for enhancement, encouragement, collaboration, and specific paths to provide the best educational opportunities for all public school students in New Mexico.

Formal Relationships

In 1891, following legislative statute, the governor appointed a Public School Board of Education which included the presidents of the University of New Mexico, the Agriculture College (NMSU), and the College of Santa Fe, a private Catholic institution. When New Mexico became a state, Article XII of the constitution created a State Board of Education. The state board included the governor, the state superintendent of public instruction, and five other members. This number included "the head" of an educational institution. The higher education member later was eliminated from the State Board of Education. A link between the two systems that continues is that the secretary of public education is a member of the board of regents of each of the universities.

⌐⟶

Town and Gown, Stage II

. . . The Socorro tale continues. In the wake of Sputnik and the push for mathematics, science, and language study in the United States, New Mexico Tech quickly became interested and successful in developing a program for providing science education at the graduate level for teachers in New Mexico, including Socorro's science and mathematics instructors. Gradually, the ties between Tech and the local public schools were strengthened, and what was of interest to one party became important to the other. Some interesting developments followed when the college leaders, administrators, and professors became acutely interested in influencing local public school policies. Individuals stepped forward to run for public school board positions; with the election of candidates representing campus interests to the local public schools' board of education came some political alliances that eventually impacted the Socorro school administrators and personnel. A new day had dawned in Socorro politics with the college now becoming a player in local politics and school issues. It was "Town vs. Gown," to use an expression used to describe the English love-hate relationship between colleges and villages. Higher education suddenly loomed large, intrusively and productively, in Socorro's schools.

⌐⟶

As we attempt to describe or record the multiple relationships of K–12 public education and higher education in New Mexico, it may be productive to briefly identify some major similarities and differences. As current planners at the institutional level and at the legislative level contemplate a seamless K–16 system (as reinforced by the Constitutional Amendment of 2003 which addresses a public education system), there are factors of the two systems that can be compared.

Compulsory vs. Noncompulsory Education

The K–12 public schools represent a compulsory system in which every child, except those attending government or private schools, must attend a public school. The public school mission is to provide an education for all K–12 students. The journey these students are required to take for some twelve or thirteen years is one that creates a high degree of dependence (may be called "handholding"). The elementary years ideally address basic academics and social skills; the middle years are touted as crucial for guidance, exploration, and social adaptation. Although high school students gain a margin of independence in the last two years of high school, the degree of independence and flexibility is minimal. Curricular offerings at the high school level are fairly standard, although some high schools have taken on an "academic flair," offering in-depth curricula within the basic disciplines, advanced placement programs, and concurrent enrollment in a college or university. Historically referred to as the comprehensive high school, the high school is subject to continuing question that it seeks to do too much, yet fails to provide necessary preparation for many seeking entrance to higher level education.

"ALL AMERICAN"

The late 1950s and '60s witnessed a re-examination of the American secondary school program. High school programs came under intense scrutiny, and everyone concerned about high schools was reading James Conant's The American High School. The so-called comprehensive high school was under fire for trying to be too much! Nevertheless, in one national report, a student named Anna Marie Fortune from an Albuquerque north valley school was highlighted as being a stellar example of what the high school in America could produce. Anna Marie was academically talented, a Girls' Stater, a cheerleader, a prom princess, member of the school newspaper staff, and belonged to key school organizations. If that were not comprehensive enough, in her senior year she was invited to have lunch with former First Lady Eleanor Roosevelt. Debate continues on high school programs, but many of that era remember those years with pride.

Universities and colleges, in contrast with the K–12 public schools, are not part of a compulsory system; they function on a more selective basis in admitting students. Lately, critics both in New Mexico and across the U.S. charge that there has been a "dumbing down" of university undergraduate programs and that universities have been forced to take on remedial programs to prepare students to handle college-level coursework. Areas most directly affected have been English, history, math, and science programs. Students at the higher education level are more likely to be viewed as primarily responsible for their work, for their study habits, and for their decisions, but higher education institutions in New Mexico have developed some support programs for entering freshmen.

Public vs. Less Public

The K–12 system, especially elementary and middle levels, may be precariously vulnerable or susceptible in the most "democratic tradition" to their publics. Parents, grandparents, and community activities are a natural part of the daily existence of these schools. High schools are no less immune to a participating public; however, the involvement of parents and community is more focused on music activities, athletics and sports programs, science fairs, and art shows. At both the elementary and the secondary level, these publics can be both a form of "boosterism" or "criticism." The contrast with higher education is, in fact, best described as a kind of detachment on the part of the public. Except perhaps for athletics and other performances, universities and colleges are somewhat shielded from the public and daily involvement of parents.

While the local public schools have a delimited constituency, universities cast a long shadow across regions of the state. Local high school graduates enjoy an occasional reunion, and some graduates may play a continuing role in the life of their schools.

Schools like New Mexico State University and the University of New Mexico impact the entire state; alumni of NMSU, UNM, and other schools can be an influential force in the active support of their respective institutions.

Goals and Public Service

The goals of institutions of higher education are basically threefold: teaching, research, and public service. The research function brings considerable prestige and funding. Universities and colleges remain heavily dependent on state funds, and these state funds account for three-fourths of the instructional budget in the four-year institutions. Gifts from foundations and donations from alumni are also factors in funding (Hain, et al. 1994, 191). Tuition and fees provide a portion of the funding for higher education. Both K–12 public schools and higher education institutions compete for legislative funding.

The public service mission takes on a philanthropic cast, which gives university personnel and the university as a whole a "magnanimous" reputation when compared with the more pedestrian, familiar role of the K–12 schools. Although the role of K–12 is also a "public service" role, universities and colleges are seen as a major resource for helping communities and the state economy.

HIGHER EDUCATION HEROES?

Heroes in the public school arena most often spring from our K–12 experiences. Higher education heroes are often recognized long after "formal" education years are completed. When we look back at those university leaders and professors later, it is easy to identify heroes; but in that hectic drama of earning professional degrees time is often not available to ponder about who "made a difference." Just a few heroes are Simon Nanninga, Richard Lawrence, Frank Angel, Sam Vigil, Chester Travelstead, John Aragon, David Darling, Harlan Sinninger, Phillip Ambrose, David Colton, Sabine Ulibarri, Mari Luci Jaramillo, J. Cloyd Miller, Donald Roush, Guy Waid, Peggy Blackwell, Malou Gonzales, Ted Martinez, Alvin Howard, Viola Florez, William Runge, Vita Saavedra,

Lloyd Tireman, and the boards of regents of our universities and colleges.

↩

Economic and Financial Differences

Even as K–12 public schools experience the proximity of their
publics, they also have a heavy dependence on funds appropriated at the state level. Anchored though they may be in their local
districts, they are creatures of the state; they are, in effect, fiscal
"wards" of the state of New Mexico. The major flexibility of the
K–12 public schools, financially speaking, is in the matter of capital outlay where they may or may not have to seek building
funds because of their local bonding capacity. Nonetheless, local
districts feel more vulnerable and more dependent than do the
institutions of higher education. Local boards of education and
administrators have enjoyed discretionary powers in utilizing
funds, but the major source of funding for operations resides at
the state level. Higher education funding, on the other hand,
comes from the state, research grants, tuition, foundations of
various types, and economic support from alumni. Two-year
institutions depend heavily upon local financial support through
tax levies.

Programmatic Difference

At the higher education level, one finds a relationship between
disciplines whereby students at both the undergraduate level and
the graduate level achieve their upper level education, notwithstanding the highly specialized departments. This assimilation of
knowledge and learning appears to elude the secondary level curriculum, although there are some secondary programs in which
subject matter articulation and mastery are coordinated. The
"academic" atmosphere of the university is more intense, more
searching, and because it is of a voluntary, not a compulsory,
nature, it is more rigorous and directed more by the student than
the school.

Notwithstanding the differences in the school and economic
cultures, the two systems share the goal of educating the students and the citizens of New Mexico. They also share some
geographic territories. For example, Highlands University and
the schools of northern New Mexico have an opportunity to
create special educational opportunities for the citizens of that

region. The same is true for Eastern, Western, and New Mexico State Universities. Those regions have needs and issues that can be addressed by the universities; they also have resources, talent, and pride in their institutions of higher education. Interestingly, both the K–12 and the higher education institutions must answer to the governing authorities at the state level, as well as to their local governing bodies. While they may be in competition for some of the same dollars, they both struggle for the cause of education; they also share the pleasure and challenge of the diversity of New Mexico's students. At the higher education level, the degree of diversity becomes greater with students from other states and countries providing special enrichment. Despite the gradations in curriculum and knowledge, both systems share in teaching and passing on the heritage of New Mexico. One final similarity is the pride the teachers, administrators, and parents share in their respective schools and in their institutions of higher education.

Preparation of Teachers and Other Professionals

A major relationship between the secretary of public education and the higher education system is in the preparation of teachers, principals, counselors, and other educators who serve the public education system. The Public Education Department accredits the teacher, administrator, and counselor preparation programs of each of the colleges of education. A system of accreditation has been established in conjunction with the National Council for Accreditation of Teacher Education (NCATE), an organization that accredits colleges of education every four years. During the 2001 cycle of accreditation, all colleges of education were accredited by both the State Board of Education and by NCATE. The secretary of public education carries out the accreditation responsibility through the Professional Standards Commission, made up of practicing educators and Public Education Department personnel. The relationship between NCATE and the New Mexico Public Education Department was strengthened when the public schools and the universities formed in essence a K–16 system of education. Some accreditation issues include articulation, teacher preparation and quality, number of courses in subject matter, and methods courses.

A crucial relationship exists between the colleges of education and school districts in the process of admission of candidates to the teaching profession and in their subsequent preparation and licensure. The extent to which teachers of content areas study the pedagogy and the methodology for teaching and learning is a concern. There is frequent debate about what constitutes a desirable balance between academic and experiential knowledge for teacher preparation. In 2001, the Educational Leadership Program in the UNM College of Education established an Educational Leadership Advisory Committee composed of experienced practitioners for the purpose of ensuring that the preparation of future school administrators is as functional as possible. Programs in the preparation of both teachers and administrators have recently appeared to reflect a greater concern for field experience and "reality" in facing classroom and community. The age-old issue regarding the number of methods hours versus the number of hours in the academic area started with the normal schools and continues today.

↩

TEACHERS OF TEACHERS

In the ranks of New Mexico colleges of Education professors and instructors we celebrate some of our outstanding colleagues: University of New Mexico—Frank Angel, Keith Auger, Ronald Blood, Ignacio Cordova, David Darling, Guillermina Englebrecht, Jim Everett, Dolores Gonzales, Marie Hughes, Wilson Ivins, Mari Luci Jaramillo, Roger Kroth, Jo Ann Krueger, Richard Lawrence, Leroy Ortiz, Paul Pohland, Steve Preskill, Bill Runge, Vita Saavedra, Joe Suina, Lloyd Tireman, Richard Tonigan, Horacio Ulibarri, George Blanco White, and Carolyn Wood. New Mexico State University—Philip Ambrose, MaLou Gonzales, Phil Hosford, John Julia McMahon, Bill O'Donnell, Donald Roush, and Jack O. Saunders. New Mexico Western University—George Baldwin, Jess Binghaman, Ray Brancheau, Robin Hunt, Arlene Kilpatrick, J. Cloyd Miller, and Hazel Sechler. New Mexico Highlands University—John Johnson, Seth Parsons, Harlan Sinninger, and Helen Walters. Eastern New Mexico University—Al Bettina, Guy Waid, and C. B. Wivel. You will remember so many others who should be honored.

↩

Public Education Department and the Commission on Higher Education

Colleges, universities, and public schools, through their many connections, have addressed the issues of articulation of academic areas and the socialization process of young people moving from the cocoon of the high school to the challenge of higher education. Sometimes the more formal efforts at articulation have not been as successful as desired; sometimes town and gown do not speak the same language. There is evidence that universities are working to introduce incoming students more thoroughly to the new culture and to encourage staying the course in college. Many students are now attending local two-year schools where they earn credit toward a degree, then transferring to four-year schools where they complete the degree.

Commission on Higher Education and State Board of Education Roundtable of 2000

The Commission on Higher Education and the State Board of Education traditionally met once a year to exchange information. These meetings were informal until 1998, when a roundtable was convened which, in effect, introduced the concept of a K–16 partnership. This meeting represented an unprecedented collaboration of approximately one hundred policy makers, educators, governing authorities, business representatives, and legislators. The roundtable had two objectives: (1) identifying strategies to strengthen the preparation and ongoing professional development of public school teachers and (2) enhancing the role of higher education in supporting and strengthening public school teachers and students (New Mexico State Board of Education 2002).

In September of 2000, the Commission on Higher Education and the State Board of Education held a second statewide roundtable on K–16 education with the focus on teacher quality. In May 2002, the roundtable met to plan strategy that would enhance collaboration on the K–16 system of education. One outcome of these collaborative sessions has been the development of the Teacher Education Accountability Council.

Teacher Education Accountability Council

The Teacher Education Accountability Council received a federal grant under Title II, Teacher Quality Enhancement State

Grant, to be utilized to examine teacher quality. One of the major
goals of the Teacher Education Accountability Council (TEAC)
has been oversight of this grant. TEAC also served as a coordinating body to help the Commission on Higher Education, the
State Board of Education, and other stakeholders ensure that
New Mexico had a quality teacher in every classroom (Teacher
Education Accountability Council 2001).

The major goals of the Teacher Education Accountability
Council were to (1) improve teacher recruitment, (2) improve
teacher preparation, (3) improve teacher induction, (4) improve
teacher professional development, (5) strengthen other aspects
of teacher quality, and (6) build capacity for shared state leadership (mechanism for teachers, administrators, and state personnel to meet and share). The TEAC has been responsible for
developing and proposing several legislative initiatives that have
become statutes, including such initiatives as mentoring of new
teachers, financial loans to teachers to encourage their remaining in the profession, and recruitment and teacher induction programs. The Teacher Education Accountability Council may be
allowed by statute to formalize the K–16 system of education,
subject to the new governance system.

2002 Joint Statement

In the spring of 2002, a joint statement, *Post-Secondary Education,*
was issued as a result of a collaborative effort between the State
Department of Education and the Commission on Higher
Education, which reflects the consensus of both agencies and indicates a material commitment as part of an overall K–16 partnership. The document spelled out the major "accelerated"
opportunities for students and encourages the following major
areas of collaborative activities and program:

1. *Adult basic education,* which is administered by the State
   Department of Education with programs located in the
   colleges.
2. *Advanced Placement* for high school students. This program provides rigorous courses at the high school level
   in preparation for university and college work. It is
   administered through New Mexico Highlands
   University (NMHU) and is under the jurisdiction of the
   State Department of Education.

3. *Area Vocational High Schools.* These are specialized programs that serve high school students on the campuses
of postsecondary institutes to provide sharing of facilities for vocational programs. There are at present four
area vocational programs.
4. *Concurrent Enrollment.* This program allows qualified
public high school students to attend public postsecondary educational institutions and simultaneously
earn both high school and/or college credits.
5. *New Mexico School-to-Work/School-to-Careers.* The purpose of this program is to support efforts to build a
system that gives the opportunity for every young
person to develop necessary academic and employability
skills for eventual entry into a challenging career path.
6. *Tech Prep.* This program offers students relevant opportunities to explore several career paths and to earn
postsecondary course credit while in high school. This
program combines high school curriculum and a minimum of two years of postsecondary education in a
nonduplicative sequential course of study. It is designed
to lead to an associate degree, a baccalaureate degree,
or a two-year certificate apprenticeship. This program
is administered through the Public Education
Department and is federally funded (Root 2002).

The Teacher Education Accountability Council has encouraged a pre-K–16 system of education and includes the goal of
improving the achievement of New Mexico students through
quality teacher and other educator preparation programs. A possible long-range outcome might be a seamless system of education for New Mexico students.

Summary and Reflections

The relationship between higher education and K–12 public
schools has been ongoing from the time normal schools were created in the 1890s. Both K–12 and higher education systems were
formalized and developed by enactment of laws in the state constitution. Higher education has its boards of regents, the
Commission on Higher Education, and policy/advisory boards
for two-year colleges; the K–12 public school systems operate

under a cabinet-level secretary of public education and school district boards of education.

The relationship between the two public school entities has been formalized recently as the two entities, the Public Education Department and the Commission on Higher Education, are scheduled to meet on a regular basis. They have developed a set of beliefs and have listed the programs on which they will collaborate for the purpose of providing special opportunities that benefit high school students, i.e., concurrent enrollment and advanced placement. This relationship has also developed a Teacher Education Accountability Council for the purpose of supporting strong training and professional development programs for teachers. The relationship has also included offering more courses via satellite and on line, provided by the recently created Distance Education (UNM, NMSU, NMHU, and ENMU) program that is "sending" courses to rural areas of the state. The variety of these courses will continue to increase.

Another major change is the creation of a secretary of public education position, appointed by the governor, to oversee education. The constitutional amendment passed in 2003 appears to be strengthening the concept of a seamless educational system. Major advantages include the financing of education on a coordinated comprehensive manner and, more importantly, developing an articulated K–16 educational plan.

The mosaic of New Mexico's higher education system offers some tantalizing contrasts that confirm and, in fact, complement or imitate some of the characteristics of many public school districts. Imagine a sparsely populated state with so many universities and two-year colleges and special institutions, and you have a picture of New Mexico higher education. It incorporates urban and rural vistas, mountain ranges, and river valleys, as well as desert mesas, and universities and colleges that serve that geography and its peoples. The richness of New Mexico's mountain ranges comes alive at Highlands University in Las Vegas, just as the fertile fields of southern New Mexico nourish and complement New Mexico State University in Las Cruces. Each college or university draws strength and resources from its locale and its peoples; each mirrors its wellspring. A continuing challenge for universities and all of the institutions of higher education in New Mexico is that of serving an increasingly diverse student population and ensuring that the higher education population indeed reflects that diversity.

Of equal importance is the need for higher education programs in New Mexico to reflect, incorporate, and offer programs of studies that compete effectively with and beyond other institutions nationwide. Notwithstanding local imperatives, universities have a historic calling that is of a higher nature and carries great responsibility to advance truth and to disseminate knowledge. A task in New Mexico, or any other state, is to find and maintain a balance between state needs and that higher sense of purpose. A simple perusal of our history suggests that New Mexico's universities and colleges have been successful in providing this balance: agricultural courses of study, engineering and mining, science and technology preparation programs, medical programs, business administration and management curricula, astronomy, and music and fine arts programs all attest to that success and that "higher sense of purpose." Dean Chester Travelstead spoke about the spirit of a great university addressing the "higher sense of purpose" in these words: "Faculty and students are supported and encouraged to think for themselves, to criticize the values, beliefs, and practices they observe around them, and to dare to design and help bring about what they think is a better society" (1976).

It is necessary to make higher education programs attractive to our high school graduates so that, instead of those students being wooed away to other exotic places, they find a home and a challenge in Silver City, Portales, Las Cruces, Albuquerque, Santa Fe, Socorro, and Las Vegas, New Mexico. To help meet the need for recruiting our students, there is an accompanying challenge to close any gaps that exist between New Mexico's K–12 public schools and its higher education institutions. A major finding in a dissertation by Langu Okal listed the need for a stronger partnership between higher education and public schools as extremely critical (Okal 1996, 284). This requisite articulation addresses curriculum or subject area coordination primarily between secondary schools and the universities; it impacts guidance counselors at both levels; and it demands the attention of secondary teachers, principals, and their counterpart professors of individual disciplines at the university level. The challenge is also to improve student orientation at the higher education level and enhance the ability of the college or university to identify and support less independent high school students through the transition years, increasingly making them more independent learners. In New Mexico as well as across the nation, providing special transitional support for minority students should remain a goal, for that talent and resource will make itself felt in the state and nation today and tomorrow.

An intriguing challenge resides in the research responsibility of the universities as they deal with public schools. A wealth of raw data relating to the public schools exists; mining that data through "parochial" research projects to provide improved, exemplary, or creative research findings applicable to local school districts is a challenge. The array of theses, dissertations, and other studies could provide practical insights for public schools in New Mexico. In fact, "parochial" research would appear to be "New Mexico style" research. Just as interesting would be the possibility of capturing from individual schools, school districts, school teaching personnel, and school administrators that area of research loosely regarded as "wisdom of practice." Clearly some "wisdom of practice" worthy of research is evident today in all our schools and universities; that research should be encouraged.

The ultimate challenge for New Mexico's higher education system and the public school system may be simply creating, maintaining, and coordinating that K–16 mechanism needed to communicate with each other. Mutual respect for the contributions of each is a reasonable and worthy goal; "traffic of professionals" between universities and colleges and public schools can only be productive.

Who will take the lead? Who will take the time? Who will provide the incentive to enhance the coordination and research possibilities that exist between the New Mexico system of public education and the system of higher education? The answer may be found in a type of statesmanlike stewardship that must emanate from both the public schools and the universities and colleges. One of the items that Okal acknowledges will impact higher education is the quality of elementary and secondary education and its ability to develop the youth "wholly and totally" (1996, 284–88). There is a need for a partnership between higher education, public schools, and community.

Chapter 8 Questions and Related Materials

Identify basic differences between the governance plans of
K–12 public schools and the institutions of higher education.

Discuss some of the needs of the citizens of the state of New
Mexico and the role of the higher education institutions in
meeting those needs.

There are differences between the purposes of K–12 education
and higher education. Identify at least three major differences
and discuss how educators might find increased commonalties
to serve more of the student population in New Mexico.

How might the institutions of higher education work to recruit
and retain more of our state's students?

Commission on Higher Education and State Board of
    Education—TEAC (2001)
Hain, Paul; Garcia, F. Chris; St. Clair, Gilbert (1994)
Root, Tom, Commission on Higher Education (2002)

CHAPTER 9

~

Future Trends

Almost forty years ago, Dr. Tom Wiley closed his book, *Public School Education in New Mexico*, by stating some of the trends he foresaw for education. Dr. Wiley predicted that "humanitarian" proposals would be given strong support in relationship to that given to the "prudential" (financial responsibility, care in planning budgets) philosophy and that cries about the needs of education were likely to be heard as plainly and as loudly as were the cries about the costs of education. Dr. Wiley supported his prediction with a list of several factors including (1) emphasis will be placed on the sciences but also on the social sciences; (2) sectional barriers will be less formidable; (3) political leaders will recognize greater importance of education; (4) there will be greater support for education on the part of the legislative body; (5) the interest groups will continue to impact education; and (6) the news media will give greater attention to education. After reviewing several of these factors, he predicted or foresaw an optimistic future for the New Mexico public education system (1965, 151–54).

To those interested in education in New Mexico, it is obvious that many of the trends that Dr. Wiley foresaw have developed. To differing extents, each of the factors he identified has materialized; most are ongoing today. Future trends will follow developments taking place across the country. Some of these trends can be fairly readily identified.

Accountability as measured by student test results and school data will continue to be stressed by the Public Education Department. New Mexico's formal accountability plan was adopted in 2001, based upon 1989 legislative action. Better assessment results will continue to be demanded by parents and by the community. The legislature, which funds education as well as other governmental entities, will continue to press for improved test results, success of schools, and enhanced utilization of

finances. The secretary of education, who oversees K–12 education, will expect improved test results in every school and in every
district. Much of this activity was stimulated by federal legislation enacted by Congress in 2002, calling for more testing of students and for sanctions for schools whose accountability
measures reflect poor performance.

Standards will continue to be refined and utilized to mark
what students are expected to learn; there will be a criterion-referenced assessment instrument aligned with New Mexico standards. (This was to have happened in 2000 and again in 2002,
but funding to develop a criterion-referenced test was vetoed by
the governor.) The State Department of Education developed criterion-referenced tests for use in the spring of 2003 for grades 4
and 8 in Language Arts and Math. Funding for this step was
made possible by a federal grant under the Elementary and
Secondary Education Act. Development of criterion-referenced
tests for other curriculum areas will continue.

Choice of learning environment by families for the education
of their children will continue. This trend began with the concept of alternative schools in the 1970s and has continued in the
form of home schooling, charter schools, concurrent enrollment,
and other alternative programs. Home schooling will continue
to grow with the possible addition of stronger ties to public
school programs on a part-time basis. Another major trend that
has started in other parts of the country and will develop in New
Mexico is the concept of having for-profit corporations and not-
for-profit organizations managing public schools. This trend is
supported by state guidelines that address the accountability program feature under which low-performing schools may be taken
over by the state as part of the corrective action plan. This plan
started during the 2002 school year, and it is a viable option that
will be put into practice. The former superintendent of instruction accepted responsibility for not going to private agencies, but
letting school districts develop plans for corrective action
together with the State Department of Education.

The concept of issuing vouchers for parents to use to send
their children to private and religious schools will develop in
New Mexico. This will follow the trend started in other parts of
the country, supported by the Supreme Court decision of 2002
in a case filed in Cleveland, Ohio. There have been efforts in New
Mexico to create a voucher system; this national movement

involving state monies paid to parents in the form of vouchers for use in sending students to private schools may hasten such a program. The issue of separation of state and church will continue to be raised; secular opponents of the voucher system may present legal challenges. The impact of a voucher system on the public schools must be studied.

Parents of Title I students from low performing schools are given the choice to have their children attend higher performing schools with federal funds providing transportation. While there appears to be a trend to remain in the neighborhood schools, indications are that this choice will continue to be a viable one. Recent news reports indicated that, while requests for student transfers from low-performing schools in Albuquerque Public Schools were not high in the first year of the schools' being classified as low performing, there was an increase in the number of transfer requests for the following year. Guidelines are indicating that a "receiving" school cannot deny the transfer of a student from a low-performing school because "no space is available." Similar patterns appear to be occurring nationwide. Choice for placement of transfer students in local public schools has been in practice for many years on a "space available" basis.

Distance Learning is a concept developed as a result of the tremendous increase in the availability and quality of technology; delivery of instruction on line or through Internet Web sites, known as virtual instruction or education, may become a norm. Much of the virtual education is presently being completed in conjunction with or in connection with face-to-face instruction. At the university level, the University of New Mexico, New Mexico State University, New Mexico Highlands University, and Eastern New Mexico University provide distance education programs.

The New Mexico Public Education Department has provided a virtual high school program for students in rural areas, accessible to any student in the state. The trend continues, and there appears to be some indication that elementary school students will be involved to some degree in the near future; home schooled students will have access to such a program. Major questions might be asked of these programs since they are not providing socialization and other opportunities for students. There are questions of equity as well as accessibility.

Financing of Education historically has been an issue in New Mexico. Despite its low per capita income, the state supports schools effectively, and it has been recognized for that effort. Until 2002, the state was making sporadic progress in raising teachers' salaries substantially, but not enough to avoid losing staff to better paying opportunities in other states or in other professions. Teachers were recruited by districts offering higher salaries and other incentives, and there are several proposals in the legislature to recruit and retain new teachers with improved salaries and lucrative fringe benefits. The 2003 legislature passed bills that provided for increased teacher salaries and will move New Mexico from its low ranking among other states in the area of teacher pay. Recruiting in foreign countries and in other states and offering bonuses for teaching in challenging schools or for bilingual capabilities have been utilized by New Mexico school districts.

A dilemma is that the cost of educating our youth continues to increase as the public education system attempts to provide increased services through health clinics, after-school programs and activities, parental education, training and involvement, and opening schools for community use. The search for increased financial resources for education and for other programs that help families provide better opportunities for their children continues to be an issue. Funds for the school and state budget are derived primarily from taxes levied across the state; funds for the public schools are distributed through the State Equalization Guarantee Formula. While New Mexico laws for financing schools are known to be the most equitable ones across the country, an insufficient amount of resources is available. Legislators, citizens, and educators are searching for additional resources and for ways to expend available resources efficiently and effectively. Access to more of the permanent fund monies was provided by a constitutional amendment in 2003, which provided for an increase in the percentage of interest taken from the Permanent School Fund to be utilized for improved financial support for school districts for a period of five years. The issue of equity in funding for school districts may be eroded by the concept of adequacy in the future.

Financing for capital outlay programs for schools has been under litigation, and the courts found the system unconstitutional; the state must devise an equitable capital outlay plan, such as has been developed for the operational part of the finance system. The legislature has developed some changes in the law so that the state will fund more of the capital outlay program.

Teacher Quality must be improved. Competitive salaries will prevent loss of teachers to other states because of income and quality of life. With strong support, inexperienced teachers may become master teachers. A collaborative effort between the Public Education Department and the Commission on Higher Education has begun to develop a system that will prepare and support New Mexico's K–12 teaching staffs. Accompanying this issue is the need for supporting a good mentoring program for new teachers so they feel supported and assisted during those crucial first years. Collaborative efforts between the Public Education Department and the Commission on Higher Education have begun to develop a system that will prepare and support New Mexico's K–12 teaching staffs. The question is: Can we accomplish this goal of higher pay and improved support before the state gets too involved with having other organizations taking over schools?

Cultural and Economic Diversity will continue to be addressed in school curricula because of the multicultural makeup of our state and because of an influx of immigrant children. The so-called minority student population has now become the majority in the state. Socioeconomic diversity will continue to be an issue, and increased diversity means changes in staff needs, curriculum, and other educational programs. Aging of the population will continue and will mirror national statistics of increasing numbers in the 60+ age group, with their special needs and interests; financing for those needs may impact education funding for students. The needs of Native American students must be addressed specifically and diligently at the state and local levels. The state legislature began this process by enacting the Indian Education Act in 2003, a major step in developing a commitment to the education of Native American children.

Governance of schools was modified by a constitutional amendment passed by the voters in 2003. The many years of discussion about who is responsible for education at the state level has been settled by the amendment that places education under the Office of the Governor with a cabinet-level secretary of public education to oversee the system. The amendment also provided for an elected public education commission. The principal role of this commission is to develop a strategic plan for the Public Education Department.

At the district level, site-based management and budgeting will place greater emphasis on making the local principal, parents, and faculty more responsible for student success with commensurate budget- and decision-making ability. Demand by parents and educators will be for more autonomy even though the Public Education Department and the legislature have worked diligently at giving greater autonomy for the local districts and schools. That involvement is now required by NM HB 212. This will be evidenced by a stronger move to increase site-based budgeting and management at the local school level, where parents, principals, teachers, and students can be involved to help make decisions for their school.

There are indications across the country and some discussion in New Mexico for a district superintendent to function as the chief executive officer (CEO) instead of acting as the district instructional leader. This signals a business model versus an instructional model and calls for the local board of education to limit its responsibilities to developing policy for the operation of schools.

Development of the concept of a K–16 school profile will continue to be explored as there is more collaboration between the state, the local school districts, and the higher education facilities in the state.

Smaller School Communities concepts and trends will boost the concept of site-based schools, and schools-within-schools will be supported by parents and educators. Research will continue on the success of students taught in smaller environments, as this concept has indicated benefits for students and teachers. New Mexico First, a not-for-profit statewide organization made up of a diverse membership, made a strong recommendation in 1999 during its twenty-first Town Hall meeting that no school should be larger than six hundred students.

Technology in the instructional program will increase as knowledge and funding increase. Examples of this impact of technology may be found in most district public schools, the charter schools, home schools, and other alternative schools within and outside the public school system. The role of the teacher increasingly may become one of mentor and guide as Internet use and online education continue to increase. Students may be provided with computers as part of the textbook allocation of school materials.

Globalization will become more evident as, increasingly, the interconnections of political and economic policies of the United

States with the policies of the rest of the world will mean more policy and curricular changes for schools. Technological advances further influence the significance of the globalization phenomenon. These interconnections will be felt in our schools as we move through the twenty-first century. Schools must develop global awareness in students and communities without losing the importance of individual and personal development. Awareness and understanding of globalization must be balanced with awareness for student, family, and country. Globalization is daily recognized in New Mexico because of the scientific and military facilities and because of the country's proximity to Mexico, Canada, and South America. Computers, television, and direct contact personalize this vast issue of globalization for students in New Mexico schools.

Civic Education will again come to the forefront in this country and in the schools. Active citizenship in America has been declining, according to both political scientists and observers of our democratic institutions. Even as America talks about building democratic institutions in other parts of the world, our own citizen participation in civic matters has become lax. A certain trend or reaction to this failing appears on the horizon for our schools. A report by the Carnegie Corporation entitled "The Civic Mission of the Schools" was recently released, which addressed the problem of the erosion of political participation by young people in this nation (2003). It suggested that, apart from the other entities (parents, churches, voluntary organizations), the schools are potentially the best "active labs of active citizenship." The implications for the social sciences in our schools are significant; a resurgence of civic education is merited.

Civic education in New Mexico could be enhanced or enriched by celebrating our multicultural roots. There has been active Hispanic participation in New Mexico for centuries in the political arena, and a lively interest in the political process has historically been a part of the New Mexico community. Increasingly, multicultural groups, not just the Hispanic population, are becoming more active and more involved in the political arena. Students, teachers, and parents in diverse communities must become aware of opportunities for utilizing this very personal and very public area of civic education to enhance the curriculum.

Summary and Reflections

New Mexico's rich and storied history will forever remain imprinted on the educational system, even as the system seeks to keep pace with trends and reforms at state, national, and global levels. Trends presented in this chapter appear to be the most pervasive of the trends dealing with education in New Mexico in the first years of the twenty-first century. The "humanitarian" concerns of Dr. Tom Wiley have materialized and continue to be paramount in future trends involving cultural and economic diversity, smaller school communities, and civic education. The increased demand for accountability and for fiscal responsibility in the future echoes, in part, Dr. Wiley's call for "prudential" educational decision making.

There are strong and pressing indicators that higher performance standards and improved teacher quality will dominate educational forums in the immediate and long-term future. Inescapable as factors for tomorrow's schools are the technological marvels available to our educational system. Impressive, but not without controversy, are those evolving new governance proposals which, in our estimation, reveal historic tensions between the centralization or decentralization of educational decision making. In New Mexico's educational history, the concept of local control and the prominent role of local school boards have been unchallenged until recently. Federal as well as state mandates vie for the power of changing and reforming our schools. Centralizing the authority to make those changes is increasingly a popular model, but it is not without opposition.

Notwithstanding the "centralization" tendencies, we are also aware that leadership in something we can call "horizontal leadership" is very real. This term suggests that school superintendents, principals, teachers, and other leaders in the educational fraternity must accept and acknowledge that parents, citizens, business and community leaders, noneducation professional associations, legislators, and community special interest groups have a stake in education, and more and more they are exercising their right to have their voices heard. Leadership for tomorrow's schools in New Mexico involves acknowledging that the teaching and instructional personnel must have center stage, but accepting the reality of many new partners. Those ideas and proposals coming from our partners may be politically tinged, philosophically different, financially challenged, and sometimes territorially compromising (i.e., the professional educator versus the lay person). As we work with these varying partners, the most stable and guiding principle directing educational personnel should be: What does this mean for children and young people?

We believe that greater cooperation among all peoples and groups concerned about the education of our young people will evolve and will reflect new forms of participation. The trends presented here suggest greater involvement and stewardship. Some trends and issues may be revisited under a different name or with a different emphasis and with new imperatives. It is important for the school community and for everyone involved to acknowledge, recognize, and appreciate our unique educational history in New Mexico and to prepare to meet the challenges of this new century.

Optimism becomes a part of the New Mexico persona, and that optimism includes positives about the future of education in New Mexico. Passion for New Mexico and for the educational system of our state can only increase as citizens learn more and become more involved.

Chapter 9 Questions and Related Materials

There are several trends identified in Chapter 9. Identify the three trends that you consider might have the greatest impact on our educational system during the next two decades.

Compare the trends that Dr. Tom Wiley identified in his work, *Public School Education in New Mexico*, and those presented in Chapter 9.

What and who, in your opinion, impact what trends are set and what the outcomes will be?

Trends in school size have existed during the history of public schools in New Mexico. Is there evidence that a specific size should exist? Cite the evidence and develop your rationale. What would be the financial, governance, and educational implications for the size you might recommend to your school community?

New Mexico First: K–12 Education in New Mexico:
    Benchmarks for the New Millennium (1999)
Wiley, Tom (1968)
Carnegie Corporation (2003)

Epilogue

We close this book with a brief review and a personal message. It has been our goal to share the remarkable cultures, personalities, events, and landscapes influencing the history of education in the state of New Mexico and the vision of free public education for all students. Our goal also has been to remind readers about the convergence of cultures and the educational manifestations of events, visions, ideas, and circumstances. The concept of free public schooling was a quest of the Spanish and Mexican governments during the seventeenth and eighteenth centuries. Those ideas of schooling traveled up the *Camino Real* and the *Rio Grande* originally; they did not arrive full-blown from across the wide Missouri. This acknowledgment of early Spanish and Mexican concern for public schools does not detract from the excitement and drama of the American territorial period and the coming of the Common School, nor can it erase and ignore the contributions of the indigenous peoples who had an established system of educating the young long before the arrival of the Spanish.

Our Personal Message

In our telling of the New Mexico education story and its status, we have tried to recognize the greatness and the outstanding and courageous contributions of a legion of New Mexicans (conquerors and the conquered, citizens, teachers, principals, district superintendents, parents, university professors, state superintendents, finance chiefs, governors, and other unknown heroes). We hope that we have done them justice. We believe that embroidering the history with the folktales, some true, some questionable, breathes life into the times and circumstances of those personalities who made history or who were, perhaps unwittingly, part of history. This short volume could not include all the support personnel who make education happen for students; it would be impossible to share the significant contributions of those untold numbers of individual heroes and leaders. We hope you, the reader, will develop your personal list of heroes and identify why or how you found those particular heroes in your mind's eye.

We have shared our ideas and opinions on many topics, based upon our personal and professional experiences in public education in New Mexico. We have, personally and as administrators, developed, lived through, and survived at least four major reform efforts and periods. To us, reform movements show that we are, as a state, constantly reviewing where we are, where we want our educational system to go, and ways to promote and provide opportunities for educational growth for our students, for our educational personnel, and for our communities.

We continue, even after all these years of personal involvement with education in New Mexico, to feel a sense of excitement when we see, experience, read, or hear about success in schools or about students who overcome hardship and handicaps to be successful participants in their communities. We are proud when we learn about communities that have recognized educators for their contributions to students. We continue to be passionate about education, about New Mexico, and about the opportunities for those professionals who follow in our footsteps, learn from our successes and challenges, and will be the leaders to implement the reforms identified as well as those reforms we don't even know about at this time. Our passion only grows; it does not fade.

We hope our readers and students have enjoyed our efforts in compiling this history and the status of education and in making observations and recommendations. Furthermore, it is our expectation that because you have shared this information, you will contribute ideas, comments, anecdotes, dreams, and visions that will help make this a living and working document. We appeal to students and educators to consider developing a sequel to this "work in progress" that might emphasize educational research and theory, as well as that concept of "wisdom of practice" related to the history of public education in New Mexico, a sequel that could also provide updates on educational practices in the field of education and educational leadership. State, national, and global trends in public education must be explored.

I was involved in my first political campaign as a
candidate during 2002, learning in a new arena,
seeing and feeling history in the making, wanting
to work for education even more after that way
of exploring New Mexico. Working on this book,
too, has made me appreciate public education in
New Mexico even more.

—John B. Mondragón

I am continuing to build a library of collectible history books about New Mexico and becoming even
more enthralled with the idea of sharing the history and stories about education in New Mexico.
Now I'm performing in my first real dramatic
stage production, *Cuentos de la Llorona*. I die real
good! I am helping to preserve one of the traditions and the folklore of New Mexico.

—Ernest S. Stapleton

Appendix 1

New Mexico State Constitution
(Educational Controls Summary)

Article XII, Section 1 and Article XXI, Section 4:
A uniform system of free public schools, non-sectarian and conducted in English, and open to all the children of school age in the state, shall be established and maintained.

Article XII, Section 5:
Every child of school age who is mentally and physically able shall attend school.

Article XII, Section 9:
No religious test shall be required of any pupil or teacher as a condition of admission into the public school or any state educational institution.

Article XII, Section 3:
The educational institutions provided for by this constitution shall forever remain under the exclusive control of the state, and no public money shall be used for the support of any sectarian or private school.

Article XII, Section 10:
Children of Spanish descent may not be segregated.

Article XII, Section 8:
The legislature shall provide for the training of teachers proficient in both the English and Spanish languages, to qualify them to teach English speaking pupils.

Article XII, Section 6:
A state board of education shall control all public schools. It shall consist of the governor, the state superintendent of public instruction, and five other members appointed by the governor, with the consent of the senate, including the head of some state educational

institution, a county superintendent of schools, and one other person actually engaged in educational work.

Article XII, Section 2:

The permanent school fund shall consist of the process of sales of certain lands and all grants, gifts and devises made to the state, the purpose of which is not otherwise specified.

Article XII, Section 7:

The permanent school fund shall be invested in the bonds of New Mexico, or of any county, city, town, or school district therein. The legislature may provide that said funds may be invested in other interest bearing securities. All investments must be approved by the governor, attorney-general, and secretary of state. All losses shall be reimbursed by the state.

Article IX, Section 11:

No school district shall borrow money, except for school buildings or school grounds, and only when approved by a majority of those voting thereon. No school district shall ever become indebted in an amount exceeding six per cent on its assessed valuation.

Article XII, Section 4:

Fines and forfeitures, net proceeds of property that may come to the state by escheat, rentals of all school lands and the incomes derived from the permanent school fund shall constitute the current school funds. The proceeds of a tax levied by the legislature shall be added to the current school fund. The fund shall be distributed on the basis of the census child, but before distribution a five-month term to every district which levies the full limit prescribed by law.

Article VII, Section 1:

School elections shall be held at different times than other elections

Article XX, Section 17:

A uniform system of textbooks shall be adopted for the public schools which shall not be changed more than once in six years.

—from J. E. Seyfried, *Analysis and Evaluation of New Mexico School Laws* (Wiley 1974, 10–19).

Appendix 2

New Mexico Superintendents of Public Instruction, 1891 to 2004

Appointed	Amado Chaves	1891–1893
	Amado Chaves	1893–1895
	Amado Chaves	1895–1897
	Placido Sandoval	1897–1898
	Manuel C. de Baca	1898–1899
	Manuel C. de Baca	1899–1901
	J. Francisco Chaves	1901–1903
	J. Francisco Chaves	1903–1904
	Amado Chaves	1904–1905
	Hiram Hadley	1905–1907
	James E. Clark	1907–1909
	James E. Clark	1909–1911
	James E. Clark	1911–1912
Elected	Alvan N. White	1912–1916
	J. H. Wagner	1917–1918
	J. H. Wagner	1919–1920
	John Valdez Conway	1921–1922
	Isabel L. Eckles	1923–1924
	Isabel L. Eckles	1925–1926
	Lois Randolph	1927–1928
	Atanasio Montoya	1929–1930
	Georgia L. Lusk	1931–1932
	Georgia L. Lusk	1933–1934
	H. R. Rogers	1935–1936
	H. R. Rogers	1937–1938
	Grace J. Corrigan	1939–1940
Appointed	Grace J. Corrigan	1941–1942
	Georgia L. Lusk	1943–1944
	Georgia L. Lusk	1945–1946
	Charles R. Rose	1947–1948
	Charles R. Rose	1949–1950
	Tom Wiley	1951–1952

	Tom Wiley	1953–1954
	Georgia L. Lusk	1955–1956
	Georgia L. Lusk	1957–1958

↩

Elected &
Appointed   Tom Wiley   1959–1963

↩

Appointed   Leonard J. DeLayo   1963–1985
                     Orlando J. Girón   1985–1985
                     Alan D. Morgan   1985–1997
                     Michael J. Davis   1997–2003

↩

Appointed by Governor: Secretary of Public Education
                     Veronica G. Garcia   2003–present

Information compiled by Dan D. Chavez, PhD, University of New Mexico.

Appendix 3

The American Association of School Administrators (AASA)
List of Responsibilities
School District Superintendent

A. To serve as the school board's chief executive officer and preeminent educational advisor in all efforts of the board to fulfill school system responsibilities
B. To serve as the primary educational leader for the school system and chief administrative officer of the entire school district's professional and support staff
C. To serve as a catalyst for the school system's administrative leadership team in proposing and implementing policy changes
D. To propose and institute a process for long range and strategic planning
E. To keep all board members informed about school aspirations and programs
F. To interpret the needs of the school system to the board
G. To present policy options along with specific recommendations to the board when circumstances require the board to adopt new policies or review existing policies
H. To develop and inform the board of administrative procedures needed to implement board policy
I. To develop a sound program of school/community relations in concert with the board
J. To oversee management of district day-to-day operations (includes the recommendation for the employment of personnel)
K. To develop a description of what constitutes effective leadership and management of public schools; take into account that effective leadership and management are the result of effective governance and effective administration combined
L. To develop and carry out a plan for keeping the total professional support staff informed about the mission, goals, and strategies of the school system

M. To ensure that professional development opportunities are available to all school system employees

N. To collaborate with other administrators through national and state professional organizations to inform state legislatures and members of congress of local and educational concerns and issues

O. To ensure that the school system provides equal opportunities for all students

P. To evaluate personnel in harmony with district policy and keep the board informed about such evaluations

Q. To provide all board members with complete background information and recommendations for school board action on each agenda item well in advance of each board meeting

R. To develop and implement a continuous plan for working with the news media

S. To develop an Educational Plan for Student Success to be submitted to the state board and to structure the district educational program

T. To recommend to the board of education a district budget for the operation of the district.

Appendix 4
Funding Formula

State Equalization Guarantee Computation

Membership/Program		Times	Differential=Units	
Kindergarten & 3- & 4-Year-Old DD	FTE	x	1.440	
Grade 1	MEM	x	1.200	
Grades 2–3	MEM	x	1.180	
Grades 4–6	MEM	x	1.045	
Grades 7–12	MEM	x	1.250	
Special Education				
Ancillary	FTE	x	25.000	
A/B Level	MEM	x	0.700	
C/D Level	MEM	x	1.000	
D Level	MEM	x	2.000	
3- & 4-Year-Old DD	MEM	x	2.000	
Bilingual	FTE	x	0.500	

SUM OF UNITS

Total Program Units

T&E Index Multiplier ──────→ Times Value from 1.00–1.500

Adjusted Program Units

PLUS ↓

D-Level NPTC

| Elem./Jr. High Size Units |
| Senior High Size Units |
| District Size Units |
| Rural Isolation Units |
| At-Risk Units |
| Enrollment Growth Units |

PLUS ←

EQUALS →

Total Units

↓

+ Save Harmless Units

Grand Total Units

Grand Total Units x Unit Value = Program Cost

Program Cost
- 75% (Noncategorical Revenue Credits)
- Utility Conservation Program Contract Payments
State Equalization Guarantee

Appendix 5

State Department of Education Public School Reform Act of 1986, Legislative Changes Summary—Effective Dates

1986–1987

- Sets requirements for high school graduation beginning with 1986–87 9th graders (adds units, courses, competency tests).
- Criteria for participation in gifted program defined; gifted programs to be studied.
- Sets academic criteria for participation in extracurricular activities.
- Parents must receive notification of failing student.
- Parents and staff to participate in textbook selection, development of discipline, and other policies.
- Increased academic requirements for teacher certification (beginning with freshman class of 1986–87).
- Increases requirements for student teaching and requires 14 weeks student teaching (some early, some late in training), in order to be certified.
- Repeals tenure rights.
- Establishes arbitration procedures: reemployment and discharge situations.
- Teachers not held liable for reports of student discipline or drug violations.
- Pledge of Allegiance required daily.
- $2200 salary increase, including employee benefits.
- Administrators must serve a one-year apprenticeship.
- Administrators must participate in training every 2 years.
- Freezes salaries for one year for administrators earning over $40,000.
- Small schools can use previous year ADM for funding.
- Districts must file 1985–86 and 1986–87 salary schedule with Office of Education.
- SDE must approve administrator training.
- SDE must develop administrator competencies.

1987–1988

- Sets maximum class size at 20 students for kindergarten and grade one (aide available with 15 at grade one), or, with approval of the state superintendent, kindergarten maximum of 26 with aide at 21; grade 1 maximum of 26 with aide at 24.
- Students must master competencies, or participate in remediation or an alternative program. (Delayed until 1989–90.)
- Sets minimum length of school day and minimum required instructional days.
- Establishes mandatory kindergarten. (Delayed until 1988–89.)
- Parents can be fined for truant student.
- Teachers are released from noninstructional duties (noon, cafeteria, ground and bus duty) (counselors excepted). Limited to noon recess—counselors included.
- Sets minimum instructional time for academic subjects, other topics of study limited.
- More alternative and remedial programs may be required. (Delayed until 1989–90.)
- Requires more student testing in reading and writing.
- Districts must develop school discipline policy.
- SDE must provide magistrate judges training on compulsory attendance laws. (Repealed.)
- SDE must provide essential competencies for students.
- Student absences for extracurricular activities limited to maximum of 10 times per semester.
- Students must have grade point average of 2.0 for grading period preceding participation.

1988–1989

- Sets maximum class size at 24 students for grade 3, or, with the approval of the state superintendent, a maximum of 29 with aide at 23.
- Sets maximum class load per day of 160 students for grades 7 through 12.
- Sets maximum class load per day of 135 students for English courses in grades 7 and 8, with a maximum of 27 students per class.
- Sets maximum class load per day of 150 students for

English courses in grades 9 through 12, with a maximum of 30 students per class.

- Student absences for extracurricular activities limited to maximum of 7 times per semester. (Changed to maximum of 10 per semester.

1989–1990

- Sets maximum class size at 24 students for grade 3, or, with approval of the state superintendent, a maximum of 29 with aide at 25; kindergarten and first grade, a maximum of 20 with aide at 15.
- Student absences for extracurricular activities limited to maximum of 5 times per semester. (Changed to maximum of 7 per semester.)

1990–1991

- Sets maximum class size at 25 students for grades 4 through 6, or, with approval of state superintendent, maximum of 29 with aide at 25.
- Student absences for extracurricular activities limited to maximum of 5 times per semester.

SDE = State Department of Education
ADM = Average daily membership

Appendix 6

Higher Education Institutions in New Mexico

Type of Institution	Legal Authority	Institutions	Scope of Program	Funding	Governance/Responsibility
University (6)	NM Constitution	ENMU NMHU NMIMT NMSU UNM WNMU	Baccalaureate degree education and possible graduate and post-graduate degree	Full I &G formula 4-year tuition credit Land & Permanent Fund revenue	Five member appointed Board of Regents (UNM-7 member) Board determines policy and manages the university Statewide mission
Constitutional Community College	NM Constitution	Northern NM Community College	Technical and vocational instruction beyond high school and not more than 2 yrs. college level academic instruction	Land & Permanent Fund revenue No local mill levy Full I & G formula 2 yr. Tuition credit Greater state support than other community colleges	Five member appointed board; not required to be local residents; no student representative Board determines policy and manages the college Local mission
Independent Community College (4)	NMSA 1978 §21-13	Clovis CC NM Junior College San Juan College Santa Fe CC	Not to exceed 2 yrs. training in arts, sciences & humanities beyond 12th grade, or a max of 2 yrs. Vocational/technical curriculum	Min. 2 levy Full I & G formula 2 yr. Tuition credit Less state support, greater local support than branch community college	Five or seven elected members of Governing Board Board determines financial and education policy, and management Local mission & control

Type of Institution	Legal Authority	Institutions	Scope of Program	Funding	Governance/Responsibility
Branch Community College (9)	NMSA 1978 §21-14	ENMU-Roswell NMSU-Alamogordo, Carlsbad, Dona Ana, Grants UNM-Gallup, Los Alamos, Valencia, Taos	First 2 yrs. of college education or vocational/technical curricula of max 2 yrs. duration	Min. 1 mill levy Full I & G formula 2 yr. Tuition credit Greater state support, less local support than independent community college	Parent institution's board retains full authority and responsibility Local school board(s) act as advisory board to regents Local mission
Off-campus Instructional Center (1)	NMSA 1978 §21-14A	ENMU-Ruidoso	First 2 yrs. of college education organized vocational/technical curricula of max 2 yrs. duration	Min. 1 mill levy Full I funding only No Tuition credit No G funding, but no tax revenue used in formula	Parent institution's board retains full authority and responsibility Local school board(s) act as advisory board to regents Local mission
Technical & Vocational Institute (3)	NMSA 1978 §21-16	Albuquerque TVI Luna CC Mesalands CC	2 yrs max vocational and technical curricula, and appropriate courses in arts and sciences	Min. 1 mill levy Full I & G formula 2 yr. Tuition credit Less state support, greater local support than branch community college	Five or seven member elected board from single member districts SBE and board prescribe course of study Local mission and control
Learning Center	NMSA 1978 §21-16A		All educational services brokered, not provided directly	Min. 1 mill levy No formula spending No state support	Local school board(s) or community college board Local mission and control

References and Related Sources

Adams, Evelyn C. 1946. *American Indian education: Government schools and economic progress.* Morningside, NY: King's Crown Press.

American Federation of Teachers. 1963a. *New Mexico Union Teacher*, August.

———. 1963b. *Why You Need AFT.*

Anderson, George B. 1907. *History of New Mexico, its resources and its people. (vol. 1).* Los Angeles: Pacific States Publishing Company.

Atkins, Jane. 1982. Who will educate: The schooling question in territorial New Mexico 1846–1911. PhD diss., University of New Mexico.

Baca, Luciano R. 1999. Impact of federal policies on the structural development of education in New Mexico. Unpublished paper.

Bachelor, David L. 1991. *Educational reform in New Mexico: Tireman, San Jose and Nambé.* Albuquerque: University of New Mexico Press.

Ball, Sharon S., Andrea Volckmar, and Nancy Flynn. 2001. *History of the New Mexico Coalition of School Administrators 1971–2001.* Albuquerque: University of New Mexico and Coalition of New Mexico School Administrators.

Ball, Sharon Smith. 2002. Equity at risk: an examination of the New Mexico public school funding system, 1974–2003. PhD diss. proposal, University of New Mexico.

Bandelier, Adolph. 1871. *The delight makers.* New York: Harcourt Brace Janovich.

Beauchamp, George. 1968. *Curriculum theory*, 2nd ed. Wilmette, Ill: The Kagg Press.

Beers, C. David. 1989. Practitioners' views of Indian education in New Mexico. Assisted by Bernard Dallas, Renee Love, Borrmil Page, Rena Oyenque-Salazar. Unpublished brochure. State Department of Education and University of New Mexico.

Bloom, Lansing B., and Thomas C. Donnelly. 1933. *New Mexico history and civics.* Albuquerque: University of New Mexico Press.

Bruchac, Joseph. 2003. *Our stories remember: American Indian history, culture and values through storytelling*. Golden, CO: Fulcrum Publishing.

Budke, Maralyn. 1977. The formation of the Board of Educational Finance: A pioneering effort. Unpublished document.

Cabeza de Baca, Fabiola. 1954. *We fed them cactus*. Albuquerque: University of New Mexico Press.

Cajete, Gregory. 1994. *Look to the mountain: An ecology of indigenous education*. Durango, CO: Kivaki Press.

Carnegie Corporation. 2003. *Civic mission of schools*.

Chavez, Dan. 1988. *College Enrichment Program: 1968–1988, 20th anniversary edition*. Albuquerque: University of New Mexico.

———. 2003. Territorial and state superintendents of public instruction and composition of territorial and state boards of education. Unpublished document, University of New Mexico.

Chávez, Fray Angélico. 1954. *Origins of New Mexico families*. Santa Fe, NM: Santa Fe Historical Society.

Coan, Charles F. 1925. *A history of New Mexico: Vols. 1, 2, 3*. Chicago: The American Historical Society, Inc.

Colton, David, and John Mondragón. 1998. School finance formula in New Mexico. *Educational Considerations*, 25 (spring): 46–49.

Commission on Higher Education and State Board of Education. 2001. *Teacher Accountability Education Council (TEAC)*.

De Aragon, Ray John. 1978. *Padre Martinez and Bishop Lamy*. Las Vegas, NM: Pan-American Publishing Company.

De Thoma, Francisco. 1896. *Historia popular de Nuevo Mexico*. New York: American Book Company.

Defouri, Rev. James H. 1930. *Historical sketch of the Catholic Church in New Mexico*. San Francisco: McCormick Bros.

Edmonds, Ron. 1983. *An overview of school improvement programs*. East Lansing, MI: Michigan State University Press.

Education Week. 2002. The State of the States. No. 17 (January 10): 71–84.

Foote, Cheryl J. 1990. *Women of the New Mexico frontier, 1846–1912*. Boulder: University of Colorado Press.

Gaddis, John Lewis. 2002. *The landscapes of history*. New York: Oxford University Press.

Gallegos, P. Bernardo. 1992. *Literacy, education, and society in New Mexico 1693–1821*. Albuquerque: University of New Mexico Press.

Getz, Lynne Marie. 1997. *Schools of their own, the education of Hispanos in New Mexico, 1850–1940.* Albuquerque: University of New Mexico Press.

Goals 2000: Educate America Act of 1994. Public Law 103-227, § 306d.

Gonzales, Phillip. 2000. *Barefoot boy from Pecos: The life and times of Phillip Gonzales.* Albuquerque.

Hain, Paul, F. Chris Garcia, and Gilbert St. Clair. 1994. *New Mexico government.* Albuquerque: University of New Mexico Press.

Hallenbeck, Cleve. 1950. *Land of the conquistadores.* Caldwell, ID: Caxton Printers.

Hammond, George P., and Thomas C. Donnelly. 1936. *The story of New Mexico: Its history and government.* Albuquerque: University of New Mexico Press.

Harrington, E. R. 1963. *History of the Albuquerque Public Schools.* Albuquerque: Albuquerque Public Schools.

Holder, James D. 1969. A View of the American Federation of Teachers, Local 1420. Unpublished paper. Albuquerque, NM.

Horgan, Paul. 1975. *Lamy of Santa Fe: His life and times.* New York: Farrar, Straus, and Giroux.

Huxel, Larry. 1973. A computer-based simulation model for public education in New Mexico. PhD diss., University of New Mexico.

Jenkins, Myra Ellen. 1977. Early education in New Mexico. *NEA-NM New Mexico School Review* (Midwinter): 5–11.

Jenkins, Myra Ellen, and Albert H. Schroeder. 1974. *A brief history of New Mexico.* Albuquerque: University of New Mexico Press.

Kane, William T. Revised by John J. O'Brien. 1954. *History of Education: Considered chiefly in its development in the Western World,* (328–47). Chicago: Loyola University Press.

Kitchens, Richard, and Diane Velasquez. 1998. *Dropout intervention/prevention in New Mexico schools with special emphasis on Hispanic and Native Americans.* Albuquerque: New Mexico Research and Study Council, University of New Mexico College of Education.

Krueger, Jo Ann. 1975. The politics of school finance: New Mexico passes a school funding formula. *Journal of Education Finance* 1 (summer): 86–95.

Lessinger, Leon M., and Ralph W. Tyler, eds. 1971. *Accountability in education.* Worthington, OH: Charles A. Jones Publishing Co.

Lummis, Charles F. 1952. *The land of poco tiempo*. Albuquerque: University of New Mexico Press.

Lynch, John. 1973. *The Spanish American revolutions, 1808–1826*. NY: The W. W. Norton Co.

Mares, Ernest A. 1983. Padre Antonio Martinez: Changing perspectives on his life and works. Paper presented at Rio Grande Institute Forum, Abiquiu, NM.

Mares, Ernest A., et al. 1988. *Padre Martinez: New perspectives from Taos*. Taos, NM: Millicent Rogers Museum.

Mort, Paul R. 1961. *Toward a more dynamic fiscal policy for New Mexico schools*. Report to State Board of Education. Santa Fe, NM: State Department of Education.

Moyers, R. A. 1941. A history of education in New Mexico. PhD diss., George Peabody School of Education.

Nagle, Conrad. 1968. The Rebellion of Grant County, New Mexico, in 1876. *Arizona and the West* 10: 225–40.

Nanninga, Simon P. 1942. *The New Mexico school system*. Albuquerque: University of New Mexico Press.

Nation at risk: The imperative for educational reform. 1983. Washington: The Commission on Excellence in Education.

New Mexico Constitution: Article XII Sections 1 through 15. (as adopted January 21, 1911, and as subsequently amended by the people in general and special elections, 1911 through 2001). Santa Fe, NM.

New Mexico Territorial Constitution of 1850.

New Mexico First. 1998. *American Indians in New Mexico and their neighbors: Building bridges of understanding*. Town Hall Conference report. Albuquerque, NM.

———. 1999. *K-12 education in New Mexico: Benchmarks for the new millennium*. Center for Teacher Education. Albuquerque: University of New Mexico.

New Mexico State Legislature. Employee Bargaining Act. 1992. Santa Fe, NM.

———. Indian Education Act 2002 and 2003. Santa Fe, NM.

———. Indian Education Bill 126. Santa Fe, NM.

———. New Mexico Accountability Report. 2001. Santa Fe, NM.

———. New Mexico Reform Act of 1986. Santa Fe, NM.

———. New Mexico House Memorial 43, 1999. Santa Fe, NM.

———. New Mexico House Bill 8. Santa Fe, NM.

———. New Mexico House Bill 212. 2003. Santa Fe, NM.

———. Public School Reform Code of 2003, HB 212. Santa Fe, NM.

————. Public School Reform Act, 1986. Santa Fe, NM.

————. Public School Code: Legislative Act of 1923. Santa Fe, NM.

————. Public School Finance Act of 1974. Santa Fe, NM.

————. Technology Act of 1994. Santa Fe, NM.

————. *Strategic Plan: Charting student success in the new millennium.* 1999. Santa Fe, NM.

————. *New Mexico State Board of Education Publication.* January 2002. Santa Fe, NM.

New Mexico State Department of Education. School Code of 1860. Santa Fe, NM.

————. Status Report on Indian Education 1998, 1999, 2001. Santa Fe, NM.

————. *Standards primer: A guide to standards based education in New Mexico.* 1999. Santa Fe, NM.

————. How schools are funded in New Mexico. 2001. Santa Fe, NM.

————. Agency Bill Analysis. 2002. Santa Fe, NM.

Noriega, Jorge. 1992. American Indian education in the United States: Indoctrination for subordination to colonialism. In *The State of Native America: Genocide, colonization, and resistance,* edited by M. Annette Jaimes, (371–402). Boston: South End Press.

Okal, Langu. 1996. Critical factors facing and influencing higher education planning in New Mexico in the first decade of the twenty-first century. PhD diss., University of New Mexico.

Palm, Rufus A. 1930. New Mexico schools from 1581 to 1846. Master's thesis, University of New Mexico.

Pino, Pedro Bautista. 1995. *The exposition on the Province of New Mexico, 1812.* Santa Fe and Albuquerque: El Rancho de las Golondrinas and University of New Mexico Press.

Priestly, Lee. 1988. *Shalam: Utopia on the Rio Grande, 1881–1907.* El Paso: University of Texas at El Paso: Texas Western Press.

Prince, L. Bradford. 1910. *New Mexico's struggle for statehood.* Santa Fe, NM: The New Mexican Printing Co.

————. 1913. *Student history of New Mexico.* Denver, CO: Publishers Press.

Pullian, John D., and James J. Van Paten. 2002. *History of education in America.* Upper Saddle River, NJ: Prentice Hall.

Read, Benjamin M. 1911. *A history of education in New Mexico.* Santa Fe, NM: The New Mexico Printing Company.

————. 1912. *Illustrated history of New Mexico.* Santa Fe, NM.

Root, Tom. 2002. *Post-Secondary Education.* Commission on Higher Education document.

Salaz, Ruben Marquez. 1999. *New Mexico: A brief multi-history.* Albuquerque, NM: Cosmic House. (also listed as Ruben Marquez.)

Salpointe, Rev. J. B. 1898. *Soldiers of the cross: Notes on the ecclesiastical history of New Mexico, Arizona and Colorado.* Banning, CA: St. Boniface's Industrial School.

Scholes, France V. 1935. Civil government and society in New Mexico in the seventeenth century. *New Mexico Historical Review.* (Vol. X).

Shea, John Gilmary. 1892. *History of the Catholic Church in the United States, Vols. 1–4.* New York: Lippincott.

Simmons, Marc. 1968. *Spanish government in New Mexico.* Albuquerque: University of New Mexico Press.

Smith, Anne. 1968. Indian education in New Mexico. Unpublished booklet. University of New Mexico College of Education.

Stanley, Francis Crocciola. 1963. *Giant in Lilliput land: The story of Donaciano Vigil.* Pampa, TX: Pampa Print Shop.

Suina, Joseph H. 2003. The Pueblo People and the dominant culture. *Encounter: Education for Meaning and Justice.* (spring: Vol. 16, No. 1).

Tobias, Henry J. 1990. *A history of the Jews in New Mexico.* Albuquerque: University of New Mexico Press.

Travelstead, Chester. 1976. *The spirit of the great university.* Albuquerque. UNM Alumni Board pamphlet. December.

Tyack, David, and Larry Cuban. 1995. *Tinkering toward Utopia: A century of public school reform.* Cambridge, MA: Howard University Press.

Walker, Randi J. 1991. *Protestantism in the Sangre de Cristos.* Albuquerque: University of New Mexico Press.

Wiley, Tom. 1949. *An appraisal of school district consolidation in Bernalillo County, New Mexico.* Albuquerque: University of New Mexico Press.

——. 1965. *Public school education in New Mexico.* Albuquerque: University of New Mexico Press.

——. 1968. *Politics and purse strings in New Mexico.* Albuquerque: University of New Mexico Press.

——. 1974. *Forty years in politics and education: Some memories, recollections, and observations.* Albuquerque: Calvin Horn Publishing Company.

Useful Web Sites

Historical Timeline of Public Education in the US
www.arc.org/erase/timeline.html

History & Facts about Indian Education
www.aiefprograms.org/history_facts/history.html

New Mexico Coalition of School Administrators
www.unm.edu/~nmcsa

New Mexico Research & Study Council
www.unm.edu/~nmrsc

New Mexico State Department of Education
www.sde.state.nm.us/

Other Web Sites

American Association of School Administrators
www.aasa.org

American Federation of Teachers
www.aft.org//index.htm

Education Week
www.edweek.org

Healthier Schools New Mexico
www.healthierschools.org

National Assessment of Educational Progress (NAEP)
www.nces.ed.gov/naep

National Association for Bilingual Education
www.nabe.org

National Association of Elementary School Principals
www.naesp.org

National Association of Secondary School Principals
www.nassp.org

National Association of State Boards of Education
www.nasbe.org

National Educational Association
www.nea.org

National Educational Association-New Mexico
www.nea.nm.org

National School Boards Association
www.nsba.org

New Mexico Commission on Higher Education
www.nmche.org

New Mexico Federation of Teachers
http://members.aol.com/nmft1/index.htm

New Mexico First
www.nmfirst.org

NM K–12 Public Schools and Districts
www.sde.state.nm.us/sde_othersites.html

New Mexico Office of the Governor
www.governor.state.nm.us

New Mexico State Department of Education
www.sde.state.nm.us

New Mexico State Legislature
http://legis.state.nm.us

Strengthening Quality in Schools
www.sandia.gov/Human_Resources/sqs.html

U.S. Charter Schools
www.uscharterschools.org

U.S. Department of Education
www.ed.gov/index.html

UNM Bureau of Business and Economic Research
www.unm.edu/~bber

UNM Center for Teacher Education
http://teachered.unm.edu

Recommended Reading

Bancroft, Hubert H. 1888. *History of the Pacific States*. San Francisco: The History Publishing Co.

Beck, Warren A. 1962. *New Mexico: A history of four centuries*. Norman: University of Oklahoma Press.

Blaisdell, Bob, ed. 2002. *Great speeches by Native Americans*. Mineola, NY: Dover Publications, Inc.

Cather, Willa. 1927. *Death comes for the Archbishop*. NY: Alfred A. Knopf, Inc. (Book of the Month Club 1995).

Chávez, Fray Angélico. 1974. *My penitente land*. Albuquerque: University of New Mexico Press.

Drumm, Stella M., ed. 1926. *Down the Santa Fe trail and into Mexico: The diary of Susan Shelby Magoffin, 1846–1847*. Lincoln, NE: University of Nebraska Press.

Encinias, Miguel. 1998. *The two lives of Oñate*. Albuquerque: University of New Mexico Press.

Feyereisen, Kathryn V., A. John Fiorini, and Alene T. Nowak. 1970. *Supervision and curriculum renewal: A systems approach*. New York: Appleton-Crofts.

Fleming, Walter. 2003. *Native American history*. Penguin Group, Inc.

Gregg, Josiah. 1968. *The commerce of the prairies*. New York: Citadel Press.

Johnson, Leighton H. 1952. *Development of the central state agency for public education*. Albuquerque: University of New Mexico Press.

Larson, Robert W. 1968. *New Mexico's quest for statehood, 1846–1912*. Albuquerque: University of New Mexico Press.

Loyola, Sister Mary. 1939. *The American occupation of New Mexico, 1821–1852*. Albuquerque: University of New Mexico Press.

Lucero, Antonio. 1914. "Early School Days in New Mexico." *Old Santa Fe Magazine*.

Lux, Guillermo. 1984. *Politics and education in New Mexico: From the Spanish-American Normal School to the Northern New Mexico Community College*. Las Vegas, NM: New Mexico Highlands University.

———. 1986. Politics, NEA, and public education. Unpublished manuscript. Las Vegas, NM: New Mexico Highlands University.

Mayfield, Thomas J. 1938. *Development of the public schools in New Mexico between 1848 and 1900*. Albuquerque: University of New Mexico Press.

McKee, John DeWitt. 1984. *Time of trouble, time of triumph, a centennial history of the First Presbyterian Church of Socorro, New Mexico, 1880–1980*. Socorro, NM: Presbyterian Church.

Melendez, Gabriel A. 1997. *So all is not lost 1834–1958*. Albuquerque: University of New Mexico Press.

Meyer, Marian. 1989. *A century of progress: History of the New Mexico School for the Deaf*. Santa Fe, NM: New Mexico School for the Deaf.

Mondragón, John. 1970. "Curriculum Development." *New Mexico School Review*.

Mondragón, John. 2002. "What New Mexico can do for its struggling Indian students." *The Albuquerque Tribune.* December 18.

Morrow, Baker H., ed. *A harvest of reluctant souls: The memorial of Fray Alonso de Benavides, 1630.* Boulder: University of Colorado Press.

Page, Jake. 2003. *The hands of the great spirit: The 20,000-year history of American Indians.* New York: Free Press.

Perrigo, Lynn I. 1985. *Hispanos: Historic leaders in New Mexico.* Santa Fe, NM: Sunstone Press.

Prather, Hugh. 2001. *A study on the effects of accountability systems on student achievement.* New Mexico Research and Study Council. Albuquerque: University of New Mexico College of Education.

Roller, Twila J. 1993. *Methodism in their madness.* Albuquerque, NM: Creative Designs, Inc.

Sanchez, George. 1940. *The forgotten people.* Albuquerque: University of New Mexico Press.

Sando, Joe. 1971. *Pueblo Indian biographies.* Albuquerque, NM: Cultural Awareness Center.

———. 1992. *Pueblo nations.* Santa Fe: Clear Light Publishers.

Stapleton, Ernest S. 1949. History of the Baptist Missions in New Mexico, 1849–1866. Master's thesis, University of New Mexico.

Steele, Thomas J., Paul Rhetts, and Barbe Awalt, eds. 1998. *Seeds of struggle: Harvest of faith.* The papers of the Archdiocese of Santa Fe Catholic Cuarto Centennial Conference on the History of the Catholic Church in New Mexico. Albuquerque, NM: LPD Press.

Stone, Rev. James M. 1961. *Lighting the candle: The Episcopal Church on the upper Rio Grande.* Santa Fe, NM: Rydall Press.

Szasz, Ferenc M., and Richard W. Etulain, eds. 1997. *Religion in modern New Mexico.* Albuquerque: University of New Mexico Press.

Twitchell, Ralph E. 1911–1917. *Leading facts of New Mexican History. Vol. 1.* Santa Fe, NM: Old Santa Fe Press.

Valdes, Guadalupe. 1996. *Con respecto: bridging the distances between culturally diverse families and schools.* NY: Teachers College Press.

Warner, Louis H. 1936. *Archbishop Lamy.* Santa Fe, NM: Santa Fe New Mexican Publishing Co.

Weber, David J., ed. 1973. *Foreigners in their native land.* Albuquerque: University of New Mexico Press (reprinted 1975).

Wiles, Jon, and Joseph Bondi. 1984. *Curriculum development: A guide to practice.* Columbus, OH: Charles E. Merrill Publishing Company.

Index

Adams, Evelyn C., 62
Albarez, Father Sebastian, 8
Albuquerque Classroom
    Teachers Association
    (ACTA), 94–95
Albuquerque Public Schools
    Board of Education, 95
American Association of
    School Administrators
    (AASA), 98, 225–26
American Federation of
    Teachers, 92–93;
    Albuquerque chapter, 93,
    94–95; collective bargain-
    ing and, 93, 94–96; New
    Mexico chapter, 92
Apodaca, Governor Jerry, 32
*Association for Retarded
    Citizens v. State of New
    Mexico,* 38
Association of Supervision
    and Curriculum
    Development, 125

Beers, C. David, 67–68
Bell, T. H., 161
Benchmarks. *See* curriculum
Bilingual education, 2, 54,
    122, 169; Article XII and,
    118; history of, 116–17,
    160, 164–65; *Serna v.
    Portales Municipal
    Schools,* 38
Board of Education: local,

28–29, 45–48, 73, 180,
    215; New Mexico state,
    28, 48; superintendents
    and, 50–51; Territorial,
    135
Box, Eddie, 81
*Brown v. The Board of
    Education,* 159
Burroughs, Governor John,
    140

Cajete, Gregory, 2, 69, 77,
    80, 81
Capital outlay funding of
    schools, 148–52; litiga-
    tion impacting, 150, 211;
    revisions to, 150–52;
    state supported funding
    and, 148–49
Carlisle Indian School, 64
Catholic Church and educa-
    tion, 37, 85 (*see also*
    Franciscan missionaries;
    Lamy, Bishop);
    Franciscans and (*see*
    Franciscan missionaries);
    Native Americans and
    (*see* Native American
    education; Native
    American students);
    Spanish and Mexican
    periods and, 9–12, 113
Charter school movement.
    See schools, charter

Chaves, Amado, 20, 22–23; bilingual instruction and, 116–17; education and, 32, 87, 136
Chino, Darva, 77, 80–81
Civil Rights Act of 1964, 159, 160; bilingual education and, 169
College of Santa Fe, 8
Commission on Higher Education, 187, 189–90; Public Education Department and, 201, 204; State Board of Education Roundtable of 2000 and, 201; TEAC and, 202
Cortes, Hernando, 7, 9
Curriculum: conflict and, 121–23, 124; content, 122–23, 124, 127–28; development, 110, 119–20, 125, 128–29; early Native American, 112–13, 128, 130; ethnic studies, 125–26, 212; formal and informal, 119–20; history of, 113–18; influences on, 112, 123–25, 129–30; models of, 81, 115; New Mexico and, 110–12, 128–30; religion and, 109, 129; school administrators and, 54, 55; school districts and, 124–26; science and technology and, 110–11, 213; standards-based, 118, 127–28, 128–29; testing and assessment and, 90,

124, 130, 177–79; vocational, 117, 120

Davis, Michael, 106
De Thoma, Francisco, 109, 113
DeLayo, Leonard, 141–42
Dixon Case, the. See Zeller v. Huff
Dropout rates, 75–76, 122

Early education programs, 122–23
Eastern New Mexico: College, 188; University (ENMU), 188
Edmonds, Dr. Ron, 173
Educate America Act, 1994, 162, 176
Education Act of 1972: Title IX and, 161
Education of the Exceptional Child (Public Law 94-142), 160
Education Reform Act of 2003, 96, 104, 179–81; teacher licensure and, 104
Educational funding in New Mexico, 9–10, 17, 19, 204, 210–11, 231–32; Article XII and, 132, 161; capital outlay funding and (see capital outlay funding); equalization formula for, 71, 138–39, 143, 144–48, 181, 211, 227 (see also State Equalization Funding Formula); federal government and, 169–70; history of, 19, 132–37,

139–44; Permanent School Fund and, 132, 181, 211; reform of, 139–40, 172; school vouchers and, 163, 209–10; taxes and (*see* taxes for education)

Educational Leadership Advisory Committee, 200

Educational Plan for Student Success (EPSS), 48, 55

Educational reform in New Mexico: accountability and, 177–79, 181; bilingual education and, 169, 170; consolidation of districts and, 166–68; definition of, 156–57; Education Reform Bill of 2003 and, 96, 104, 162, 179–81; funding and, 181, 182, 184; impact of, 181–83, 219; influences on, 157, 179–80; legislation and, 166, 180–81, 182; national reform and, 157–62, 162–64, 184; New Mexico Reform Act of 1986, 178; Public School Finance Act and, 168–69; Public School Reform Act, 1986 and, 171–72, 228–30; San Jose/Nambé reform project and, 164–65; School Code of New Mexico and, 164, 181; special education and, 169–70; teachers and, 170–71, 180; technology and, 174–75; testing and curriculum and, 170, 171, 178, 184; the state and, 164–81

Educational testing, 176, 178, 209; curriculum and, 124, 128, 177; educational reform and, 170, 171, 178; Native American students and, 60, 75

Elementary and Secondary Education Act (ESEA) (No Child Left Behind), 20, 45, 125, 159, 181; Native Americans and, 71; reauthorization of, 162, 163; testing and, 177, 179, 209

Emergency Assistance Act, 1970, 163

Employee Bargaining Act, 96

Fergusson, Erna, 121

Franciscan missionaries: education and, 3–5, 8, 9–10, 14–15

Gaddis, John Lewis, 23, 26

Gallegos, Bernardo P., 113

Getz, 116, 117

Golden Apple Foundation, the, 193

Governance of public education in New Mexico, 231–32; Commission on Higher Education and, 189–90; Common School model of, 28–29; federal role in, 29–30; local boards of education and, 28–29, 56–57, 213;

Public Education Commission and, 28, 29, 189; role of, 28–29, 56, 124; State Board of Education and, 29; State Constitution and, 28, 181; the state and, 56–57, 183, 212–13
Governor's Citizens Taxpayers Committee, 138

Hadley, Hiram, 19, 97
Harrington, E. R., 119–20
Harwood, Thomas and Emily, 19, 85
Haskell Institute, 64
Higher education in New Mexico, 197–98; funding for, 197, 198; history of, 187–88; public education and (*see* public and higher education in New Mexico)
History of education in New Mexico, 8, 11, 23, 25–26, 218, xii; American occupation and, 12–13; colonial period, 3–5, 6, 9, 133; diversity and, 23, 25; federalism and, 14, xii; financing and, 13–14, 16–17; Franciscan order and, 3–5, 6, 8, 9; Mexican period of, 8–12; Native Americans (*see* Native Americans and education); nonsectarian schools and, 16–17; poverty and, 7, 23; territorial period and, 13–18,

133–37; textbooks and curriculum and, 10, 15
Hodgin, Charles, 22–23
Home schooling, 176, 209

Improving American Schools Act, 1994, 175
Indian Education Act, 69–70, 72, 73, 76, 80–81
Individuals with Disabilities Act (IDEA), 160
Institute of American Indian Arts, 67

Jenkins, 10, 11, 115
Johnson O'Malley Act, 66
Joseph Institute, 116

Kearney Code, 12–13
Kearney, Stephen W., 12–13, 116
King, Governor Bruce, 32, 142

Lamy, Bishop Jean Baptiste, 8, 15; education in New Mexico and, 15, 19, 85, 134
Lau v. Nicols, 160
Lessinger, Leon, 177–78
Licensure: superintendent, 49–50; teacher (*see* teacher licensure)
Local school councils, 55–56; New Mexico House Bill (NM HB) 212, 55; purpose of, 55
Loretto Academy for Girls, 15, 116, 134
Los Alamos v. Wugalter, 38
Lummis, Charles, 111

Martinez, Father José
  Antonio, 15; school in
  Taos and, 10, 19, 133
Menaul, John and James, 19
Mission schools, 3–5, 6;
  Native American students
  and, 59, 61–62, 67; secu-
  larization of, 9
Mondragón, John B., 220
Mort, Dr. Paul, 140
Moyers, R. A., 3, 4, 9

Nanninga, S. P., 3, 7, 8, 118
Nation at Risk report, 1983,
  161–62, 171, 172–73,
  178
Native American education,
  25; boards of education
  and, 72–73; cultural sensitivity and, 79–80; federal government and,
  70–72, 79, 80; funding
  for, 70–71, 72, 80; governance of, 70–75; Indian
  Education Act and,
  69–70, 72, 73, 76, 80;
  Johnson O'Malley Act
  and, 66, 71, 72; Native
  American culture and, 77,
  79; schools for, 70, 77,
  79; state government and,
  71–73; treaties and, 59,
  61, 63, 70, 71, 79, 133;
  tribal government and,
  73–75
Native American Student
  Success Conference,
  73–75
Native American students:
  BIA schools and, 59, 64,
70, 77, 79, 80; boarding
  schools and, 64–65;
  Christianization of,
  61–62, 64; Common
  School concept and,
  65–66, 81; educational
  needs of, 67–70, 72,
  75–76, 81, 158, 160,
  183, 212; enrollment of,
  59, 66–67, 70, 74, 79–80;
  federal government and,
  60–61, 70–75, 79–80;
  funding for, 70–71, 80;
  graduation rates of,
  59–60; history of, 60–67,
  109; issues of, 67–70, 72,
  75, 76–77; Johnson
  O'Malley Act and, 66,
  71; learning styles of, 61,
  75–76; legislation and,
  69; mission schools and,
  61–62, 109–10; parental
  involvement and, 77–79;
  present status of, 75–79;
  public schools and, 66,
  70, 72, 76–77, 79–80;
  school districts with, 61,
  73, 74, 79–80; state-mandated testing and, 60, 75;
  teachers of, 68, 69, 70,
  109; treaties and, 59, 61,
  63, 70, 71, 79
Native American(s): culture
  of, 2, 25, 61–62; educational responsibility to, 2,
  68–70; educational
  system of, 1, 2–3, 61,
  112–13; mission schools
  and, 3–5, 6, 63; pueblos
  and reservations of, 60
Nava, Cynthia, 180, 184

NCATE (National Council for Accreditation of Teacher Education), 199

NEA (National Teachers Association), 89–92; - New Mexico, 89–92, 94–97; collective bargaining and, 94–97

New Mexico Coalition of School Administrators, 53

New Mexico Constitution, 22–23, 28, 221–22; amendments to, 40, 44–45; Article IV, 33; Article V of, 32; Article XII, 39–40, 132, 221; Territorial, 43–45

New Mexico First: town hall on American Indians in New Mexico, 68–70; town hall on education, 179–80, 213

New Mexico Highlands University (NMHU), 202

New Mexico House Bill (NM HB) 174, 180-82, 212-13: local councils and, 55

New Mexico Institute of Mining and Technology, 188

New Mexico Public Education Department, 44–45; Commission on Higher Education and, 201, 204; funding and, 138; Indian education and, 69–70, 73; Reform Act of 1986 and, 178, 228–30

New Mexico Reform Act, 1986, 178, 228–30

New Mexico Research and Study Council, 192

New Mexico School Administrators Association (NMSAA), 98–100

New Mexico School Boards Association (NMSBA), 99

New Mexico School Code, 164, 180–81

New Mexico School-to-Work/School-to-Careers, 203

New Mexico Standards for Excellence, 128

New Mexico State Board of Education, 28, 39–43; Article XII and, 39–40, 193–94; Native American education and, 72–73; Public Education Commission and, 41; structure and role of, 32–33, 41–43; teachers and, 93, 199–200

New Mexico State Department of Education: Indian Education Division of, 67, 72, 73, 80; testing and, 209

New Mexico State Legislature: education and, 33–37, 124; educational funding and, 34, 35–37, 38 (see also educational funding in New Mexico); Legislative Education Study Committee (LESC) of, 34–35, 184; NM HB 212, 55, 174, 180–81, 182, 212–13

New Mexico State University,
188
New Mexico Territorial
Education Association,
187
No Child Left Behind. *See*
Elementary and
Secondary Education Act
Noriega, Jorge, 61–62
Northern New Mexico
Community College, 187,
188
Northern New Mexico
Normal School, 90–91
Northwest Ordinance, 63

Okal, Langu, 205

Palm, Rufus, 3, 113
Partners in Education, 106
Permanent School Fund, 132,
181, 211
Pestalozzi, Johann Heinrich,
114, 115
Pino, Pedro Bautista de, 7,
14, 114
Post-Secondary Education,
202–3
Prince, Governor Bradford,
19, 22, 23; education
and, 30–31, 136; State
Board of Education and,
39; state superintendent
of public education and,
44; Territorial Education
Association, 86
Principals of schools, 51–55;
duties of, 51, 52–53; professional organizations of,
53–54, 100; qualifications
for, 51–52, 53

Professional Standards
Commission, 199
Protestant missionaries: education and, 13, 15–16,
25, 134
Public and higher education in
New Mexico: concurrent
enrollment and, 203; dif-
ferences between, 198–99;
formal relationships
between, 193–203; K-16
system and, 187, 195,
199–203, 204, 206, 213;
programs between, 190,
192–93, 205; relationship
between, 190–93, 194–95,
196, 204–6
Public Education
Commission, 28, 29, 189;
New Mexico State Board
of Education and, 41,
181; secretary of public
education and, 33
Public education in New
Mexico, 56–57, 113,
133–34; accountability
and, 177–79, 208–9; as a
profession (*see* teaching as
a profession in New
Mexico); bilingual educa-
tion in (*see* bilingual education); Catholic Church
and, 9–10, 11–12 (*see*
also Franciscan missionaries); curriculum and (*see*
curriculum); diversity and,
1, 116–17, 158, 164–65,
214; Equalization
Funding Formula for, 36,
37; federal role in, 14,
29–30, 31, 154, 162–63,

xii; funding for (see educational funding in New Mexico); future trends in, 24, 208–14; governance of (see governance of public education in New Mexico); governor's office and, 30–33; higher education and (see public and higher education in New Mexico); history of (see history of education in New Mexico); K-12, 187, 189, 195, 196–97, 198, 203–4, 205; K-16, 187, 195, 199–203, 204, 206, 213; legislation and, 1, 29–30, 32–39; multicultural, 1, 71, 121, 158, 160, 214; Native Americans and, 1–2, 3–5, 21, 68–70 (see also Native American students); religious and ethic issues and, 2, 3–5, 6, 8, 9, 25, 37 (see also Zeller v. Huff); standards-based, 127–28, 173, 176–77, 209; statehood and, 18–22, 137–44; taxes and (see taxes for education); TEA and, 89–91; U.S. Constitution and, 29–30
Public Education in New Mexico (Little Hoover Commission Report), 139
Public Law 874, 122
Public School Capital Improvements Act (PSCIA) (NM SB 9), 149, 151

Public School Capital Outlay: Act, 148, 151–52; Council (PSCOC), 148–49, 150–52; Improvement Fund, 151–52
Public School Code, 41, 138; of 1860, 86; of 1923, 164, 181
Public School Finance Act, 1974, 144, 168–69
Public School Reform Act, 1986, 147, 171–72
Pueblo Revolt: Popé and, 5, 6, 113
Pueblos, 4, 6–7, 60

Quality Education Awards Program, 192–93

Read, Benjamin, 7, 9
Read, Hiram, 116
Rodriguez v. San Antonio, 142, 168
Rodriguez, Father, 3

Scholes, Dr. France V., 4, 9
School administrators, 97–102, 225–26; accountability and, 54, 100, 179; curriculum and, 54, 55; district superintendents and, 54–55; duties of, 55, 124; professional organizations of, 54–55, 100
School Budget Office, the, 137–38
School districts: budgets of, 48, 142, 151; conflict between, 17–18, 166–68;

consolidation of, 166–68; curriculum and, 124–26; map of New Mexico, 24; teacher education and, 199–200; with Native American students, 61, 73

School Improvement Act, 151

School vouchers, 163, 209–10

Schools, 3, 112, 120, 174, 176, 209; accountability and, 208–9; BIA, 59, 64–65, 67, 70, 79; Catholic (*see* Catholic Church and education); charter, 55, 163, 174, 175, 209, 213 (*see also* charter school movement); home, 176, 209, 213; mission (*see* mission schools); normal, 90, 187–88; private, 7, 17, 59, 116, 133–34, 209–10; public, 11, 21, 59, 73, 96, 133–34; religious, 15, 67, 116, 134, 209; rural, 17–18, 122 (*see also* urban/rural educational conflicts); urban, 17–18, 70, 122 (*see also* urban/rural educational conflicts)

Secretary of Public Education, 204; State Accountability Plan and, 45; superintendent of public education and, 44–45

Serna v. Portales Municipal Schools, 38, 169

Serrano v. Priest, 142, 168

Severance Tax Bonding Act (STBA), 151–52

Southwestern Indian Polytechnic Institute, 67

Spanish period in New Mexico: education and, 3–5, 6, 9

Spanish settlements: free public schools in, 6–7

Special education programs, 169–70

St. Michael's College, 15, 85, 116, 134

Standards Primer, The, 127, 128

Stapleton, Ernest S., 220

State Equalization Funding Formula (*see also* educational funding in New Mexico), 71, 138, 143, 144–48, 152, 153, 211; cost of, 144–45; National Finance Project model and, 144

State Equalization Guarantee, 145–47

State Severance Tax Bonds (SSTB), 151

Stewart, Mimi, 180

Students in New Mexico, 9, 120, 173, 202; by ethnicity, 78, 158, 165, 173; diversity of, 158, 160, 199; high school, 190–91, 202–3, 204; Hispanic, 76, 158, 160; minority, 158, 160, 206, 212; Native American (*see* Native American students); with special needs, 38, 158, 160, 169–70, 182, 210

Suina, Joe, 65, 68, 79, 200
Superintendents of schools,
    223–24; Board of
    Education and, 50–51;
    district, 49–51, 54–55;
    duties of, 50–51, 213;
    licensure for, 49–50; state,
    39, 43–45, 179

Taft, President William
    Howard, 23, 137
Taxes for education (see also
    educational funding in
    New Mexico): gross
    receipts, 138; property,
    19, 134–36, 138, 140,
    141, 147; railroad, 135;
    reduction in, 172; tax
    base and, 153
TEA (Territorial Education
    Association), 89–91, 97
Teacher Education
    Accountability Council
    (TEAC), 201–3, 204
Teacher licensure: framework
    of, 103–5, 170–71; his-
    tory of, 86–88; Native
    Americans and, 69; TEA
    and, 90; three-tiered, 96,
    104–5, 171, 180
Teachers, 3, 21, 93, 212;
    accountability and, 106,
    201–3, 204; American
    Federation of (see
    American Federation of
    Teachers); collective bar-
    gaining and, 93, 94–96;
    Franciscan missionary
    (see Franciscan missionar-
    ies); from religious organ-
    izations, 37, 85, 139;

licensure for (see teacher
    licensure); minority, 11,
    77, 78, 91, 106; National
    Education Association
    and (see NEA); of Native
    American language and
    culture, 68, 69, 71, 77;
    professional organizations
    of, 87, 88–89, 106; rights,
    92, 93, 94–96; salaries of
Teachers' salaries: AFT and,
    92–93; cost of, 7, 21;
    levels of, 87–88, 140,
    147, 154, 211–12; licen-
    sure and, 105
Teachers' training, 122,
    199–200, 204; history of,
    86, 90, 187–88; licensure
    and, 102–5, 170–71
Teaching as a profession in
    New Mexico: early
    Native American educa-
    tion and, 84; Mexican
    territorial period and, 84;
    Spanish colonial period
    and, 84; statehood period
    and, 87–88; the American
    occupation and territorial
    period and, 85–87
Tireman, Dr. Lloyd, 164–65
Title I. See Elementary and
    Secondary Education Act
    (No Child Left Behind)
Title II, 201–2
Travelstead, Dean Chester,
    205
Tyler, Ralph, 177–78

University of New Mexico,
    188; College of
    Education, 192–93, 200

Urban/rural educational
conflicts, 17–18

Vigil, Donaciano, 13, 19,
22–23

Wiley, Tom, 215; *An
Appraisal of New Mexico
School District
Consolidation in
Bernalillo County*, 167;
as state superintendent,
140; educational history
of New Mexico by, 17,

23, 118, 120; *Politics and
Purse Strings in New
Mexico*, 33, 136, 164,
166–67; *Public School
Education in New
Mexico*, 208
Wisdom of practice, 206, 219

Zeller v. Huff, 37, 139
*Zuni, Gallup-McKinley,
Grants-Cibola County
School Districts v. State
of New Mexico*, 38–39

About the Authors

John B. Mondragón is a native New Mexican born in the village of Holman in the northern part of the state. His parents are members of the early Spanish families who settled some of the original land grants; his great-grandparents settled in the villages of Trampas and Chamisal. His parents, though not highly formally educated, encouraged their offspring to get an education. John attended Mora High School with Sisters of Loretto as his teachers (in a public school). He served in the United States Army and returned to receive a BA and an MA degree from New Mexico Highlands University. He holds a Doctorate from the University of New Mexico and has taken postdoctoral work at Stanford University.

In his thirty-three years of public school experience, John served as a teacher in the East Las Vegas Public Schools and in the Albuquerque Public Schools. In APS, he served as teacher, assistant principal, principal, deputy superintendent, and area/regional superintendent. As South Area Superintendent in APS, he worked with the first cluster in the district utilizing the Effective Schools Model.

At the University of New Mexico, he has served as Educational Leadership faculty member and has been the program coordinator for three of the ten years. He also serves as an Outreach Coordinator for the College of Education. He is the Executive Director of the New Mexico Research and Study Council, a consortium of NM school districts providing research, professional development, and other services member districts need. He teaches School Finance, School Business Management, Human Resources, Public Education in New Mexico, and Federal and State Policies in Educational Administration. John also serves as an advisor on Doctoral and Masters Student Committees.

His work at the University of New Mexico has included coauthoring a textbook on public education in New Mexico. He has just recently been inducted into the New Mexico Coalition of School Administrators' Hall of Fame. John is passionate about New Mexico and the education of its youth.

Ernest S. Stapleton is a native New Mexican born in Albuquerque. He attended school in Socorro and graduated from Socorro High School. His father was a teacher and principal in the Socorro Public Schools, and both his father and his mother modeled for him the value of an education and respect for others and helped to establish a direction and goal for his entire future. That future included a term with the United States Marine Corps during World War II. He holds BA and MA degrees from the University of New Mexico, doctoral studies at Columbia University, and holds an Honorary Doctorate from the University of Albuquerque. Ernie's beloved wife of fifty years, Elsie, had a wonderful and profound influence on his career and his life.

In his thirty-year career in the Albuquerque Public Schools, Ernie was a teacher and administrative assistant at Jefferson Junior High School; principal at Mark Twain Elementary School; counselor, teacher, and principal at Valley High School; director of instruction, assistant and associate superintendent, and Superintendent of the Albuquerque Public Schools. He served thirteen years as the Executive Director of the New Mexico Association of Elementary School Principals. Over twenty years at the University of New Mexico included serving as special assistant to the president, coordinator of the administrative internship program, academic director of LAPE (Latin American Programs in Education), and faculty member teaching courses in the principalship, educational reform, public education in New Mexico, curriculum development, and others.

He proudly supports Ernest S. Stapleton Elementary School in Albuquerque/Rio Rancho, his namesake, and he was recently inducted into the New Mexico Coalition of School Administrators' Hall of Fame.

Ernie has published some articles over the years; he is a book collector with a collection of over 10,000 volumes. He loves New Mexico, its landscapes, its people, and its food. Coauthoring *Public Education in New Mexico* has been one of his latest challenges.